ANGELS WITH DIRTY FACES

Three Stories of Crime, Prison, and Redemption

By Walidah Imarisha

AK PRESS
EDINBURGH • OAKLAND • BALTIMORE

PRAISE FOR *ANGELS WITH DIRTY FACES*

"Walidah Imarisha has written a brave book. It demonstrates both the universality and distinctiveness of three lives enmeshed through the US prison system. Imarisha pushes us to give up easy distinctions between innocence and guilt, good and evil, and to experience punishment and imprisonment as the messy, complex systems they are. And she reminds us that, while there are no winners in this game, it is one replete with compassion, care, and resistance enough to permeate walls and cages."

—Rachel Herzing

"Some authors approach the subject of incarceration from a great distance, but with *Angels with Dirty Faces*, author/activist Walidah Imarisha goes as deep as any writer can without actually serving time. The result is a highly personalized and intimate portrait by a courageous writer who goes beyond clichés and platitudes. This book is a bracing, clear-eyed exploration of one of the most important issues of our time: the growing incarceration rate in the U.S., and the consequences of this for citizens both inside and outside prison walls."

—T.J. English, *New York Times* best-selling author of *Where the Bodies Were Buried* and *The Westies*

"*Angels with Dirty Faces* is a powerful exploration of America's prison nation. Using three disparate yet interconnected stories, including her own, Walidah Imarisha gives us an unvarnished take on prison abolition. Beyond slogans or strategy, we are left with people, in all our imperfections and possibilities. This is a bold, beautiful, and absolutely necessary book, told with urgency and passion."
—Dan Berger, author of *Captive Nation: Black Prison Organizing in the Civil Rights Era*

"We live in a violent state, run by a violent economic trap, that a violent prison system perpetuates and hides. The reality of violence in the US is so pervasive that the state has all the mirrors in the house covered up. *Angels with Dirty Faces* is a memoir of a reality so crucial and transformative that the state is desperate to keep it locked out of our collective consciousness. And yet we live it.

Here, Imarisha is doing the work that we all must do if we are going to have the world we deserve. She is looking deeply at the violence of prisons and the lives and impact of people who have engaged in violent acts with a love that never stops believing that we are *more* than the violence that structures our days. There is hope, love, and honesty here. And a model for the conversations we need to have right now, right here in hell."
—Alexis Pauline Gumbs

"Walidah Imarisha relates the experiences of crime, punishment, and victimization, not as abstractions, but as lived human tragedies. She shows us how they diminish and distort—but never define—the lives of those who suffer them. Writing with sorrow, and anger, and courageous hope, she forces us to reconsider what we mean by 'justice,' and by what endeavors its cause might be advanced, if never finally achieved."
—Kristian Williams, author of *Our Enemies in Blue: Police and Power in America*

"A brave, honest search for answers regarding incarceration."
—*Kirkus Reviews*

"*Angels with Dirty Faces* is actually three biographies in one, a 'triography' so to speak, of the lives of Mac, Kakamia, and Walidah converging at a California prison. In the beginning they all thought they would just be telling a story... until they made the decision to tell the truth.

Angels with Dirty Faces is a superbly written, shocking, sensuous, sometimes sadistic and even scandalous binding of biographies struggling with the question: What does redemption actually mean? It is impossible for one to engage this work and not emerge on the other side profoundly affected."

—Sundiata Acoli

"I read *Angels With Dirty Faces* in one sitting, mesmerized by what Walidah Imarisha has accomplished: a daring dive into the real deal about why prisons don't work, filled with love for hustlers, rebels. and the criminalized, imperfect survivors that the prison-industrial complex locks up. Written in such lyrical, fierce poetry it takes your breath away."

—Leah Lakshmi Piepzna-Samarasinha, author of *Dirty River: A Queer Femme of Color Dreaming Her Way Home*

Dedicated to Hasan Shakur

and James McElroy

Angels with Dirty Faces: Three Stories of Crime, Prison, and Redemption

ISBN 978-1-84935-174-4 | Ebook ISBN: 978-1-84935-175-1
Library of Congress Number: 2015942525

© 2016 Walidah Imarisha

This edition © 2016 AK Press and the Institute for Anarchist Studies
Cover design by John Yates | STEALWORKS.COM
Interior Design by Margaret Killjoy | BIRDSBEFORETHESTORM.NET
Printed in the USA on recycled, acid-free paper.

AK Press
674-A 23rd Street
Oakland, CA 94612
WWW.AKPRESS.ORG
AKPRESS@AKPRESS.ORG
510.208.1700

AK Press UK
P.O. Box 12766
Edinburgh EH8 9YE
WWW.AKUK.COM
AK@AKEDIN.DEMON.CO.UK
0131.555.5165

Institute for Anarchist Studies
PO Box 90454
Portland, OR 97290
WWW.ANARCHISTSTUDIES.ORG
ANARCHISTSTUDIES@GMAIL.COM

CONTENTS

ACKNOWLEDGMENTS

THANKS TO MY MOTHER AND MY FAMILY, KAKAMIA, MAC, MUMIA, Haramia, Hasan (Rest in Power), and to everyone else who let me borrow their stories and lives for this book.

Thanks to Bayla, Turiya, Elijah, EKela, Pete, Nadia, John J., Kodey, Alexis, Leah Lakshmi, adrienne and the Brood, Hasan Salaam, Ian, Seth, Aishah, Sham, Leah Yacoub Halperin, Khalil, Jasmin, David W., Amelia, Gabriel, Eliana, Jordan, fayemi, Joy, The TARDIS Collective, and every friend/heart family who listened to me about this project, gave feedback, or just hugged me after a hard day of writing.

Thanks to Sundiata Acoli, David Gilbert, all political prisoners, all prison organizers in and outside of the walls, and especially thanks to the Human Rights Coalition.

Thanks to the Institute for Anarchist Studies, to Lara for being such a thoughtful and supportive editor. Thanks to Nick for copyediting. So much thanks to Charles, Zach, Suzanne, and everyone at AK Press.

Thanks to Critical Resistance, Ari, Molly P., Molly and Chela, Chris F., Claude Marks and the Freedom Archives, INCITE, Scott Handleman, Juanita, Gaby, and Graciela. Thanks to Kristian, Dan, and Max for reading and helping to keep me honest, while telling me the project was worth finishing. Thanks to Matthew Shenoda for his mentorship when this book was a thesis. Thanks to Aimee Liu,

Michael Klein, Jennifer, and Patricia. Thanks to the Blue Mountain Center, to Ben, Alice, Nica, and Jamie. Thanks to Cloee, Center for New Community, Favianna, Culture Strike, Jason, Oriana, Lisa, Sophia, Eduardo, Sesshu, Gan, Andrew, Jesus, Azul, Cesar, Siddhartha, Naeem, Julio, Imin, and Manisha. Thanks to Fred Bryant (Rest in Power), Alyssa, JoAnn, and the Justice for Keaton Otis Coalition. Thanks to Kent Ford and Dr. Haynes. Thanks to TJ English for his amazing scholarship and writing. Thanks to Stefan and Marion and the Mayfair Retreat Center.

THROUGH THE GATES

"Ma'am, you're going to have to check the underwire from your bra, or I'm not letting you in."

She was a squat woman, bleached blonde wisps leaking out from her California Department of Corrections baseball hat. The mud brown uniform drew color from her face. In the unforgiving fluorescent lighting of the prison processing center, her features bled away, leaving only razor-edged eyes that bored into me, a mouth twisted with impatience.

The people waiting behind me in line, shoes and belts in hand, shifted irritably. I understood. We had all been on our feet for an hour and a half, up early enough to see the sun crack dawn over the lonely highway that, for us, dead-ended at a wall wrapped in concertina wire.

In the bathroom ten minutes earlier as I hurried into a stall, I passed two women who had the movements of birds, faces heavy with make-up too hastily applied. Using the box cutter with the chipped orange handle given to me by the dour-faced guard, I ripped the seams out of my new black bra, the metal skeleton underneath as exposed as I felt. Meanwhile, the women preened in front of the warped bathroom mirror, one reapplying the dark stain of lipstick every few minutes. The other spoke of her man's sentence as though it was a communal one they shared: "Girl, we only have 148 days left!" One woman, red-faced from her obvious hangover, laughed too loudly as her friend pointed to the hickie on the side of her neck. She murmured an embarrassed "thank you" and re-adjusted her collar to cover it.

I took in the processing room that never had enough chairs as I walked back towards the counter after the dissection of my bra. White faces dotted the institutional green. Even when it wasn't their first visit, they always looked like it was. Most faces, however, reflected me back as I met eyes briefly: Black and brown, female. Tired. No men by themselves; only women alone, shifting on swollen ankles they had spent all week on. Many were mothers of the men warehoused here. On their faces was stamped the dogged resignation that comes from going to see your child week in and week out in a place surrounded by razor wire.

Some waiting were like the young woman in line next to me. Her carefully ironed shirt, laid out lovingly the night before, was now creased like the frown on her face as she tried to manage three wild-as-weeds children, who shot questions about seeing daddy in rapid fire succession. The wide-faced baby in her arms shifted fitfully as the mother separated out the six diapers and two clear baby bottles allowed in.

Two bright-faced and dark-skinned boys tumbled past me, giggles streaming in their wake. Before their mothers had a chance to rope them back under control, one of the guards behind the processing desk boomed out, "No running in the waiting area!" The boys' faces froze more than their bodies—eight-year-old bodies that would soon grow into young Black men bodies: dangerous property, to be handled only by professionals.

As an anti-prison organizer, my work takes me behind the walls, into cages where dignity is stripped and humanity denied, where rehabilitation is nonexistent and abuse is a daily practice. I have spent years visiting political prisoners, which this country denies having. Most of them are from the hopeful, chaotic, and turbulent 1960s and 1970s, when they believed revolution was a single breath away. Now they strain to draw each lungful in the stifling atmosphere of incarceration. Many of them have spent more years in prison than I have on this planet. I have been to the white-hot hell of Texas's death row, and to the stainless steel brutality of Pennsylvania's most infamous restricted housing unit. I have gone behind the walls, and I have the heartbreaking privilege to walk out of them every time.

That day's prison in California looked like so many of the newer institutions: sprawling three-story concrete buildings, windows like slitted eyes squinting in the harsh sunlight. All new prisons look the same from the outside. And thanks to the prison-building boom in the 1980s and 1990s, almost all prisons are relatively new.

California prisons spread faster than a forest fire during a drought and became a symbol for prison growth across the country. 1852 marked the first California state prison, San Quentin. In the first hundred years of California penal institutions, nine new prisons were constructed. That state now operates thirty-three major adult prisons, eight juvenile facilities, and fifty-seven smaller prisons and camps, the majority of which have been built since 1984. The prison-building brushfire of the 1980s often relied on the same corporations and the same plans to build institutions quickly, quietly, and profitably. The corporations profited in dollars, and the state profited from the control of potentially rebellious bodies. There wasn't time for creativity to grow in the shadow of gun turrets.

Now over 2.3 million are incarcerated across this country. One in one hundred adults are living behind bars, according to the Pew Charitable Trusts, and over seven million are in prison or on parole. This means one in thirty-one adults is under some form of state control or supervision, by far the highest rate in the world. American prisons account fully for one-quarter of the entire world prison population. Is this the "number one" people are always shouting about?

At the California prison where I was, there had been an attempt at beautification. Art pieces decorated the sterile visiting room, including a piece from my adopted brother, all flames and burnt black tree limbs. A garden was planted along the walkway to the visiting building. The inmates tended it. It was, my adopted brother told me, a coveted job, because you got to be outside, working with your hands, instead of washing someone's dirty underwear or scraping meatloaf off 3,769 plates each dinner service. The prison's designed capacity was seventeen hundred, but three times as many people are crammed in: 7,538 feet in shoes three sizes too small. This meant triple bunking: three prisoners lived in a cell designed for one. The gym was no longer used to release frustration; it was used as dormitory-style sleeping, where two hundred people lived on top of each other. Fifty-four people shared one toilet.

This is not unique to this prison. The majority of prisons across the country are filled until the seams are bursting, but California is an extreme case. The entire system warehouses almost double the number of people it was designed to hold, and the federal government has been forced to intervene. In May 2011, the U.S. Supreme Court upheld a lower court's ruling: California's prison system violated the Eighth Amendment, the prohibition of cruel and unusual punishment, though not so unusual in this nation. The Supreme Court ruled the state must parole or transfer thirty thousand prisoners in the next two years.

Thirty thousand: everyone with a loved one in California began dreaming it would be them. One in five: much better odds than the lottery. We were so busy whooping with cries of celebration, the second word of the ruling was drowned out: transfer. California argued the whole time that it could solve the overcrowding issue by new construction (during an economic collapse) or by transferring prisoners to be held in other states' prisons. Ultimately they only had the second option. They brokered deals; they sent prisoners to Texas, Arkansas, Missouri. The State of California will still continue to pay for these prisoners, but technically the California prisoner population will be reduced—for now. Yet this is only a stopgap measure.

This is not how we stop the hemorrhaging.

* * *

A visit to a prison requires precise planning and a keen attention to detail. For the honor of standing in the visiting room at that California prison, I had flown from Philadelphia to the Bay Area, rented a car, and driven two hours to stay at the local motel. This trek was not by any means the longest taken—so many drive eight, twelve, or more hours to see their loved ones. These are fraught journeys worthy of immortalization by Homer: millions of epic quests that go uncelebrated, even unnoticed.

In my more dramatic moments, I imagine myself and others challenging the prison system to be Cassandras, cursed by the gods to foretell the future to deaf ears, while our predictions of the destruction of Troy by the Spartans slowly drives us mad. There are thousands of Cassandras waiting in prison processing rooms right now.

I consider our visions of devastation just as dire as Troy's fate, in a country with the highest incarceration rate in the world. Prisons are this society's Trojan Horse, proffered as an end to the "war on crime." We have taken it in and accepted the horrific ramifications that come with it; we are one of the few countries with a death penalty, and one of the few countries that tries juveniles as adults. Our country executes many who are deemed too young to drink, to buy cigarettes, to vote. There has been a continual siege of our senses, the nightly news telling us to be scared in our skin (to be scared of darker skin). This Trojan Horse of more prisons gives a solution to our purported (and mostly fabricated) crime problem and to our perpetual economic crises. It is a solution for which we have flung our gates wide open. But rather than signal the end of a war, it has wreaked destruction we as a society do not acknowledge, do not see. Family members load into cars, climb onto van services while it is still night outside, and make a day's drive across desolate states to see a glimpse of a loved one. For federal prisoners, this hardship may not even be an option for their families; a federal prisoner can be shipped to any federal prison in the country, and a continent is sometimes too much to cross. In order to raise money for the state budget, Arizona now charges families twenty-five dollars to see their loved ones. Families are devastated, communities rendered, and futures without bars are extinguished. Children left behind, growing up in the shadow of walls, are five times more likely to end up in prison themselves.

This cure has proven far more dangerous to the body than the disease, and that is because it was never meant to be a cure. Prisons are not about safety, but about control and containment of potentially rebellious populations. Our current prison system mushroomed after the end of legal slavery. As Angela Davis wrote, at the very time that Black people broke the shackles of slavery, the shackles of prison snapped tight on their wrists. It happened in the Thirteenth Amendment, which outlaws slavery and involuntary servitude "except as a punishment for a crime, whereof the party shall have been duly convicted." This exception was coupled with the Black Codes, a set of state crimes that only applied to Black people. Davis explained in her book *Are Prisons Obsolete?*:

> Thus, former slaves, who had recently been extricated from a condition of hard labor for life, could be legally sentenced to penal servitude. In the immediate aftermath of slavery, the southern states hastened to develop a criminal justice system that could legally restrict the possibilities of freedom for newly released slaves. Black people became the prime targets of a developing convict lease system, referred to many as a reincarnation of slavery.

Davis quoted Mary Ellen Curtin's study of post-emancipation Alabama prisoners to show that before the abolition of the state's 400,000 enslaved Africans, ninety-nine percent of Alabama's prison population was white. Scant years after the end of slavery, Alabama prisoners overwhelmingly took on a darker hue. Scholar Michelle Alexander has shown there are now more Black people in prison then there were enslaved at the height of slavery.

The plantation haunts us, as a living specter, not a past dead and buried. The foundations of our justice system are rooted in enslavement, in the concept of white supremacy as law. The template for the modern police force is the slave patrol, as Kristian Williams shows in his book *Our Enemies in Blue: Police and Power in America*. The foundation was only to serve and protect those who were white and wealthy. For those who lived in Blackness, the predecessors to the police were there to ensure our obedience to chattel slavery. Slavery to prisons. Slave catchers to police. After Black youth organized and rebelled in the streets to bring attention to it, we heard the names last year of Black people murdered by the police, in rapid fire, with no end in sight: Michael Brown, Taylor Garner, Tamir Rice, Darrien Hunt, Akai Gurley.

There were the names from the same time we did not hear as well—Tanisha Anderson, an unarmed Black woman killed by Cleveland police. Aura Rain Rosser, killed in Ann Arbor. Black women and Black trans people are subject to state and police violence as well as intimate violence in their own homes and communities, and they are often erased from the public outcry. In this way, we lose the connections between state violence and the violence we inflict on one another, which serves to uphold the state.

Another name is added to this litany of death and mourning every twenty-eight hours. Every twenty-eight hours, a Black person is killed by law enforcement or white vigilantes, according to the Malcolm X Grassroots Movement's *Operation Ghetto Storm: 2012 Annual Report on the extrajudicial killing of 313 Black people by police, security guards and vigilantes.* The FBI's own 2012 data admits that white police killed a Black person almost twice a week for a seven-year period. And during Jim Crow segregation, a Black person was lynched every four days in this country. History is not just the past, but a living legacy, continuing to crush the breath from our lungs.

We say we prepare our children for the future. But really, we lie to our children about the present, shield their eyes from looking directly into the sun. We know they would never willingly emerge from the womb if they knew the truth. And once they learn the truth, it becomes a struggle to keep them here, on this planet. Black children, especially, seem to be born with terminator seeds planted deep in their bellies, seeds activated by lack of resources, decent education, adequate housing, lack of jobs, opportunity, dignity, respect, freedom, self-determination—lack of their faces reflected back at them in anything other than a mug shot shown on the 5 o'clock news. We tear at the faces we are told are the enemy's. We tear at our own faces.

And while prisoners are overwhelmingly Black and brown, prisons themselves dominate all of our landscapes. Rural white towns devastated by the flight of capital overseas, by a globalization that too often makes the world tight as a noose around working necks, have looked to prison developers as prophets. Blue-collar industrial workers based in U.S. urban settings used to be necessary for the stability of the U.S. economy. But corporations have gone global, exploiting communities of color across continents, enacting a typhoon of monetary destruction that sends waves of economic refugees to our shores. As Chicano emcee Olmeca rapped, "You must be stupid/ No one crosses a desert cause they want to. It's a necessity/ A sacrifice for the family/ You don't call 'em illegals/ Call 'em economic refugees."

The working class here in the U.S. has shifted faces. No longer white male factory machinists with lined faces and heavy gloves; now they are immigrant, brown. Often women. Cleaning the messes we do not see, which we work so hard not to see. Robin D.G. Kelley wrote in his contribution to *Race, Class and Gender: An Anthology*:

> In a world of manufacturing, sweatshops are making a huge comeback, particularly in the garment industry and electronics assembling plants... These workers are more likely to be brown and female than the old blue-collar white boys we are so accustomed to seeing in popular culture.

Communities of color that are not being exploited for their labor are left with double and triple rates of unemployment when compared to the national average. Ruth Wilson Gilmore wrote in *Golden Gulag*, "Convicts are deindustrialized cities' working or workless poor." Black unemployment is more than double that of whites. In devastated urban areas, it is much higher. Kelley stated, "The ghetto is the last place to find American workers." Contrary to the message that things get better for Black and brown, this is the highest rate of unemployment in almost thirty years. As reggae prophet Bob Marley warned us, "A hungry man is an angry man." So what is to be done with this surplus, unneeded labor, this hunger simmering into rage?

America used to make cars. Now we make prisoners.

"Not in our backyard!" was the past response to the faintest whiff of a prison near rural white town limits. Now towns clamor for an institution, outbidding each other to provide the most enticing package. Prisons mean jobs, economic stimulation, normalcy returned to downsized lives. That's what the brochures say. They don't read the fine print. They don't know the majority of people building the prison will be out-of-area contractors, most of the guards will be hired from surrounding areas, and those who are "lucky" enough to land a job will bring violence home. Prison is not something you clock out of, you cannot hang it up at the end of the night next to your uniform shirt. The increased rates of intimate violence, drug and alcohol addiction, assaults and suicide in prison towns bleed that truth.

There was a time I believed prisons existed to rehabilitate people, to make our communities safer. I thought they might need tweaking now and then, but what system didn't? I thought bad apples sometimes infiltrated, but there were ways of rooting them out. The prisons I have been to, the hands that have held onto mine a moment longer than necessary, the stacks of prisoner mail that crowd my desk no matter how many I answer, all contradict that belief even more than the books I have read and the lectures I have attended. When I saw for the first time (but not the last) a mother sobbing and clutching her son when visiting hours were up, only to be physically pried off and escorted out by guards, I knew nothing about that made me safer. This is the heart of this country's prison system. And the prison system has become the heart of America.

* * *

I got to my California small town motel room late the night before my visit. I robotically unpacked my small bag. Though I would be visiting both days it was allowed, I had only brought one pair of pants: my black pinstriped interview pants. They were the only pair of pants I owned that weren't jeans. At this prison, you weren't allowed to wear denim. That was what the prisoners wore, and the administration feared—I was told—a clothing swap under the ever-present eyes of the guards and the all-seeing gaze of the surveillance cameras, allowing the prisoner to make a break for freedom. It was a security risk, and the regulation was necessary for the smooth running of the institution, and for the safety of the larger community. But only in Oregon, New Jersey, and California. In New York, Pennsylvania, and Texas, security and safety wore a completely different outfit, so my jeans were regulation approved there.

These arbitrary guidelines, which must be followed to the smallest detail, have all blurred in my mind, until I forgot where I am allowed to wear open-toed shoes and which metal detector was set off by my lip ring. For the sake of my sanity and for simplicity, I developed one outfit that worked at every prison I have visited (so far): black tank top with a red button down long sleeved shirt, the pinstriped pants, black tennis shoes, and no jewelry other than my lip and ear piercings

(I found if I don't add additional metal, the detectors won't go off). Like the prisoners, I created my own prison uniform; I wear it summer or winter, sun or hail.

At the motel, I finished packing. I lay down in bed, flipping through the endless chatter of cable television, my mind crowded with thoughts of the two disparate individuals I would see the next day: my adopted brother Kakamia Jahad Imarisha, and James McElroy, nicknamed Jimmy Mac, a New York Irish mobster (I will refer to him as Mac in this text, for clarity). I would see Mac first, then my brother.

Mac was a hit man who worked for the Gambino family, a part of the nucleus of what then U.S. Attorney for the Southern District of New York Rudolph Giuliani dubbed "the most savage organization in the long history of New York City gangs." Mac was a member of the feared Irish Mob, the Westies. The Westies ran Hell's Kitchen from 1966 until 1988 with a brutal yet simple motto: "No corpus delecti, no investigation." They cut up the bodies of their victims, stuffed them in plastic black garbage bags and tossed them into the Hudson River on a small island they dubbed "the graveyard."

This was the man I was interviewing, thanks to Kakamia, who was doing time with Mac in this maximum security institution where Mac, a federal prisoner, had been transferred "for his protection." Mac was in California rather than closer to his home of New York City because he and the other Westies had worked for the Mafia, specifically for John Gotti, the most powerful don in the underworld at the time. Mac testified against Gotti after his and the other Westies' convictions. The federal prison system shipped him west to ensure he would not become a body to be hidden, himself.

Mac turned down an interview with *60 Minutes* and the *New York Times*, but agreed to talk to me because I was "almost family," as he said in his letter letting me know I had been approved for visitation. I was excited to write a piece about him. The idea of being his family made me more than a little uneasy.

* * *

"What did you say?" I said, my embarrassment and exhaustion making me as curt as the blonde guard glowering at me.

"That underwire I made you cut out of your bra when it made the metal detector go off—you can't just throw it away in the bathroom like you did. I need you to get it, bring it to me. I will give you a slip that shows you checked it in, and when you leave, it will be returned to you." The guard clipped her words, as if not to waste any more breath on me than was absolutely necessary.

"But I don't want the underwire back!" My voice peaked with frustration. And it was true: I didn't. I was angry at myself for forgetting the most basic component of my prison uniform: a sports bra, sans underwire. I had already ripped up a brand new bra to meet regulations. I did not relish the thought of going back into the cramped bathroom, rummaging around in the trash with the used tampons and dirty crumpled tissue paper to pull out two small Us of metal, just so I could get them back at the end of the day. What was I going to do, sew a whole new bra just to put them in?

"This is prison policy." Her tone, laced with a hint of malice, suggested she was addressing an unruly and slow five-year-old. "If you do not follow procedure, you will not only not be allowed into this facility at this time, I will flag you so that you will not be allowed back in the facility until we know that you will properly follow the rules established for your safety and the security of this institution."

I swallowed the anger and rebellion that rose up. I reminded myself that every time any prisoner came to the visiting room to see me, they were strip searched and sometimes body cavity searched upon entering and leaving. I'm getting off easy, I told myself.

I marched stiffly to the bathroom, not making eye contact with any of the faces watching. Unlike the guards' hostility or detachment, the other visitors' faces showed understanding, fear, and relief—they knew next time it could be them. Setting my mouth in a hard line, I reached into the garbage can, willing myself to actively not think about what my hands might be touching. I finally brushed the thin metal strips, pulled them out. After burning the top layer of skin off my hands with the scalding hot faucet water, I returned to the wooden desk, the underwire from my bra clipped wings digging into my palm, and unceremoniously plunked them down on the table.

The guard swept them into a plastic bag and paper-clipped it to my ID, which went back in a drawer. She took her time writing out a yellow slip that would entitle me to reclaim my valuable property. As she handed it to me, she said, without a trace of a smirk, "Welcome to this correctional institution. Enjoy your visit."

* * *

After walking through three locked metal doors and showing my ID four times, I entered the prison visiting room. It resembled a school gymnasium with linoleum floors and stucco walls. The room was full of dingy white plastic tables and chairs. Visitors crowded into the space looked like they were on a picnic gone awry. A guard sat lazily at the front desk, elevated so you had to look up as you handed him your paperwork. He assigned me table number six, in the middle of the room, then promptly went back to staring off into nothing.

I sat, nervously smoothing the front of my "uniform." I tried to look like the professional and experienced journalist I was—not the easiest task, given my multiple piercings and streaks of blue dye crowning my large afro. A punk rocker in my high school days, I had decided there were additional ways to fight the system that existed outside of mosh pits, but I still clung stubbornly to my counter-culture roots.

The metallic sound of bolts sliding from the roller pounded like thunder, signifying a prisoner was coming out. From the ugly flaking blue door stepped someone who could only be Mac: late 50s; short but wiry; light, thinning hair combed stylishly. He walked like the former boxer turned enforcer he was, jawline set hard and penetrating baby blues sweeping the room. They fell on me, and his mask melted into a smile.

I stood awkwardly and went for the handshake, which he promptly swept aside in favor of a brief hug. "Ah," Mac said as he sank into the plastic chair. "I woulda known you anywhere, you look just like your brother." We get that all the time, which is funny since Kakamia and I aren't related by blood. Instead of correcting Mac (not the best start to an interview I decided), I offered to buy him something from the vending machines with my plastic bag full of quarters. He accepted a coffee. As I stood up, hefting the baggie, he joked, "I coulda used that real well in my old line of work." I walked away, gingerly feeling the weight of the makeshift weapon I had unwittingly carried in. Thank goodness they made me check that underwire, or I could have done some real damage.

* * *

We, the general public, take prisons for granted, and at the same time we try our very best not to think too hard about prisons themselves: what happens inside of them, what leads up to someone going into prison. We allow ourselves to be lulled to sleep at night by the fairy tale that only bad people end up in prison: as long as we are good, we don't have to worry about what goes on behind the walls. In this tale, it is only individual bad decisions that land people in prison; there are no larger forces at work. As Angela Davis wrote, "The prison…functions ideologically as an abstract site into which undesirables are deposited, relieving us of the responsibility of thinking about the real issues afflicting those communities from which prisoners are drawn in such disproportionate numbers."

If we begin to get troublesome thoughts, looking at the statistics that show that seventy percent of those incarcerated are people of color, wondering about communities left with gaping wounds where people once were, we always have the nightly news to comfort us. The news obliterates centuries of inequality and oppression, leaving only Black and brown hands in cuffs, shown at higher rate than whites, despite the fact that whites commit more crimes because they are the majority of the nation's population. Eighty-one percent of Americans get their understanding of crime from the media, rather than personal experience, according to "The News Media's Influence on Criminal Justice Policy," and Americans believe corporate media, especially television news, to be reliable and credible.

Over the past twenty years of doing work around incarceration, I have learned many things first-hand about prisons, things not shown in the news. I have learned rules and regulations. I have learned tension and despair. I have learned brutality and monotony. Most of all, I have learned many prisoners' lives were cages before they ever stepped into a prison. I have learned that poverty confines, hunger contains, homelessness chokes, powerlessness restricts, and oppression destroys.

I have learned we all have prisons in our lives, and most of us are too frightened to look directly at them.

And I have learned people do not stop being people when they are issued a prison ID number. The images we are given of prisoners are so dark, we can no longer distinguish the features anymore. But each person in prison has a face, a story, and a heart that hurts in the night and has the capacity to expand beyond ribcages.

In the summer of 2004, my sister died after back surgery. The doctors gave her a clean bill of health after the operation and discharged her. While she slept, a blood clot traveled through her body to her brain and killed her. A few months earlier, she and I went to visit my mother, diagnosed with breast cancer. My sister and I did not know if it would be the last time we spent time with her. We wanted to make sure she saw her children all together again before she left this world. Little did we know we would suffer a crippling blow as a family, just not the one we feared then.

When I received the call, I was stunned into immobility. My family was devastated, my mother inconsolable. I was thousands of miles from her and the rest of the family. My friends rained love and support down on me.

But the gentlest care I received came in envelopes stamped "Inmate Mail." Letters already slit open and read by authoritative eyes, they were sent to me only after being deemed safe. They were not safe, though. The words of support were subversive. They continued the fundamental shift of how I felt about the prison system, and the prisons all of us live under.

This book is my attempt to draw back the faces erased in the flashing red of squad cars, shaded by gun turrets, and stamped out by the letters "DOC."

If the prison system is a cure worse than the disease, or not even ever intended to be a cure, then what else is there? How do we as communities react when someone harms another? How do we set up systems to make whole what was broken, beyond clanging locks?

There is a growing movement of organizations and communities exploring alternatives to prisons. Alternatives that keep the community safe while recognizing the humanity of those who have done harm. Many of the alternatives to prisons focus on drugs. Drug courts.

Addiction treatment services. Counseling. Decriminalization. This is not surprising, given that almost half of all people in federal prisoners are there for nonviolent drug offenses according to the Federal Bureau of Prisons' own statistics. The astounding explosion of the prison population, up 700 percent since 1970 says Pew Charitable Trusts, is disproportionately due to the War on Drugs. The American Medical Association argues that drugs and drug addiction should be understood a health crisis, not an invading army.

The majority of people who are in prison are there for nonviolent offenses. In fact in 2006, thirty-five percent of all folks going into state prisons were there on parole violations, not because they had committed new crimes, says the National Conference for State Legislatures. For states like California, that number is closer to two-thirds.

The reality is that the vast majority of people in prison were never tried in front of a judge. Over ninety percent of people in prison took a plea bargain. With harsher sentencing laws and mandatory minimums to wield like flaming swords, prosecutors stand over defendants, who often have not even glimpsed their defense attorney, and offer them the lesser of the most evil. Less than ten percent of prisoners were tried by a "jury of their peers"; the rest had trial by prosecutor, and rather than risk ten, twenty-five, or life in prison, they take a plea. Innocence or guilt did not even enter into this equation.

What the nightly news does not show is that crime rates have steadily declined for decades. We are told by media and law enforcement we are less safe now than we have ever been. The truth is, crime rates are closer to those of the 1950s, according to the FBI's own statistics, though we definitely are not being shown images of *Leave It To Beaver* when we turn on news programming.

Prisons are overflowing with folks there for nonviolent drug offenses, who were not convicted in a court of law. That is the reality. But the reality is also that humans do harm one another. This harm is often horizontal violence enacted upon the tender flesh of those who are already marginalized, with the least access to institutional resources. The majority of this harm, against those who are poor, of color, young, women, and trans and queer (and especially those who live at the intersections of these identities), is never reported. It would not be taken seriously by law enforcement if it were. Much of this harm is caused by law enforcement and other agents of the state. For harm done within oppressed communities, convictions would only result in more Black and brown people being stolen from already-destabilized communities.

So sometimes people hurt each other. Horribly. And then what? What of those who have done damage—sometimes unimaginable—to others? When do we stop seeing a human being and see only a monster, only a prisoner?

For this book, I have not chosen stories that fit easily into our preconceived societal notions of "good" and "bad." I know many innocent prisoners, wrongfully convicted. It would be easier to argue for their release, and to challenge prisons solely based on their experiences. Harder, however, is to take stories of people who are in some way guilty by their own admission.

There is my adopted brother, who denies being responsible for the crime he was convicted of. He does admit to being involved, at the age of sixteen, in a plan to commit murder. There is Mac, who fully admits to engaging in the heinous act of ending another human being's life (in fact, many human beings) for money. Mac especially is one of the stories that fuels the prison system, what prison abolitionist Ruth Morris called "the terrible few" that politicians reference to push forward more "tough on crime" legislation. Anyone who believes in exploring and creating alternatives to incarceration will eventually be hit in the face with people like Mac, perhaps even with people like my brother. Rather than run from it, these are the stories we have to explore, the transformations and the redemptions, if we are to fundamentally shift how we think about crime and punishment in this country.

I have also included my experiences in this book, experiences of working to build alternatives, specifically around sexual assault, the most common violent harm done and the most underreported. I've included my experiences of being wounded by someone I trusted, of attempting to put my politics into practice, and finding out how much messier and more painful real life is on your skin than on paper. I've included my struggles with the meaning of redemption, accountability, and forgiveness.

These are the stories of Mac, Kakamia, and myself, but we are characters. In this book, the we I write about is not us; we are not fully ourselves. As much as we try, no writer can ever capture the fullness of complexities that is a human being. These are the Mac and Kakamia I see, the histories I have learned, have imagined based on countless hours of interviews and research. These things I believe to be true, well aware that in reality nothing is true, and even our own memories can be fiction. Any nonfiction book must be read partially as fiction, for we all tell ourselves stories to make sense of our lives. And so the same is true for me. For my stories and the people in them. I have tried to be as honest as possible, with myself as much as everyone else.

In the spirit of accountability, I have also changed some names in this book, of people, places, and events. I struggled with this as a writer. Haven't I, in writing a creation of nonfiction, sworn to "tell the whole truth and nothing but the truth"? But I realized two things finally: sometimes we get shackled by too much fact, unable to break free and see the larger truths. Secondly, our stories are never just our own. I am, through this book, telling dozens of people's stories tangentially, the majority of whom did not agree to that. In my quest to have difficult, complex, and painful discussions, I do not want to cause more trauma than necessary. Rather than the courtroom oath, I have taken the ethos of the Hippocratic oath: either help, or at least do no harm. In this spirit, I have worked to tell these stories responsibility, while still maintaining honesty and accuracy.

As part of this, I have included myself, which was not the original idea of this narrative. I do not know how to write people not in relation to myself. Every story I was told, every emotion I saw flit across someone's face, I used myself as a sounding board for human connection. How would I have felt? What would I have done? Who would I have become under different forces of gravity? This is ego most certainly, but also an attempt at honesty. I do not want to knowingly lie. And I believe objectivity to be the worst lie of them all. I am not objective. But I am deeply, completely and wholly invested.

I did not want to just recount dry facts from newspaper archives; I wanted to make these stories breathe, and when necessary, bleed. From extensive interviews with Kakamia and Mac, and through mining my own memories, I have reconstructed scenes from all of our lives. And reconstruction is just another way of saying imagining with its foundation in fact. As much as we research and retell history, we imagine it as well. I have tried to imagine with the fewest factual errors possible.

The title of this book, *Angels with Dirty Faces*, comes from a 1938 James Cagney film. Cagney plays Rocky Sullivan, a young man growing up in early 1900s Hell's Kitchen. Together with his best friend Jerry Connolly, Rocky got into the kind of trouble poor kids in a city got into. They stole to eat. Then they robbed a railroad car. The police gave chase. Rocky saves Jerry's life by pulling him out of the way of a steam train. Rocky gets caught by the police. His friend Jerry, who could run faster, does not. Rocky goes to reform school, graduates to more crime, spends more time in prison, and becomes one of the most notorious gangsters. Jerry stays in the neighborhood and becomes a priest.

Eventually, Rocky returns to the old neighborhood. He and Jerry spend time together. Rocky meets a woman. He becomes a hero to a group of young boys. But the life he was dealt pulls him back in. He kills another gangster. He is tried and sentenced to the electric chair.

Jerry comes to visit Rocky before his execution. He asks Rocky for one last favor before he dies: to pretend to die as a "rotten sniveling coward." Jerry asks for the group of young boys who look up to Rocky, and for the young boys across the country. Jerry asks Rocky to destroy the image of heroic outlaw they have created in their head. He asks Rocky to show himself as human and broken, so that they will not follow in his footsteps.

Rocky refuses. "You're trying to take away the only thing I have left." All he has to hold on to is the image of himself he created out of his pain.

And yet, after Rocky is strapped into the chair, he begs. He pleads for his life. He dies crying. Begging. The reporters capture it. Write it in the paper:

> At the fatal stroke of eleven p.m. Rocky was led through the little green door of death. No sooner had he entered the death chamber, than he tore himself from the guard's grasp, flung himself on the floor, screaming for mercy. And as they dragged him to the electric chair, he clawed wildly at the floor with agonized shrieks.
>
> In contrast to his former heroics, Rocky Sullivan died a coward.

The boys are disillusioned. Rocky was not the icon they thought. In the last scene of the film, Jerry reads the account of Rocky's execution to the young boys. The priest tells them, "Pray with me. Pray with me for a boy who couldn't run as fast as I could."

Rocky Sullivan is the most human and complex portrayal of a gangster I have ever seen in popular culture. The character allows nuances to live next to contradictions. The film allows for a priest to love a gangster, and for a gangster to show nobility and sacrifice in his last moments of life. Most importantly, the film tells us no one is born a gangster. It is through circumstances that gangsters are forged. And sometimes the smallest thing, like whether or not you can run faster than your friend, determines the course of your life.

But even more important, no one is beyond a taste of redemption. While some believe Rocky just broke at the end, and was truly pleading for his life, I in my heart know this not to be the case. I know Rocky instead did the bravest thing he had probably ever done in his entire renegade life. He made a decision to tell the truth. To remove the façade. To show the pain he carried, masked as bravado. To beg, not truly for his life, but for the lives of those boys who looked up to him.

That is what this book is about.

Who among us is beyond humanity? Can we hear another's pain and trauma, and still think of them only as evil? And if not, how will we deal with it, when we learn the monsters are themselves frightened, bruised children?

During Kakamia's 2008 parole hearing, where he was denied for the fourth time and given a two-year hit after eighteen years in prison, he looked at the parole board and said,

> I'm not the best. I'm not going to come in here with this shining record. I've been incarcerated over half of my life. I do the best that I can. And every day I strive not to become that individual walking that track.
>
> Every day I strive not to become just another number.

Kakamia

WHAT I DIDN'T KNOW ABOUT MY BROTHER

MY ADOPTED BROTHER KAKAMIA JAHAD IMARISHA IS CHARMING, charismatic, and complicated—riddled with gaps of darkness and pain that twenty-five years in prison have carved into him. These chasms have been left by being arrested at sixteen and charged as an adult. A sentence of fifteen-to-life hanging like a broken arm. Slowly, these gaps are filled in with fear: the thought of dying in prison floods into the void left as each passing year drains away.

During one visit Kakamia, who never seems to change in my eyes, pointed to his head. "I'm getting old, Wa," he moaned. For the first time, I saw swathes of gray glistening in the black. It scared me more than it scared him.

Survival in prison is a stroll on a razor blade. Kakamia calls it "a warehouse for people society does not want. *Amistad* for today," referencing the famous slave ship where the captured Africans rebelled. You are not meant to survive—not whole, not sane, not with a loving heart. Those who do survive find whatever means they can. To make it, you have to rebuild yourself: rebuild the old you, whatever flaws and weaknesses you brought in, mortar in the gaps of the wall. It's a never-ending job. Each day new holes are smashed in by the confinement, the inhumanity, the unnaturalness of everything that touches your skin or your tongue, that reaches your eyes or your ears, that lives under your skin and comes out when you're sleeping late at night, the lights from the tier burning behind your eyelids.

My brother recreated himself so fully, for years I did not know where the renovations took place. In the shadow of prison, I have had to confront my assumptions, my own weaknesses. I have had to force myself to see the person Kakamia was, the person he has become, and explore the fault lines between what is fact and what is true. I've had to learn these are not always the same thing.

My brother…even to call him that is a lie that speaks to a deeper truth. Our status as family is not born out of blood or bound by legal documents. Instead, it was a creation we constructed, two lost children in search of a heart that would understand.

Kakamia and I adopted each other as siblings when I was fifteen years old. We'd found each other through a progressive California newspaper I subscribed to. He was advertising his artwork, trying to earn some extra money for the overpriced prison commissary, trying to connect with a world beyond the walls. I was searching for a connection to my Black heritage, living in a small Oregon town, the child of a white mother and an absentee Black father. I thought I was just buying some Afrocentric work to decorate my room. I ended up mail-ordering a brother.

The first art piece he sent me was an African warrior, spear and shield in hand, outlined by the continent of Africa. He called me "my African sista" when he closed the letter. It was one of my first real connections to a Black cultural context. And even our racial identities are complicated. At the time I wondered if I was "really" Black, while his mix of Irish-mutt whiteness and convoluted Puerto Rican Black lineages marked him firmly as "other."

I have seen pictures of his mother. I saw my own mother staring back, the smiling folds of blonde white womanhood hardened by poverty and decisions made to carry and care for brown children of their making, our color staining and tainting their whiteness.

I have seen a picture of his father. One. Same trim frame, though Kakamia's has been built up through countless hours of dips and pushups while in solitary, free weights and chest presses when he had access to the yard. They have the same jaunty way of throwing a leg forward and leaning back, as if daring the world to step over the line they've drawn.

His father's skin glows much lighter than Kakamia's, undarkened by the ever-present California sun. Biology being the convoluted creature it is, I cannot help but wonder at the combinations that produced him.

My own birth was the controlled test group, not the variant. My family is a color test used in elementary school: "Here is what happens when you take white and black: You get brown." Vanilla/chocolate swirl, no sugar added. That was the sign I stole from a Baskin-Robbins and tacked up under the only picture I have of my mother, my father, and me. No sugar added. Kakamia always teased me, saying I prove girls are made of salt and steel and everything real.

I loved his easy connection with our shared complicated Blackness, and his acerbic humor. We wrote for years, sharing more pieces of ourselves, or whatever pieces we had to offer. He sent me letters in elaborately decorated envelopes. I sent him poems about Black history and alienation. We argued about politics sometimes, but agreed serious change was non-negotiable.

We were young Black mixed-race artists who believed in something larger than ourselves. How could we not end up family?

I feel more strongly connected to Kakamia than many of my actual relatives. When people say to me, "your brother," I think of Kakamia before I think of my brother born to me of blood. That is the truth. The fact is that our kinship exists only in our minds. We reshaped the world we lived in, re-imagined it to fit our needs. When Kakamia tells stories to people about what I was like as a child, recycling tales I have shared with him and inventing new ones, I do not contradict him. It is true—even when it is not a fact.

Our narrative is something we have constructed together. It is a story we are both writing together, but we can not look at each other's notes, and are left to guess at what comes next. As the years passed, and I reached out to more people to support Kakamia's art and poetry, support his appeals for parole, his growing activism, I faced questions that drew blank stares and screeching wheels in my mind. I realized I could not speak of my brother's story, because I honestly did not know it.

My brother created fictions that were truth—not to steal or to dominate, but to keep pieces of himself alive and whole through the darkest nights. This makes him utterly like every other human on the face of this grasping planet.

Kakamia wrote a poem called "Memories":

> Damn, the memories
> No matter how real or made up
> They sustain me.
> They have become my reality regardless.
> The touch, smell, feel, passion, pain
> They are now the truth.

My brother has survived so many traumas, most of which began long before he walked through a prison door, or perhaps every door he walked through has been a prison door. Memories can be the bars that cage you in. Like runaway Africans before us, he moved swiftly, under the cover of night, escaping the shackles of memory, following the North Star's promise of a clean dawn. Its commandment: you must build anew.

When I spoke openly to Kakamia of his puzzle piece past, his response was vitriolic. "You are calling me a liar," he said. Shocked, I did not understand the erasure of voice by race and poverty welling up in him. The bile of a society that tells him he has no control over his past, and even less over his future, that says he is only what they say and nothing more.

"I thought I was calling you a survivor," I responded helplessly.

"You're asking all these questions now, making me pull up things I buried away. Why now? Why after all these years?" he asked.

I told him I had been scared before, that in some ways I still was. I did not explain of what. I didn't have the words to express the complexities of the creeping fear in my stomach—the fear of hurting him, of offending him, of learning something I couldn't unlearn. The fear of seeing my chosen family disintegrate like ash under my touch.

"I was scared," I repeated again, because there was nothing else to say.

Kakamia breathed deep, exhaled forgiveness at my ignorance, my privilege, my judgment. He gave me the gift he has always given me:

unconditional support. He told me to go in search of the truth. To ask any questions I wanted. That he would do his best to answer them, as well as he remembered.

"I don't know what the fuck I remember anymore," his voice thick on the scratching phone line. "If I had to live with everything that had been done to me, I wouldn't be here talking to you, Wa. It wasn't enough to deny it—I had to obliterate it."

"You made yourself into the man you want to be," I responded, nodding, though there was no one to see me.

"Is it that simple?" his question full of doubt. "Is it that noble?"

"No," I said. "But it's that human."

"Then ask."

"*You have sixty seconds remaining on this call.*"

The recorded message came abruptly, telling us our fifteen minutes had bled away, too quickly as always. We rushed to get in our good-byes and I love yous and we'll talk soons.

After taking a week or two to reflect and work up my courage, I began simply, in a letter to him, hesitantly. What were you convicted of exactly? When? Where? How old were you?

I felt as if I were interviewing a stranger rather than someone I considered closer than blood.

People who have not done work supporting prisoners, who do not have loved ones behind bars, probably cannot believe that I had called this man my brother for more than fifteen years, but had never asked these questions. But behind the walls, you do not ask what someone has done. If someone volunteers, wants to talk about their case (usually the ones who believe themselves to be innocent), then you listen and provide support. But you do not ask. Because whatever they did to get there, it does not change the conditions they endure. Whatever they did, it does not change the fact that they are human, and that if they actually did harm to another human being, they have no doubt been paid back in full and then some for it. Most of the prisoners I interact with are involved in organizing behind the walls, and are being even more harshly punished for doing so. Like my brother, they have worked to be reborn behind walls, so they might make sense and use of their life.

I can tell Kakamia's mental state from his handwriting. When you rely so much on letters for communication, you become adept at reading more than just words on a page. Hastily written back, curt but caring, loving wrapped up in irritation and frustration: "Why didn't you just check the paperwork I sent you years ago? That's all there."

I reread the short response. And again.

I did not believe him.

If he had sent me anything, I would have remembered it, I thought incredulously. Why would he tell me something he knows is not true? How could I possibly forget receiving the answers to all these questions?

But before I shot off a reply full of emotion and short on intellect, I cracked open my filing cabinet, crammed to the brim with letters from prisoners, faded articles on new criminal justice legislation, legislation that was now as musty as the paper the article was printed on.

I pulled out the immense manila folder marked "Kakamia," stuffed to overflowing. I rifled past notes and cards, poems and envelopes decorated in pencil drawn roses.

It was there.

It was all there, just as Kakamia had said. The transcript from his sentencing trial, part of the arrest report, pieces of his crime discussed at a parole hearing. He had worked hard to share the truth with me, and I had worked just as hard to push it away. Pushed it so far I could not even remember the act of erasure.

"Why didn't you just ask me, Wa? Why do I have to wait until now to find out you have all these questions?"

Why didn't I ask?

It was not only that as a rule I do not ask people the details of their crimes, or even what they were convicted of. It was not only the fact that even as a journalist, it was still difficult to ask the hard questions, to see fear or pain or anger invade someone's eyes as I jot down notes.

Honestly, I did not want to know the answers. I did not even want to know the questions. I had done Internet searches on Kakamia Jahad Imarisha (a name I gave to him); his artwork came up, his poetry, the art opening I planned for him, his portrait of us. I had searched for the reborn him. I had never done a search using his birth name. I did not want to see what might have come up: bloody crime scene photos, my brother's mug shot. Accounts of the destruction he helped create.

"What are you in for?" We do not ask this. But I understand now that for those of us who love people on the inside, not asking those questions protects us as much (or more) than the prisoner. It kept me from seeing my brother through the eyes of his victims. I did not know if I could see him through those eyes, and feel the same way about him. I wanted and desperately needed to see Kakamia as the prisoner who, against all odds, worked to turn his life around, who was committed to changing himself and this world, who used his art as an instrument to implement that change. And he is that.

The truth is always more complicated.

THE TRUTH AND
NOTHING BUT...

"First, I would like just to make a brief statement on behalf of my client, and I think it's very important for the Court and for the family who's present, to know that I've had an opportunity to spend time with the defendant, at times when he's been much more quiet, much more remorseful, much more insightful."

Kakamia watched his lawyer pleading for his life. With his big Santa-like beard and thick glasses, he didn't look like your typical lawyer, but he had worked for years as both a prosecutor and a criminal defense attorney. Kakamia's mother had hoped his years of experience would change the course of her son's disintegrating future.

"I just want the Court to realize that this is a person who came into this system, quite frankly a boy, a child. A very immature young man that did a tremendous wrong, and he has learned a great and hopefully a life-changing lesson, here," Kakamia's lawyer continued.

Funny, Kakamia didn't feel like a child. At nineteen, he felt like a grown man. How many men could say they had already done three years in jail at the age of nineteen on a conspiracy to commit murder charge?

While he swaggered hard in the jail about his time in, when he was alone in his cell, it wasn't pride he felt. He missed his family, despite his fractured past. His mom had tried so hard to raise the bail. But it just hadn't been enough. Seems like it was never enough. Innocent until proven guilty, he snorted mentally. Even if they had decided to let him go, he still would have lost three years of his life. But of course, he wasn't going home. After all the things he'd done, and been through… He looked down at his forearms. He saw the kiss of razor-blade to his skin, old faded lines crossing his flesh, along with new red intersections. He'd done them himself. Not deep enough to cause damage, but enough to feel. To control the pain. Be in charge of it for once. Be in charge of his own body. Scars on the outside to match the scars on the inside. Maybe then someone would notice.

Just surviving growing up in Crown Heights, Brooklyn in the 1980s had been an accomplishment, though they didn't hand out certificates. He had heard some of the older Jewish people in the neighborhood reminiscing about when it was a good place to live—clean, safe, friendly. He knew that meant before Black people moved in. By the time he was there in the 1970s, the neighborhood was mixed, and the Jewish residents were the only whites stubbornly holding on. There were clashes between the different groups. He had been involved in more than a few himself.

The neighborhood fell from comfortable to dirt poor. It had to be that way for him, his mom, and his sister to live there. His mom worried about him so much, gave him a curfew and strict instructions. She held down two jobs his whole life, and when she wasn't working, she was trying to find a way to block out the pain.

His eyes in the courtroom looked over to his mom, who sat in the first row, twisting the banister with her hands, as if trying to wring some compassion out of the court. She was short and solid, with a hearty laugh and gold brown hair that curled like sunrays around her head. He always teased her that she must have some Puerto Rican in her Irish heritage, to get hair like that. "I don't know, ma, you know they're always talking about Black Irish—there might be something to it."

He got so tired of having to explain to people that yes, that was his mom, yes he was mixed, yes it was Puerto Rican and white, but Puerto Ricans were Black too, don't you know? Didn't enslaved Black people get sent from Africa to Puerto Rico? Wasn't there voluntary mixing happening between the Indigenous folks and the Africans, and less-than-voluntary mixing between those two and the Spanish? He felt Black folks in his neighborhood looked at him with suspicion, because of his white mother and his light skin. And the Puerto Ricans looked at him with suspicion because of his lack of Spanish and his white mom. It would have been easier if his father had been around to point at for verification. Hell, it would have just been easier if his father had been around. He could have helped with the bills, which crushed his mother to the floor so hard, the only way she could lift herself up was with a drink or a snort of something.

But his dad was locked up. Again. He had been out all of five years of Kakamia's life. Most of the time he was at one of the maximum prisons in upstate New York, and they didn't have the money to travel up to see him. And by the age of thirteen, Kakamia was no longer interested in him. He left us, he had told himself, so he can go fuck himself for all I care.

What would his father think of him now, Kakamia wondered, looking down at the orange prison jumpsuit the state gave him. He had been in jail for almost three years, first awaiting trial and now awaiting sentencing. If he had money, he could have been bailed out. If he had had money... So many of the thoughts throughout his life had started with those words.

Three years. 1,059 days. That was three birthdays. He could now vote, he thought sarcastically. Smoke legally. Die for his country. And kill. Only for his country though. If he had done what he'd done on the battlefield, he would be a hero right now, instead of this... The shackles on his ankles clanked dully.

Kakamia tuned back to the sentencing trial swirling around him. He wasn't really part of it. He was like this table: a thing, to be moved around. That's what he'd felt like, moved from jail to jail, from the California Youth Authority to the adult jail when they decided they would try him as an adult.

They had tried both of them, him and Bobby, as adults, even though at the time of the crime Kakamia was sixteen and Bobby was seventeen. Sixteen years old. Joining the ranks of too many smooth faces that have never been touched by a razor, living life with shadows of bars on their soft cheeks. Mike Males recounted the story of the first youth sent to the electric chair, tried and convicted as an adult in his book, *Framing Youth: 10 Myths About the Next Generation*. The youth asked for a cigarette as his final request. The guard admonished him, saying he was too young to smoke. Then the state electrocuted him.

Kakamia and Bobby were facing murder, attempted murder, and conspiracy. It was the conspiracy that really scared Kakamia. It woke him up with cold sweats at night, hoping with his eyes squeezed tight that he would open them and be back home. Conspiracy carried a sentence of life without parole. No chance of going home again. That's it. First strike and you're out.

After all, this was his first charge. Of course it was a big one. It hadn't seemed real at the time, not while he stood in the entryway of what Bobby's parents called "their dream home." Kakamia had never been in a house so nice before. He thought of the bedroom he, his mother, and his sister shared back home, and worse, the car they had shared for a few weeks when the bills got the best of them.

It hadn't been real to him until he heard the first shot rip the air. And another. And another. It had not been real until he saw Bobby's face emerging from the bedroom. It was real when Bobby dropped the gun into Kakamia's hand. It was real when Kakamia felt the heat from the recently fired barrel. The gun curled up in his hand, warm like hot blood was rushing through its casing. The air smelled like burnt metal and closed doors. That's when it began to feel real. And that's when it was too late.

Kakamia remembered his friend Eric approaching him in school with this deadly proposal. He knew both Bobby and Eric, who the prosecution had described as the little devil on the shoulder, telling everyone to do it. Kakamia was much closer with Bobby: as close as he was to anyone. People liked Kakamia well enough; they thought he was charming, engaging, funny. But they also thought he was crazy. They thought that about him in New York as well. And he was proud of that—he had worked hard to cultivate crazy. After all, when you're a scrawny mixed Puerto Rican kid with a white mom addicted to drugs and alcohol in a racially charged neighborhood—shit, a racially charged country—you gotta do something.

The something he did was pick up a two-by-four during a fight with another Black kid to prove something, if only to prove he existed.

The funny thing was, Kakamia couldn't recall what the argument was about now. It seemed like so long ago, even though it was only a few years away. What Kakamia did remember was the blood that poured out of the kid's ear, how he looked lying unconscious on the ground. Mostly Kakamia remembered how everyone treated him later, nicknaming him Lumberjack. They gave him some real respect after that.

Soon after, his mom decided they needed a change of scenery, him and his four half-brothers and -sisters. Different daddies, same mom, but they were all family as far as they were concerned, regardless of the fact they looked like a color wheel, lightest to darkest.

So mom chose Sacramento: sunny California, a place of new beginnings. Everyone goes west to strike their fortune.

This is where it got them, Kakamia thought as his eyes took in his mother's face, creased and worn with stress as she stared at the judge.

When Eric approached him in the hallway at school with a proposition, he listened with an open mind.

"Hey, you wanna make some big money, I mean real easy?" Eric started out.

"Sure, who doesn't? What would I have to do?" Kakamia replied.

"Simple. Help Bobby kill his parents."

To most people this would have been a shocking statement to hear at school. And it was…the first time they heard it. But Kakamia was the third person to be asked to join in on this contract over the past week. It was a high school, word got around. Kakamia had wondered if they would approach him. He already had a speech prepared, having played the scene out in his head many times; he was kind of excited to get to use it.

"What's the plan?" He spat out the line like he was in a movie.

"They have a gun in the house. It'll be easy. Bobby will take the gun earlier and hide it. I'll drive you out there, and he'll let you in. We'll steal a TV or something to make it look like a burglary. Then you'll sneak up into the bedroom, put pillows over their faces, pull the trigger. You won't even have to see the blood. I'll drive you home, and that's it. We just wait for Bobby to collect the insurance money."

"And how much is that?"

"It's gonna be like a million for both of them, can you believe that?"

Kakamia thought about it. No more struggling, no more going without heat in the winter like when they were in New York. No more spaghetti for dinner for weeks on end. No more hearing his stomach rumble.

Kakamia already knew his options were limited. He felt like he had so much talent, but none of it saleable. He was always working on the scheme that would make them rich. His sister teased him about it constantly. His mother told him the only way to get rich was to go to school and go to college. But school had never worked for him. They moved around so much, he spent more time fighting and establishing his reputation than actually going to classes. His reading and writing weren't so good. In fact, they were awful. He had gotten this far by faking it. By the time they settled in Sacramento, he was so far behind the other students in his class, he was embarrassed to go: scared the teacher would call on him and show him up in front of the class.

He ran through the moneymaking options he'd tried as an alternative to school. It was the golden era of hip hop, and Kakamia was in the middle of it. He tried breakdancing, and he was good at it too —for once his long limbs and lighter weight were an asset, instead of a detriment like in boxing. But breakers weren't making any real money —you could put a can out and break on the street for folks walking by, but that was almost as bad as school. He had been able to get some loot out of DJing parties, but he didn't have any money for his own equipment and you couldn't borrow someone else's turntables forever. Graffiti just landed you a one-way ticket to jail, which was too bad, cause he was actually a great graffiti artist.

He'd tried to sell drugs, gotten down with the Bloods. But he knew unless he moved up fast, he'd just be a low level gangster working harder than if he had a 9 to 5, and barely scraping by. Until someone put a bullet in the back of his head.

All of this made him wide open to Eric and Bobby's plan. Plus, Kakamia really loved gangster movies. He liked to imagine himself as a Mafioso, like the ones he used to see in Little Italy in New York. And suddenly, one of his favorite movies had come to life. After all, this was a contract. He'd be a contract killer, a hit man. If that didn't sound dangerous, he didn't know what did. No one would dream of fucking with a hit man. Hit men got real respect. Hit men didn't have to worry about a cousin's wandering hands in the middle of the night, about their mother's boyfriends' heavy boots on flesh.

Kakamia had tried everything to block it all out before. Alcohol when he was eleven. He graduated to pills, cocaine, meth, crack, heroin: anything to erase his past and his present; anything to open a door in his head so he could finally escape.

None of it worked. The next morning, he would be right back in his body, track marks on his arms, eyes a little more vacant in the mirror.

Perhaps blood would finally wash him away.

"All right," Kakamia declared, "I'm in."

"But I got some terms." He steepled his fingers and leaned back. He felt so Marlon Brando in *The Godfather*. "I want $25,000 in cash when the insurance money comes in. And Bobby has to buy me and my mom a house. And a car.

"And anything else we need," Kakamia added, proud that he had thought to cover future expenses like that.

Eric and him shook hands solemnly.

"We'll be in touch soon," Eric turned to walk away.

"Hey," Kakamia called out as an afterthought. "Why does Bobby want to kill his parents? Is it just the money?" Frankly, Kakamia couldn't really imagine this being Bobby's idea. He definitely had an explosive temper, but he didn't seem like a planner. More like a "fly into a violent rage and damn the consequences" kinda guy.

Eric stopped and turned around. "Man, you know he's been grounded for almost two years cause of his grades. And they make him give them almost his whole check from his after school job to go towards household expenses. They say he'll get it back when they pay for college, but you know that's wrong. And you know his mom's the worst. She's a real bitch. She goes through his mail, listens to his phone calls. I know whenever I call over there, she's on the other line, listening to every word we say. He came to me saying he just couldn't stand to live with them anymore, he wasn't going to be able to make it to his eighteenth birthday. So I suggested he have them taken care of. And that's where you come in."

Kakamia was a little shocked. Could this kid really want to kill his mom over something so trivial? Kakamia's gangster mask faltered. He thought of his mother. Sure, things had been hard. Sure, he wished she'd been there more, that she'd protected him more, that she'd believed him more. She was the first one to tell him he was making up stories when he finally showed her the wound he had been carrying around for years.

He had wanted to leave home so many times, and had run away half a dozen. He had vowed to never talk to his mom again after particularly bad fights. But he had never imagined hurting her physically. In fact, just thinking about it now drew tears to his eyes.

Kakamia's mind and heart hardened. Yeah, but this wasn't his mom. In fact, it was better not to think of her as a mom at all. It was just a woman. No, just a...thing. Just a job to get done, a task to be completed. Nothing else.

The only way this is connected to him, Kakamia thought decisively and almost feverishly, is that it was going to make him rich. It was going to make him important. And no one will ever hurt him again.

Eric clapped Kakamia on the shoulder, and left.

* * *

Kakamia looked over at Bobby's father, sitting on the opposite side of the courtroom from Kakamia's mother. Bobby's father had a small scar on his cheek, where a bullet had bruised it deeply, but not penetrated. It was actually a miracle he lived.

Bobby's father had come to court to see Kakamia sentenced, and wanted him to get murder in the first degree. Since Kakamia was underage when the crime was committed, they couldn't give him the death penalty. But they could give him life without, which Kakamia felt was worse in some ways than the death penalty.

Kakamia fantasized about what it would be like going to the chair (he wasn't sure if that's how they did it in California, but it sounded the most dramatic). He would set his jaw and walk with confident unhurried steps. They'd strap him in, and ask if he had any last words. Sometimes in his fantasy he'd imitate one of his favorite rappers Ice Cube from the album *Death Certificate*, which came out a year after he was arrested: "Yeah, yeah I got some last words. Fuck all y'all!" Sometimes he'd smile and say, "I regret that I have but one life to give." He couldn't remember where he'd heard that line before, but he liked the sound of it.

He'd been thinking of that over and over when he was arrested, the day after the murder. Maybe that was what prompted him to tell the cops that he was the one who pulled the trigger. There had been two cops, and they had him in a room asking him a lot of questions. They called his mom but the phone had been cut off that day. She wasn't at home anyway.

They kept asking him who did it, and he wasn't saying nothing. He wasn't going to rat on anyone. At first he kept saying he didn't know, but it sounded like a burglary, if things were missing.

"I heard that burglars often shoot people if they think they could ID them later. I saw it on a TV show," Kakamia offered. That had been the story they agreed on: after Bobby shot his parents with the gun he stole from them, Kakamia would take the gun and run out. Bobby would hurry back to his room and pretend to have slept through the "burglary."

Unfortunately, Kakamia and the others hadn't studied those crime shows closely enough. There were only minimal signs of forced entry; they had barely broken the front door lock. Not enough to convince the police. And they had only taken the TV and VCR; with a house full of so many other valuables, the cops ruled out robbery gone wrong quite quickly.

Kakamia was momentarily at a loss for words after the cops interrogating him told him this. They *hadn't* thought about that. They figured it would be enough if stuff was missing and Bobby was in his bed. What were they going to do now? He started to panic.

Then he had a flash of imagination: him standing over the sleeping couple, dressed all in black with a black ski mask on, the .38 revolver in his hands. He walked to the edge of the bed, extended his arm and burrowed the bullet into the back of Bobby's mother's head, firing one shot, then swung expertly to the father, and did the same. He wiped the gun down, and threw it in the corner. Without a backwards glance, he slipped out of the house, walked around the corner, pulled out a wad of cash, counted it and started laughing.

It's already done and they already had both of them, so why not go out with style? So that's what Kakamia told the police. All of it except the cash. He knew that wasn't true, cause the insurance money hadn't come in yet. One of the cops got ecstatic. But the second wasn't convinced. "We know about you, kid, we asked around. Talked to your friends."

"Yeah," Kakamia tried to put some bass in his voice to sound tougher. "And what did they say about me?"

"They said you live in a fantasy world. That you like to be a big shot. You boast and brag about doing all kinds of things, but in reality you're just a little nigger who comes to school in worn out shoes and eats mayo sandwiches for lunch. By yourself."

Kakamia's rage flared inside him like a gun going off. "You don't know shit about me! I did it!"

But the cops continued questioning him on different aspects of the crime, trying to trip Kakamia up, confuse him.

"So you say you put the gun to both of the victims' heads while they slept in their bed at 1 AM?"

"Yeah, right up against their heads, just like they did in *The God-father*," Kakamia replied.

The cop wheeled on him fast. "Then how do you explain Bobby's father still being alive? The only reason he didn't die like Bobby's mother is because the bullet got caught in the pillow and slowed down. When it hit his cheekbone, it didn't penetrate his skull," he finished triumphantly.

Kakamia sat quiet. He had forgotten that was part of the plan, he had gotten so caught up in his own imaginations. Since Kakamia hadn't been in the room, hadn't seen what Bobby did, he didn't have that point of reference. He had waited downstairs in the darkened entryway, his hands raining sweat into his gloves.

But it was too late to turn back now, and in truth, he didn't want to. He liked the image of himself holding money, handling business, stone cold. Hurting other people before they hurt him. He liked it as long as he didn't think about Bobby's mother, didn't wonder about what her last thoughts were, or whether she knew subconsciously, as she lay there sleeping, that her own flesh and blood was about to end her life. He held that thought out at arm's length, dripping red, so it wouldn't stain him.

"Well, I did it," Kakamia said stubbornly. "That's all you need to know."

* * *

Kakamia tuned back in to his sentencing trial. The judge was talking about probation. For half a minute, Kakamia's hope flared. "According to the law, the defendant is eligible for probation for this charge. This charge, however, is one that clearly calls out for denial of probation, despite the fact that the defendant is so young and has no prior criminal record. The crime is just too enormous—there's two separate victims, with loss of life and near loss of life to the second person—to allow for grant of probation, and therefore probation is denied." His voice had the finality of a banging gavel.

Kakamia sighed. He knew he wouldn't be getting probation; it was just an empty hope. He also knew they wouldn't be sending him back to the California Youth Authority to finish his sentence. CYA could only hold him until he was twenty-five, and everyone involved, including his lawyer apparently, felt that wasn't enough time for his crime.

No, Kakamia knew exactly what he was getting. After Bobby pleaded guilty a couple months before, he was given twenty-five to life. Bobby got out of the conspiracy charge by saying he wasn't the trigger man. He blamed it on Kakamia, which of course went along with Kakamia's earlier confession to the crime. So everything was hanging on him, and he was looking at life without. Kakamia used to think prison wouldn't be a big deal. His dad had been in prison damn near his whole life. His whole life felt like a prison, like there was no escape. He was locked in, and no matter how hard he rattled the bars, no one came for him.

But when he was actually facing life in prison, he knew if his life had been a prison, it had been minimum security, grooming him for this next step, the big time. He had heard so many stories of prison from the other guys in his set, or gang. He would have to get deeper into the gang to survive, or he'd be left to fend for himself, always watching his back, always wondering where a shank was going to come from…

Kakamia couldn't breathe. His throat was just as constricted as when he had tied the bed sheet around it. Wound it around and jerked the knot. Tied the other end to the top bars of his cell door. He thought it would be fast. One of the other guys in the jail told him it would be quick, a snap and then nothing. This guy, he'd seen other guys do it, and he said they didn't feel nothing. But Kakamia hung there, no air. His eyes felt like grapes being squeezed. His legs jerked like a broken wind-up toy. They took him to the jail infirmary after they cut him down. The court had to push back his next court date, because he couldn't walk. The doctors said it did permanent damage to his lower back and neck. He still couldn't turn his head to the left or the right in the court room. He had to shift his whole upper body to look at his mom, eyes full of tears and frustration.

Kakamia leaned forward, rested his head on his folded hands. Why, at nineteen, did he feel like his life was over?

* * *

Kakamia had had a meeting with his lawyer right after Bobby pleaded guilty.

"This isn't good," his lawyer told him. "In fact, it's very bad."

"Yeah, I figured that," Kakamia spit back sarcastically. "Look, can't you just tell them I didn't do it?"

"The problem is you already told them you did. I tried to tell them that it should be disregarded, but it's on record. Now we have Bobby saying you pulled the trigger. And quite honestly, a jury is going to be inclined to believe a nice young white boy from a stable family, than a newly arrived Puerto Rican from a broken home with a disciplinary record."

Wasn't that the story of his life?

"Well, what can I do?" Kakamia said, an edge of pleading in his voice. "I don't wanna die in prison, I'm only nineteen years old."

"You could always cop a plea, make a deal. But you gotta have something to trade for a deal. If you could give them the other guy involved, I am sure I could get you fifteen to life. I've already talked to the prosecutor about it, and he assures me the deal will hold. That means you'd definitely be out in fifteen, maybe sooner if you're on good behavior. You'd have seven years probation after that and have to pay some restitution, but you'd be out in fifteen at the most."

Little did Kakamia know that his lawyer's word wouldn't mean much of anything soon. His lawyer himself would be arrested a few years later, for torturing and killing his wife. There would be no deals for him. Life in prison, sitting alongside people he had both prosecuted and defended.

Kakamia balked at the idea of snitching; he hated squealers. It was ingrained in him almost from birth, passed down genetically from his parents. It went against the gangster code—he knew that from every movie he saw. He knew it from the gang. He knew snitches get stitches.

But on the other hand, this was all Eric's fault; he got Kakamia involved. He should have stepped forward to take some of the heat off of Kakamia. It wasn't fair he carry this on his own.

Fifteen years did sound like a long time. But life was even longer. And like the lawyer said, he could be out in less time. All he had to do was act right; he could do that. Maybe he'd even be out in five.

"You promise I'll be out in fifteen?" he asked Hamlin.

The lawyer nodded his head decisively. "It's a done deal."

Kakamia sighed. "Then I'm ready to play."

* * *

The judge had given Kakamia murder in the second degree, which carried a sentence of fifteen to life, and was now setting the sentence for his second count, attempted murder in the second degree. The judge set it at the highest possible time, nine years.

"I don't necessarily know at this point, since the jury never got to the point of resolving who is the person that pulled the trigger on that gun," the judge admitted. "But it doesn't matter in terms of the sentence, because at least these three individuals who have been convicted, now, joined together in agreement to carry out the sophisticated plan of attack on a very vulnerable victim and those very aggravating circumstances far outweigh the only mitigating circumstances of a youthful Defendant without…"

Kakamia's mother shot out of her seat, and said in a tearful but still strong voice, "Excuse me, Judge, I don't mean to interrupt the court but you have to take into account the circumstances around this…"

"I'm sorry, Judge, could we have a moment," the lawyer interjected.

"You just can't call this justice in any form, though, you just can't," his mother wailed.

Kakamia's lawyer pulled her closer to the defendant's table. "You are not helping your son with these outbursts," he said sternly.

Kakamia held out his hands to her. "C'mon, mom, it's going to be okay, just calm down."

"Okay? What about fifteen to life and nine years is going to be okay?" Her tone escalated. "I just don't know how we got here. I just don't know how this happened."

"I know, mom, I know," was the only thing he could get past the lump growing in his throat.

His mother slumped back to her seat. The judge looked down at the defense table sternly, waited a moment and then continued with sentencing.

When he was done, Kakamia got what he expected: fifteen to life for murder in the second degree and nine years for attempted murder in the second degree. Luckily, the sentences would run concurrently. He would get seven years probation once he was paroled, and he would have to pay restitution to the victim, $7,469, and a $10,000 restitution fine to the state of California.

Damn, Kakamia thought. Ain't that fucked up? The state gets more money than the people who actually lost something. You'd think he'd injured the state or something.

The judge raised his gavel. "If there's nothing further, then I remand the prisoner to the custody of the Department of Corrections." The gavel sounded louder in his ears than the three shots Bobby fired that December night three years before.

And may God have mercy on my soul, Kakamia intoned mentally as the prison guards walked toward him. He felt that tight feeling in his throat again. He couldn't breathe. He thought of his cell, of twisted sheets. Maybe this time it would be quick. The drop, the snap, and then silence.

WHAT I KNOW ABOUT MY BROTHER

KAKAMIA CREATED A PIECE OF ART, A BIO/PROSE/POEM HYBRID, "Frayed Subconscious." A handkerchief, stained in paint, kisses and rips of ink. He told me it was part of the evidence against him, and it was. Perhaps it was not evidence from his legal trial, but it was evidence by the state, brought against him at the time of his birth, and at the time of his indictment. The poetic vulnerable masculinity of the piece was part of the mounting case that would eventually sentence him to life in poverty: a life in racism, a life spent more behind prison walls than outside of them.

"This handkerchief was the last piece of freedom," the art piece reads. "It held the forensics to convict and heard the whispers of innocence to acquit a sixteen-year-old accused hit man. It traveled through county jails, courthouses, and state prisons. It consoled the fears of California's most infamous criminals and masterminds, and has soaked up the blood of prison riot victims."

Poetry can exquisitely change lives. It can sustain life in the worst of circumstances. And all poetry is a lie. Facts are not poetic enough to reveal the rhythm of a human heart. We thank poetry for its inaccuracies—imperfect cracks on the face of beauty through which the light is able to shine through—word to poet Leonard Cohen.

So when Kakamia told me he met Mac—whom he called his god-father— in New York, through his uncle who had connections to the Westies and numbers rackets, I understood the need to create ties and community. When Kakamia said he would leave his Crown Heights, Brooklyn neighborhood to run errands for his uncle, I understood the desire in him to be tied to something more powerful, more terrifying, than his own thin brown body.

I asked Mac about my brother the first time I met him.

"Great kid," he replied, beaming. "He's got a good heart, Kakamia does."

Kakamia was a man of a thousand names as well. Names are a precious and powerful part of your identity. Knowing a name means you have a piece of that person. He had his birth name, signifying the child who continued getting up, mouth tasting like dirt and metal, when life knocked him to the ground. A prison ID number, an absence of self so a system can get on with its business of making commodities out of human beings without guilt. He was known as "New York" to people a continent away, where a Puerto Rican was a novelty item. "New York" shared in the cool of power, tinged with danger, that the city embodied. He was Kakamia Jahad Imarisha to those who wanted to see the man he so desperately tried to be, the man that, most of the time, he succeeded in being.

"Have you seen his art?" Mac continued. "Phenomenal, just amazing. I wish I could draw like that, I'm telling you."

"Was he always like that?" I asked tentatively, eggshells crunching under my voice. "Was he like that in New York?"

"Oh I didn't know him in New York. I only met him when I came out here. But we've known each other a long time out here. He's a really good kid, not like some of these knuckle heads around here."

I have come to learn everything I need of the truth I have now. It lives in my brother's eyes, in his strong talented hands flaked by sun and harsh soap. I gather pieces of my brother's truth and string them like beads to create a necklace, a talisman of protection.

* * *

I know prison is harsh, brutal, soul-crushing, and above all monotonous. The sheer boredom of being trapped with the same people every day, of having limited options—do I watch TV, listen to music, work out, write a letter, read a book, then do it all again tomorrow?

A prisoner told me upon his release, "It's not the guards that got to me—I learned to shut myself off from them. It wasn't the other inmates; most of them were cool and you learn early how to avoid the ones who aren't. What got me lying in my bunk at night—staring at the ceiling scrawled with drawings and messages from past prisoners—was knowing that I had to get up and do the same thing every day, for 2,237 days. That's when I felt myself slipping away: when I thought of it like that."

* * *

I know the name Kakamia chose for himself, because I am the one who picked the name for him. I know what a sacred gift that is. A new name reshapes who you are and who you are to become.

I was given my name by my mother's boyfriend at the time, a Black prisoner in California as well, in a relationship that consisted almost wholly of written correspondence with an occasional phone call thrown in. It was not the first, nor the last, relationship my mother would have with someone incarcerated. My mother has never been overtly political (except in her very vocal patriotic support of the U.S. military, in which most of our family is or was enlisted) but has always worked to support the voices of those who were marginalized and oppressed. Perhaps this is where I get my contradictions.

My mother's boyfriend wrote to me after getting permission from her, wanting to introduce himself. We wrote to each other over several years, even after he and my mother were not together anymore. He was a Black father, filling the void of my own absentee father, whose yearly Christmas cards had long ago dried up by that point. My mother's boyfriend was my mentor: my sensei in the ways of Blackness. He introduced me to deeper understandings of organizing in the U.S. by Black folks, and brought me the vastness of Africa. For once, I did not feel caught between two worlds, the white and the Black, as alien and foreign to both. For the first time, I felt I could claim my Blackness easily. There was a community waiting for me and finally I had found a guide to show me the way.

Even though my mother did not understand my need, she supported it as best she could. She felt my hunger for an identity I could carry comfortably in the crook of my arm, and she knew I would have to find that on my own. But while I searched history for my identity, a huge part of who I was stood in the kitchen on tired feet, cooking me dinner every night after working long hours, and praying quietly at night for me.

When I was fourteen years old, in honor of Kwanzaa, my mother's boyfriend sent me my gift: a choice of three African names—a chance to be reborn. It was no contest for me. I slipped on Walidah Imarisha. Walidah means "newborn" in Arabic; Imarisha is "strength" in Swahili. I felt the name slide against my flesh like a second skin.

Like so many of us stolen children of Africa, searching for names and birthrights, I was trying to find something to make me into more than I was, to see what's been inside of me all the time.

I have since learned the importance of names in prison, and of being able to choose what you answer to, in a place where you are a string of numbers barked at you all day long. One prisoner I wrote was incarcerated under the wrong name. He had someone else's ID on him at the time of his arrest. That name (the false one on the ID) was the name under which he was arrested, tried, convicted, and held for fifteen years. He tried, every step of the way, to tell them who he really was. To this day, if you send a letter to his real name, instead of his alias, it will come back "No Such Inmate." He has been stripped of the name his mother sang softly to him when he was a child.

So I took the responsibility and honor of renaming my brother seriously: as serious as the grave. I studied my Swahili name list, rolling words around in my mouth, reading and rereading definitions, and juxtaposing different combinations for the flavor of culture they brought.

Kakamia Jahad. The staccato of the hard consonants with the healing salve of rolling vowels. Kakamia: Swahili for "tireless," never giving up, obstinate. Stubborn muthafucka. Jahad: derived from *jihad:* a word that strikes fear into Western populations. Misunderstood. It does not mean holy war. It means to struggle, to strive, to try one's hardest to do what is correct.

Three years ago, Kakamia added my last name, Imarisha, to his. "It would be an honor to carry your last name, Wa. We're family, after all, and this will show the world," Kakamia's voice crackled through the static of the prison phone line.

* * *

I know he moved to California, with his mother, his brothers and sisters—full siblings with different daddies, like my own. I know he was a manchild when he came to a state full of sun, where his mother hoped that the absence of concrete might help him grow straight and tall.

* * **

I know my brother's body is landscaped with tattoos.

You can read his history, lived and reimagined, on his skin. He is a book written by an illegal prison ink gun made out of a hollowed-out broken pen tube, a needle pricked into one end. Blood clots around every word and image.

A grim reaper, scythe in hand, dominates his left arm. From his gang days he told me, when he was "Mr. Grim." I have a picture of him at his junior prom. He is fifteen years old, body jutting out at all the awkward angles of that age, stuffed into a black tuxedo with a pink cummerbund and tie, to match his date's Cinderella dress. His arms are wrapped around her, and his square jaw juts forward with a toothy grin. Her eyes dancing with a pink smile that matches the bows in her curly hair. I stare at this picture and wonder if the grim reaper is there as well, swathed in the pink cummerbund. Is he smiling for the picture too?

Bruce Lee is on his leg—"That's one baaaaaad nigga!" Kakamia bellowed. He was completely unfazed when I reminded him Bruce, though amazing, was in fact Chinese, and also he should stop using the word "nigga" so much.

Another tattoo features an amateurish portrait of the rapper Da Brat, a now-forgotten splash in the pop culture pool. The original ink bled; the tattoo has faded over the twenty years it has lived on his skin. "Yeah, it's gotten all fucked up... I'm gonna get that covered up; I just gotta come up with something," he mused.

Like his life, he revises his tattoos, keeping the images and ink that still breathe true, and erasing facts that have turned into lies through the insistent passage of time.

Many of my brother's tattoos have come after his incarceration. It is illegal for prisoners to tattoo themselves. I have met multiple men that have let my brother paint their flesh while on the inside. Some prison tats are crude and simplistic. Others, like Kakamia's, are elegant and full of life. Kakamia brings the lightest part of him to his work, his imagination skimming their skin: sunlight on a warm lake.

Kakamia does his own tattoos when the only other tattoo artist he trusts gets sent to the hole. He feels the bite of the needle, creating hours of tedium where attention cannot wander, the stinging kiss a penance and a gift.

He bleeds for his art. He bleeds to remake himself.

The ink is created from a ballpoint pen if you want the quick and dirty way. The "professional" prison ink is composed of soot from burning toilet paper, wood, Styrofoam, and something like black chess pieces. These are mixed with rubbing alcohol and water; small stones are added in the mixing process. It is the introduction of extreme heat that pushes a metamorphosis to occur. This furtive prison cell chemistry experiment is more complex than any class tests I conducted in college courses.

The expanse of Kakamia's skin has become crowded with the remains of things burnt. It is full body armor: arms to back, legs to tops of feet. Ivy curls around fingers, the eyes of a portrait of a political martyr stare out of the top of Kakamia's skull. The martyr chose death over jail. *When I die, I wear nothing but the tats on my back.* From Kakamia's poem "Last Stand." The tat on his back screams, "Fuck the World" across his shoulder blades in Old English (malt) lettering.

Almost a decade ago, doctors cut out cancer that had settled near his heart, two inches under his right nipple. It had been growing in him for some time, they said—it was just now big enough to notice. They do not know how he got cancer. "The environment you grew up in probably contained toxins in large quantities," the doctor said, telling him something he knew his entire life. His whole life has been carcinogenic.

His scar is camouflaged by the West African Adinkra symbol for eternal energy. Kakamia no longer hides his scars, but paints them brightly.

In the middle of his chest is a bullseye, and an edict: "No warning shots."

Kakamia has the symbol for the revolutionary Puerto Rican indepentistas, Los Macheteros, swaddling his Adam's apple. Their blood-red star has a machete through it, surrounded by an outline of the island of Puerto Rico.

"Cuz you know how your hermano get down!" he shouted joyfully the first time I saw it.

Kakamia and I share a tattoo—the Adinkra symbol for change and adaptability—his at the base of his neck, mine on my left shoulder. It was the first tattoo I ever got, a reminder to me not to fear what the future brings—that change is constant, and rigidity is the enemy. The tattoo is a reminder to Kakamia that such a thing as change exists beyond the same three walls and set of barred teeth greeting his eyes every day. As sci-fi writer Octavia Butler wrote, "*God is change.*"

I do not believe in god. I struggle to believe in change. When I got my tattoo I was terrified. I wasn't scared of leaving permanent marks on my body—the multiple cigarette burns and shallow razor slashes on my forearms, breasts, and abdomen were evidence of that. When I pushed the smoldering mouth of the cigarette to my skin, it was power I smelled burning. That was pain I could control as a teenager: scars I chose to carry rather than those that had been forced upon me. I was scared of uncontrollable pain.

In the tattoo parlor, I shook in the chair. The woman, covered almost completely in dayglo tattoos and endless piercings, readied her instruments. My friend was there, holding my hand, breathing for me. I had planned the design small, slightly larger than a dime, stacking the odds in my favor of making it through.

"You ready?" the artist asked, needle already purring.

The first kiss was like the sensual gnawing of my first lover's teeth on my skin.

"Is that it?" I asked her, incredulous.

"Yep, that's as bad as it's going to get," she said over the hum of my identity being etched onto me. I started laughing.

Kakamia loves to tell the story of me laughing through my first tattoo. It proves how tough and baaaad his little sister is. Like Bruce Lee.

"Now we're connected by ink."

Kakamia has a portrait of me tattooed over his heart, two afro puffs perched like dark planets on the side of my head. I have seen a photograph of this tattoo. I am not allowed to see the tattoo itself, of course, because we only meet in visiting rooms, under the watchful eyes of guards.

I hate the picture of me he chose. Taken in my friend's car when I was eighteen, I was preparing to step out into the rain, back into my apartment, into the relationship I wanted so desperately to escape— the one I finally did escape—with a bruised wrist and a fear of eyes watching me through windows. I turned to say goodbye and got a face full of flash. The picture is a torn girl trying to paste herself into a woman, all unfinished edges and messy wet glue.

I love living on my brother's skin; I just wish it was a wholer me that resided there.

Kakamia's name is a bracelet encompassing the span of my wrist. My third tattoo and my last. So far. A birthday surprise for Kakamia. After he immortalized me on his skin, every time we would talk, he would joke, "So when you getting my face tattooed on you? Only fair you know."

I did not want his face frozen. It would be only one of the countless hims I have seen over the years. It would be a fact, and it would be a lie.

So I chose words, as I always have: the letters I gave him, strung together with poetry.

I ventured deep into North Philly to an art studio, up rickety, dusty stairs to a room plastered with pin-up girls on cars and death metal bands thrusting their manhood out. The artist was a dread-locked Black man with heavy eyes, I hoped, from lack of sleep and not weed.

He tried to talk to me while I gritted my teeth, the needle digging into the delicate bone of my wrist until it felt like sawing tendons. My boyfriend Dovid was with me. We had broken apart but we were still pretending to be whole, not so much for outsiders—they could all clearly see our cracks—but for ourselves. He put his hands on my shoulder and I jumped, causing a tiny line coming down from the second "a." Permanent. Like so many little mistakes.

On the next visit, I proudly rolled my sleeve back and held my illustrated wrist in front of Kakamia's face. These were ties more than blood: ties of choice.

He dragged me by my arm, showing everyone in the visiting room—prisoner, visitor, and guard alike: "Look at that, that's my name, fool! I told y'all my baby sister loves her big brother, didn't I? Look at that, what did I tell you? That's my name!"

My brother was a graffiti artist, which is to say an outlaw. If you could read the wild styles of his youth, you could speak the words of the kamikaze graffiti tattoos on his flesh. Growing up in New York, where graf artists hung out of windows to put their names in gravity-defying places, Kakamia has become his own blank wall, readied for bombing (the graffiti term for covering a wall that isn't yours).

I can see him, tagging his name on walls, scaling fences into train yards to spend hours sucking in paint fumes, the only sounds the *shhhh* of the aerosol can, the rattle of the Krylon and your own hot breath in your ears. It is a way to leave your mark on the world: proof you were there. An undersized, skinny ghetto mule-atto mixed-up kid who never had enough money to get by. They can't erase you. Even if they sand blast you off, you'll come back. Immortality.

As he dragged me around and showed off my flesh, I was proud to realize I was his latest tag, his latest cry of resistance to a world intent on scrubbing him clean out of existence.

* * *

I know my brother sent me a clip from a paper several years ago of a high school senior—a promising star basketball player—who was killed in a car accident. *My seventeen-year-old son,* the words wept: *Thearon.* I had never heard of a son before. Kakamia's brother had raised Thearon as his own son. I had never heard of a brother before.

Thearon had not seen Kakamia; he had only heard of him as an uncle gone bad, an example not to be followed. My complexly beautiful, wonderfully frustrating, and infinitely loving brother was reduced to a convict stereotype. His son was reduced to a grainy picture in a paper, a list of accolades, and overwhelming regret. Thearon had Kakamia's wide jaw, his big forehead, and his clear eyes.

I know so many family members who have stood by their incarcerated loved one for decades. Unwaveringly sending much-needed packages, traveling hours for visits, accepting exorbitant collect phone calls. They redefine words like commitment, sacrifice, and love.

But sometimes blood family step back when the police knock at the door, or they wander during the trial, or they run after the sentence is handed down. They collapse under the biggest loss, already on the ropes from continual body blows. They drift through years that move so slowly behind bars, and so quickly out here. They run from the shame society force-feeds them, as if prison is a contagion, a plague; as if the whole family—the whole house—must be quarantined to stop the disease from spreading. They bear the tedium of not even being able to answer simple questions about their loved ones: "Where in California does your son live?" There is no way to answer this. No one truly "lives" in a prison; they are just there, marking time.

In other cases, birth families were never there to begin with, and this is part of the reason for the bars and the rage, which seem to go together for too many young people of color.

Family is a precious and scarce commodity in prison.

The next time I saw Kakamia, he had *Thearon* tattooed on his forearm in bold poignant strokes. I know he did it with his own hand, picking his scars to carry and his sins to atone for.

* * *

I know Kakamia thought he lost his mother while in prison. The smiling woman with Ireland at the corners of her lips and in her halo of dusty curls. The prison callously told him she died. Kakamia mourned for lost time and unspoken words.

He added her name to the tally of losses on his skin.

Then the impossible call came years later: she was actually alive. The prison had informed him incorrectly when she had a heart attack.

She told Kakamia when they did speak that she wasn't able to write or visit him and let him know she was alive, because she had severely advanced arthritis. While this is true, I think a lifetime of tension, two decades of bars, and years of silence between them were also the cause.

Kakamia called me, in a hushed voice said, "My mom's alive, Wa, she's alive. These bastards have been lying to me all this time."

I could imagine him touching the tattoo he had added of his mother's name, written in the same urgent, heartrending strokes as Thearon, right above it.

It is an incredible story—an unbelievable story—only if you have not been in close contact with the prison system, and do not know the capriciousness, the callousness, and the incompetence with which things are run. I have seen a guard cut a visit short because he did not like the "aggressive" look the prisoner gave him when the guard walked by. Guards search cells for contraband, crumpling children's pictures, ripping pages out of books, demolishing letters from loved ones, only to find nothing. I have seen a woman wait for two and a half hours to visit her husband, only to finally be told that he had been transferred to another facility inextricably, for no reason, the night before. She had driven six hours.

Prison is a site of pain, and unnecessary psychological games justified by the need to "keep the inmates on their toes, so they don't know what's going on." It is like a vase, jarred by running careless hands, toppling to the floor and spraying a pattern of heartbreak underfoot.

* * *

I know Kakamia was convicted of conspiracy to commit murder. I read his paperwork, read about the mother murdered, the father who miraculously survived, and the two older white co-defendants. I know when he was convicted, sentenced to fifteen to life. I know he has done ten more years than the minimum, which he was promised by his trial lawyer. I know the uncertainty of when, of *if*, is potentially fatal. There has been a countless string of parole hearings, all stamped *denied*. Not this time; try again in two years. Better luck next time, in three years. Fifteen to life is counted in decades, not years, months, or days.

When a friend of mine came home from prison, he told me that when he had a year left, he placed a deck of cards on his bunk. Every week, he would move one card over to a new pile. One week down, 51 more to go. For his last month and a half, he moved a card a day. For his last two days, it was a card an hour: anything to see time move, the end approaching, hope growing as the stack of cards shrinks.

Fifteen to life. No deck of cards. No countdown in my brother's future.

Preparation for the parole hearings is always the same: gather letters and secure job offers, housing offers, and drug and alcohol support programs. Who do I know that would impress a parole board with their support? What can I say to make them see the man I know my brother to be? Every time, I go in search of the secret magic words. I spend hours drafting my letter to the parole board, a letter they probably never even read. The immense responsibility I put on myself is comforting; if I have the power to say the right thing to set him free, then I at least have some kind of power.

But the decision is the same. It is always the same. And it always feels worse than imagined.

The state of California passed new laws around parole. The longest denial they could give before was two years. Now the shortest denial they are allowed to give is three years. Prisoners are being denied parole and given 15 year hits, the slang for the time a prisoner has to wait until their next parole hearing. Hit: slang that is so true, it hurts. It is being told you will not even have a chance to walk outside of prison walls for a decade and a half, and that your dreams must be put on hold while graduations and births and deaths pass you by. It is a blow to the face and a punch to the gut.

It is a hit not just to the prisoner. We all take that hit: loved ones, family members, and communities that will eventually welcome back the vast majority of people in prison right now—ninety-five percent, says the Bureau of Justice. Many of these people will be permanently scarred black and blue from so many hits.

Because of this terrifying change, I and others hired a lawyer for one of Kakamia's parole hearings. I begged and borrowed, saved and skimped to pay this lawyer, who only existed as a sweet deep voice on the other end of our calls. It was a committed voice that called me back on weekends. It was a dedicated voice; the lawyer went out to the prison to see Kakamia twice more than he originally agreed to. He was a steady voice that calmly quoted legal precedent for hope, and current policy for pragmatism.

This sweet deep voice called to tell me Kakamia had been denied, and that he'd been given another three year hit. That voice had to say to me, knowing the horror of it, that this hit was "lucky." With "get tough" mentalities permeating all levels of the system, it was the least amount of time the board was giving. Some had gotten five, ten, even fifteen year hits. *It is our belief you need fifteen years before you will have any possibility of being ready to return to society.* Parole board membership endows one with the power of clairvoyance.

Kakamia stayed strong for me. He wrote a letter immediately, telling me to keep the faith. It was a setback; we would continue on. He worried about my well-being in the light of this decision. He took care of me as he was shoved back into a cage.

We rallied: another lawyer, more letters, more plans. The hearing loomed.

"My chances are good, Wa, real good." I heard the hope flavoring his voice.

I held myself back. "Yes, hopefully."

I could not bring my heart out from behind the wall I had constructed to protect it from the arbitrariness of this system. Not one more heartbreak. They had made us both live behind walls.

Then the most unbelievable news: *suitable for parole.*

It was actually happening! My heart leapt from behind the wall, dancing in the shadow of gun turrets.

"You gotta be ready at any time to come get me," Kakamia reminded me for the millionth time. "They only give me forty-eight hours notice to roll out, and then they open the gates. So you gotta be here to pick me up two days after I tell you."

The twelve hour drive, my overfull schedule with commitments that had been written in ink for months—none of that mattered. It would all fade away in the light of the sun rising on my brother, finally walking through the gates with me for the last time.

In California, the governor has to approve all paroles. *Just a formality*, everyone told me. *If the parole board approves, he signs off on it.*

Imagine then when we heard the governor rejected his parole. Refused to sign off. Sent us back to the beginning of the line, to suffer the labyrinthine parole process all over again, this time with the soul-crushing knowledge that even if you make it to the end, you can open up a door you think leads to the outside, and instead fall off the top story, smashing on the pavement below.

And there is nothing to do except collect your pieces, glue them back together as best you can, and get back in line at the beginning, waiting to be called up.

* * *

I know my brother is able to create joy in a place of sorrow. I know he is able to accept love as it is given, raw and unfinished, regardless of societal edicts.

At a time when intimacy between male prisoners is seen as either a violation or the punch line of a homophobic joke, my brother claims relationships with men, women, and trans folks.

This is not something prison engendered in him. In the 1980s, his desire was far too fluid for labels. In that climate and culture—which only had room for eithers—Kakamia transgressed all boundaries, and refused to live inside any box constructed for him.

Now, his body exists in a box constructed for him. But over the past twenty-five years, his heart has flown on broken angel wings to roost where it might find warmth.

He found it with a transgenderwoman, Terra, housed in the same prison as Kakamia. She has a warrior spirit, sad eyes, and handwriting that looks like bubbles. Terra was a part of the fight that resulted in transgender prisoners at that facility receiving their hormones, hormones that allow them to look in the mirror and recognize the person they see when they look inward. "The denial of access to hormone treatment has profound effects, including extreme mental distress and anguish, often leading to an increased likelihood of suicide attempt, as well as depression, heart problems, and irregular blood pressure," according to *Queer Injustice: The Criminalization of LGBT People in the United States.* She knows all too personally what the denial of your ability to define yourself leads to.

Kakamia supported Terra in her work whole-heartedly, full of pride.

Terra and Kakamia are cellies, and have been for over a decade, at two different prisons. They have chosen to share space, to make a cell as much of a home as is possible. They have been many things to each other as the pressures of prison have caused fissures to flare up. They have not always been lovers—my brother is engaged to a woman on the outside, so that part of their relationship has ceased—but Kakamia and Terra are always working to be loving to one another.

"Your brother drives me so crazy sometimes," the bubbles floated across Terra's lined notebook page. "He always thinks he's right, and he's so arrogant. I still love him, though."

A few months later, I received a large manila envelope from Kakamia. I unfurled a small canvas, splattered in deep rich colors. His artwork is beautiful and bold, and he has done many abstract paintings over the years. But I knew this was not his.

"This is her first attempt at a painting. I've been trying to get her to try for years, but she didn't think she'd be any good. Obviously she was wrong, which I told her already, cause this is great!" the accompanying note crowed.

"Anyway, she wanted you to have it. She knows you keep all of my artwork safe. She wanted her painting to live next to mine." Away from cell shakedowns and midnight prison transfers, away from the uncertainty of steel.

* * *

I know Kakamia has been engaged to three different women on the outside in the quarter century he has been incarcerated. One of them twice. But the woman he is with now is different. She is the only one who knew him before he was locked up, when they were both teenagers, both in gangs. She came back into his life a few years ago. Kakamia calls her his wife, her two daughters his children. I have talked with them, and to hear them say "my dad" and mean my brother brings tears to my eyes. He was so young when he was arrested, barely older than his newly found teenaged daughter. So much taken from him. I have seen him shine under the light of this woman, this family, reshaping pieces of his past like clay, to get it right this time.

I also know years before this current relationship, Kakamia considered himself married to a man for over five years. Shannon was a tall, chocolate-brushed veteran from a small town in Texas, who talked incessantly, quickly, and lovingly.

They met through a dating service for prisoners. Shannon saw Kakamia's ad, and decided to write. I don't know why—I never asked. I also never asked why Shannon was on the site in the first place. With a memory of carrying extra weight and a pronounced limp that began as wheel-chair bound, Shannon's vision of himself was through murky water. He couldn't see the sparkling rivers others did when they looked at him.

They wrote continuously, pages upon pages flying back and forth. Shannon wracked up hundreds of dollars of telephone bills accepting the collect calls Kakamia put through every day.

At first, I did not pay much attention. Kakamia has often introduced me to people he was "dating," if that is the right term for folks locked down. Sometimes they last a month, sometimes a year. Like Kakamia, I am here for the long haul, and these peoples' presence in my life is just the ripple after a pebble is dropped.

But unlike others, Shannon called me regularly, and not just to get updates about my brother, but to talk and exchange stories, laughter, and advice. He asked questions about prison, about parole possibilities, about restrictions once someone came home. More than information, he was asking for hope.

It was an honor to watch love bloom in the most unlikely places.

Shannon was hopeful at Kakamia's next parole hearing. Not wanting to stain him with my cynicism, I spoke plainly but little. I mostly listened to the plans he was making for them when they came home.

Denied.

Then came the day when I called Shannon and his phone was shut off. Mildly worried, I asked Kakamia the next time I spoke with him. He too had not spoken to Shannon, which was unheard of.

I was prepared to scour hospitals and morgues in Texas, until I received a call from an unknown California number. Shannon's warm southern drawl greeted me. He knew one of the main reasons they gave for denying Kakamia's parole was his living situation; his mother had offered to house him, but because they were both recovering addicts, the state didn't think this was a healthy environment.

That's why, Shannon explained, he had moved to California, an hour from the prison, gotten a small apartment on his even smaller disability check. He knew it would be another two years before Kakamia was up for parole, but he wanted to be ready.

They had never met in person.

Normally, this level of devotion would have frightened me. But truthfully, I was in awe of it.

It also felt so good not to be alone, and to have someone else who understood the arbitrariness of the prison guards, and of Kakamia's temperament. Like a campfire not properly put out, he could flare up without warning. It felt good to have someone else who understood Kakamia beyond a number, beyond "prisoner," "convict," "felon"—someone who saw how gloriously beautiful he is.

Shannon lifted weight off me: financial, emotional, and spiritual. He bought Kakamia his quarterly packages when I had a negative bank balance. Shannon took Kakamia's calls when I was out of the country for months at a time. Shannon answered letters with love when I let time slip through my fingers and unopened envelopes stamped "inmate mail" piled up on my desk.

I have seen many prison romances bloom over the years, flowers growing in bombing zones in defiance of everything. Most often it is women counting down on calendars to the day when they don't have to drive away from the prison without their man. I have gone with these women to pick up their beloveds. I have driven the same women back to another gate a year later. The weight of no access to work, and more poignantly, no access to the image of manhood embedded into all of our minds by a patriarchal society, had taken their toll on her man. They were at the whim of arbitrary parole officers, capricious in their god-like power. *You had a dirty UA. You were an hour late to our appointment. You moved without telling me. You haven't gotten a job yet.* This is the reality for two-thirds of the people in California prisons: back into a box not because of a new crime, but because of rules that are designed to be impossible to fulfill.

I live in fear every day that this will happen to Kakamia when he gets out. And after he met Shannon, that fear wasn't just for me.

On a visit to see Kakamia, Shannon insisted I stay with him; he wouldn't hear of me getting a motel room. *And no, no you take the bed, I like sleeping on the floor better anyway—it's good for my back. Please finish eating up; I'm not even that hungry, I had a big meal before you got here.*

We had one of the best visits with Kakamia I'd ever had. I saw a new facet of him. He played Connect Four with Shannon, because Shannon said Scrabble made his head hurt. Kakamia smiled when Shannon rejoiced at winning, without a trace of sarcasm or condescension.

When I visit Kakamia on my own, it's a different story—the incessant nagging to play Scrabble starts almost the moment I sit down. It was only a few years ago that we played our first game of Scrabble against each other. I don't particularly enjoy playing Scrabble; my mother was a fanatic, even playing in tournaments. She never went easy on me when I was younger, beating me by a hundred points or more, and not letting me lay down any made-up words.

"That's not a word, get it off the board and play a real word."

"Mom, I don't know all these words. I'm like ten."

"Then you're old enough to know it's not a real word," she said. "Now play a real word."

The result is I don't like to play Scrabble but, to my mother's credit, I am quite good at it when I do allow myself to be roped into playing.

So when Kakamia challenged me to play, I expected to more than hold my own. In fact, I thought to myself, *Well, just don't beat him too badly.* Imagine my surprise when he lay down words I've never heard of, that would have made my mother glow with pride. Imagine my shock when he laid down all his tiles not once but *twice* in one game. Imagine my chagrin when he beat me by more than two hundred points.

Kakamia turned to every table within speaking distance to us excitedly: "This is my sister. She's a college professor. She teaches English and Literature. She's also a writer and a journalist. And I just beat the shit outta her at Scrabble!"

Anyone who knows me knows I am not a good loser. I have worked hard to be a little more restrained than flipping the board over as I did when I was a child, but it is still not something I take easily. But that day, watching my brother—who went into prison without a high school diploma, who taught himself how to read behind the walls—I just smiled at everyone, nodding my head.

"Yeah, he did. I didn't have a chance."

During my visit with Shannon, Kakamia boldly introduced Shannon to everyone in the visiting room as "my wife." Though Shannon later had a conversation with Kakamia (after some prompting) about using the term "partner" rather than "wife," Kakamia's desire to claim Shannon in that place of all places brought tears to my eyes. Prisons are locations where the policing of bodies and genders is strictly enforced. According to *Queer Injustice*, "Arguably, prisons and jails are the locations within the criminal legal system in which queers are most visible and punishment of sexual and gender nonconformity through endemic sexual and physical violence is most obvious and egregious." Of course, prisons are nothing but a reflection of our larger society, the state of which we can judge, as writer Fyodor Dostoevsky wrote, by entering its prisons. By claiming Shannon and their relationship in that place, Kakamia showed clearly that he would not allow gender binaries to bind or shame him.

Shannon never memorized Kakamia's prison ID number. He wrote it at least once a day for years, and he spoke it multiple times during a visit. He saw it on the envelope of every love letter, every card, and every note Kakamia sent him. But he refused to memorize it—he said he just couldn't hold it in his head.

Instead of a prison ID number, Shannon saw my wonderfully, beautifully, tragically complex brother standing in front of him.

So when Shannon asked me if I thought he and Kakamia would really be together when he got out of prison, I didn't answer right away. I clutched the wheel as I ran through the advice I gave every woman who told me of promises made under the watchful eyes of guards: *Don't believe it.*

The shocked, pained look of the women indicated they expected better from me than to fall into the old "he's a con, he must be scamming you" mentality, and I would have to clarify: "Don't believe *it*, not him. He believes everything he is telling you right now. He means it with all of his heart. He wants to come home to you, to make a life with you, to make the years of waiting up to you.

"But you don't know who he will be when he steps through those gates, because he doesn't know. He does not know what he will be beyond prison walls facing other walls, often just as confining. He does not know who he will be when he is released with a few dollars in his pocket and a set of cast-off clothes. He does not know who he will be when he is denied a job for the tenth time because of his record; when rent and electricity and water are due; when old friends turn their faces away on the street; when family refuse to let him in the house; or when strangers still see him as nothing but a number.

"Yes, he believes what he's saying. But he can't promise you what shape he will take, under the weight he will be forced to carry."

This is the speech I give, and it is the speech I gave Shannon, even though nothing inside of me wanted to. I didn't want to see his face fall, see the doubt creep at the corners of his mouth. I didn't want him to question who my brother is, who the man he loved is.

But because I loved Shannon, I told him the truth, which was crueler than a lie ever could have been. And I prayed to be wrong.

And maybe in a way I was.

Shannon and Kakamia did not stay together. They split after trying so hard to reconcile calendars and hope, expectations with reality, visions of the future with getting through today.

But the fact that they found a love like that at all is a triumph.

It was a love so bright that it was able to light the dark corners of Kakamia's cell and let him sleep peacefully at night for the first time in years.

COMMUNITY EVERYWHERE

"For prison life with its endless privations and restrictions makes one rebellious. The most terrible thing about it is not that it breaks one's heart—hearts are made to be broken—but that it turns one's heart to stone."
—Oscar Wilde, *De Profundis*

EVERY TIME I VISIT KAKAMIA, EVERYONE KNOWS HIM. AND I MEAN everyone: guards, prisoners, other visitors. People walk up to me and say, "Oh you're New York/Kakamia's sister, aren't you? I would have known you anywhere, you look just like him!"

As Kakamia says, that just proves we were meant to be brother and sister and a glitch happened somewhere along the way.

He and I have a number of visiting room rituals. Everyone I know who regularly goes to see a prisoner develops them. Humans are creatures of habit; routine brings control out of chaos.

One particular habit of ours involves singing New York-based rap group Black Sheep's song "This or That," specifically the lines, "Engine engine number nine/ On the New York Transit line/ If my train falls off the track/ Pick it up pick it up pick it up!"

One of us will start it off quietly, the other will jump in on the next line, and we will gradually get louder until the others in the visiting room shoot us looks ranging from amusement to irritation. Another ritual we have developed is singing snippets of show tunes. Believe me, you have heard nothing until you hear Kakamia's falsetto version of "How Do You Solve a Problem Like Maria?" from *Sound of Music*.

We were engaged in our Black Sheep ritual one visit when a young Black woman from another table interrupted us.

"I just had to tell you how beautiful that drawing of the elephant you did for my mother is," she said shifting the packaged chips from the vending machine from hand to hand. "We still have it hanging on the wall and people comment on it all the time."

My brother reacted with grace and humility. He didn't say much, just a few stark words of appreciation.

Once she turned to go back to her table, I picked up where we left off: "If my train falls off the…"

Kakamia interrupted me, "Hey, Wa, can I just have a moment? You know how sometimes folks recognize you from your poetry performances, like that woman in Philly in the bodega, and you called those your superstar moments? Well, this is my first superstar moment ever. I kinda wanna savor it."

So we sat and savored it, until the PA crackled, telling us it was time for count.

* * *

It didn't start off this way for Kakamia when he was first transferred to prison. Though he has always been charismatic and charming, he came into the California corrections system full of rage at the world, and mostly at himself. He was shipped to Folsom State Prison, the second-oldest prison in California, and one of the most dangerous. It was an all-out war, and Kakamia's side had already been chosen for him. Because of his affiliation with the Bloods on the street, he mobbed up with Bloodline behind the walls, another Blood set.

The original Bloods formed in the early 1970s to provide protection from the Crips street gang in Los Angeles, California. Both gangs have branched out nationally and even internationally. According to the documentary *Bastards of the Party*, produced by Blood Cle "Bone" Sloan, the Crips, the most notorious gang in the world, actually began at the

Community Revolution in Progress (C.R.I.P.), and became a city-funded community center and organization in South Central in 1969.

The Black youth who founded the Crips saw them as a direct continuation of revolutionary Black organizations like the Black Panther Party, reflecting the unrest and burning desire for change embodied in the 1960s. As first generation Crip Danifu Bey said, this was "the spirit that the Crips were created [in,] the climate of the Watts Riot... Black people being awakened to freedom and tired of being treated like slaves... The Crips and other gangs were being nurtured in that type of environment where Black people were basically rebelling and expressing themselves."

The original Crips recognized the criminalization and state repression they experienced as Black folks in general, and Black people working to change society specifically. They saw very clearly that the tools used against the Black Panther Party were the same used to control and contain communities of color: police, courts, and prisons. This is echoed by Angela Davis's analysis of the transition from slavery to prisons, and slave-catchers to police. The war waged on radicals in this country by the U.S. government eliminated—or in the words of FBI Director J. Edgar Hoover "neutralized"—an entire generation of Black leadership, who could have given guidance to Black youth looking to make a change, but without concrete political strategies. George Percy Bargainer III shows how this deterioration of forms of resistance came from the lack of direction: "With the neutralization of the Black Panther Party, the conceptual framework that they had provided to youth to interpret and understand the multiple streams of domination shaping their lives in Black Los Angeles dissipated."

Political prisoner, former Black Panther, and scholar Sundiata Acoli wrote that, while the Crips started as a space for community change, because of that lack of guidance and support owning to the arrest, exile and murder of so many Black radicals, "a sinister twist developed... [where Black] people were targets of the young hoodlums." Without an organized ideology, Bargainer argues, "the essence of Crippen became a rebellious lawlessness rather than collective subversive political activity." The Crips gang kept growing, expanding territory and ranks, and attacking all who refused to join them. In response, the remaining gangs who wouldn't join banded together and called themselves the

Bloods. Thus did these youth create organizations that are some of the most feared organizations nationally, claiming countless in their ranks as soldiers.

Kakamia didn't know any of this when he got to Folsom. Before he came to prison, he had been only loosely associated with the gang on the street, more an affiliate than one of the street soldiers. But in prison, gangs became survival—until the day when they invariably became the end of survival.

If he and other gang-affiliated youth had had programs such as CeaseFire while he was on the streets, one wonders how different Kakamia's life would have been. Started in Chicago, CeaseFire created "violence interrupters" who are themselves former gang members. They work to defuse conflicts and gang violence before it escalates. In 2013, the organization had about three hundred outreach workers and violence interrupters. Despite the fact that the two neighborhoods CeaseFire worked in, in 2012, had a nearly thirty-eight percent drop in shootings, and an almost twenty-nine percent drop in killings, the city of Chicago chose to cut funding to the program, according to a 2013 PBS article. Some say this is because the organization was too effective at stopping gang violence, that the police aren't interested in the end of the War on Gangs or the War on Drugs, because this has now become an ingrained way that our economy and our society functions.

First used by Richard Nixon in 1971, the phrase "War on Drugs" has become a foundational part of the criminal legal system, not just in this country but globally. Tens of billions of dollars a year are spent on this policy. Scholar Michelle Alexander writes that "millions of dollars in federal aid have been offered to state and local law enforcement agencies willing to wage the war." Behind bars, the massive increase in prison population over the past few decades is largely due to the War on Drugs. At the end of the day, this war is as much or more about social control than economics, and it is heavily racialized (Alexander shows eighty percent of those in prison from War on Drug-related convictions are people of color). Noam Chomsky in his essay "Drug Policy as Social Control," writes, "The so-called drug war was started in the 1980s and it was aimed directly at the black population. None of this has anything to do with drugs. It has to do with controlling and criminalizing...."

But on the street, answers aren't as clean as they are in textbooks. Kakamia had only his family telling him to stay away from gangs and drugs, and no one telling him that inside. So when he first went to prison, he kept his head down and did what he had to do. Using his anger in service of his set, he released his rage on faces that looked too much like his own. Lumberjack from New York was back with a vengeance.

For a while Kakamia embodied the mentality of Sanyika Shakur, formerly "Monster" Kody Scott, once of the most feared Crip leaders: "Certainly I had little respect for life when practically all my life I had seen people assaulted, maimed, and blown away at very young ages, and no one seemed to care. I recognized early that where I lived, we grew and died in dog years. Actually, some dogs outlived us."

Black life has always been an expendable commodity in this society, a message that has been beaten into DNA.

Kakamia tried not to remember much of anything, and during the day he almost succeeded. He worked to numb his brain, day and night. It was easy enough to do in prison. Alcohol and drugs were available; both made in-house and couriered by guard. You just had to have the money or the connections. As always, Kakamia was dead broke, but he was real good at making friends.

All the running caught up with Kakamia at night. Specters rose, pulling and biting at him. Kakamia tossed and turned in his bunk. He felt the same suffocating feeling. Years streamed by like polluted water. He turned twenty-one and barely noticed. Visits, always in short supply, began to dry up completely. There were bills, there were responsibilities, there were jobs, his family said. But he also knew they felt that since he got himself into this situation, he shouldn't expect anything from them. *We're not in prison too*, their actions screamed at him, *we don't have to do your time*. He thought about ending it all. He thought about ending it all every night. The same dark waters he battled his entire life raged into a tsunami inside of him. Why should he continue to fight to keep his head above water? The shore was too far away; he'd never get there. The release of muscle, the quieting of limbs, the soft retreat of light sounded so sweet. It sounded almost like poetry.

Kakamia had to remind himself he already tried that way out twice: once during his trial, and once right after he was sentenced.

The burning around his neck, the sudden deprivation of an essential part of life. And he was still here. Nothing changed afterwards, except his back was fucked up and everyone looked at him a little differently.

When he thinks back now to that time, Kakamia can't believe he made it out. "Everything embedded into my head said, 'You're never going home. You'll never get a date. No one cares. You might as well either do this or do that—either start stabbing, and get a SHU [Special Housing Unit] term and make a name for yourself, or just die.'"

During Kakamia's three years held in jail waiting for trial and sentencing, the doctors poked and prodded him. They had a psychologist or psychiatrist (he could never remember the difference) examine him to "assess his state of mental health." The doctor came back with a litany of disorders, from Attention Deficit to medical depression. Kakamia thought it was just being brown and poor in America.

Trapped in prison, gang members' positions are similar to those Sanyika Shakur describes for those on the street. He compares gang members to military veterans of the Vietnam War, saying that when those soldiers were injured, they were shipped back home. But no option like this exists for those fighting on frontlines in ghetto communities—underresourced and overexploited—or for those fighting in prison. "Where do we go when we've been wounded bad, or when our minds have been reduced to mincemeat by years, not months, of constant combat?" asks Shakur, who became a revolutionary organizer while in prisons. He argues gang members like Kakamia should be seen as suffering from post-traumatic stress syndrome: "… I contend that gang members who are combat soldiers are subject to the same mind-bend as are veterans of foreign wars."

After Kakamia went to prison, they felt his behavior was too erratic and unpredictable, and diagnosed him with bipolar disorder. The prison doctor prescribed him a liberal dose of lithium. It quieted everything inside of him when he took it—like a dead sea, the waters became still as glass, and he could see beyond the horizon. But it also made him feel like he was adrift on those waters in a rowboat with no oars: out of control, like he'd been his whole life, floating aimlessly and at the mercy of uncaring and unmovable forces.

Even though he didn't stay on the lithium for long, the calm he experienced inside gave him hope. He spent nights free from nightmares for once. He remembered what it was like to breathe again. Like tectonic plates shifting under the surface, things began to change. It was not something visible, but a movement shifting the very ground under his feet: a rumbling not heard so much as felt in his bones.

He realized that his life had to change. If he continued like this, in the gang, he would end up either catching another case—one that would keep him in for the rest of his life without a doubt—or bleeding out in the prison yard, his blood smearing the gang's color over the asphalt. He realized he actually did not want to be dead. He could see hope again, faint but there, like the sun's weak glow behind storm clouds.

The prison administration regularly pulled in gang-affiliated prisoners for "chats," to see if they'd be willing to flip and snitch. Because Kakamia was young, newer to the prison and because he had informed on Eric during his trial, they leaned on him more. He resisted; he justified in his head the situation with Eric by saying it was Eric's fault Kakamia was there anyway. It was just the luck of the draw Eric got away clean and he didn't: just the case of one boy who could run faster than the other.

Besides, he knew if the gang even thought he was an informant, that would be it. Even if he got through it alive, which was a big if, he would forever be labeled a snitch. There would only be a handful of prisons in California where he would be safe; at the rest he would be killed on sight. Friends he'd known for years in prison, who he fought side-by-side with, who he had been ready to die for, would never speak to him again. Other prisoners who found out would back away from him, the look of disgust emblazoned on their faces. He would become the second-worst thing you could become in prison, right above child molester.

And worst of all, he would always have that feeling of disgust inside himself, for working with the same system that held him caged like an animal.

As the months and years wore on, though, it became less and less of a choice for Kakamia. He felt his mind being reduced, as Sanyika Shakur had written, to mincemeat by the constant reality of living in a warzone. He would either die very soon, by his hand or someone else's, or he would make this decision to give up the life he had scraped together for himself here. He would burn up Mr. Grim, burn up Lumberjack. If he did that, maybe he could be reborn anew from their ashes. Maybe he would be able to find on his own that sense of peace he had felt through lithium, as more than a fleeting dream.

So he did it: he "debriefed." He met with the prison officials finally. As they listened intently, he told them where the knives were, where the dope was stashed, who was bringing it into the institution. Kakamia went straight from the office to protective custody, isolated in segregation. He was transferred before anyone knew what he'd done, to one of the few prisons where he'd be safe. There he would soon meet another man struggling with his decision to cooperate, James McElroy.

Kakamia lives with this decision every day. He still questions whether it was the right one. When the Stop Snitching campaign spread throughout the hoods, he watched rappers on BET and MTV wearing the shirts stamped with the saying in bright red. He listened to older prisoners discussing it, saying to cooperate with a system that was oppressing you was to participate not only in your own destruction, but in that of your community as well. And he agreed. It has haunted him ever since.

These issues were brought to the forefront of national consciousness starkly in 2011 and again in 2013 when prisoners across California went on hunger strike. The first time in 2011, twelve thousand prisoners from eleven different prisons participated. The second strike, which started July 8, 2013 and lasted sixty days, involved more than thirty thousand prisoners. The strike was led by the Pelican Bay Short Corridor Collective, a multiracial group of prisoners held in the indefinite SHU, in solitary confinement, some of them for decades. They and the majority of prisoners there were thrown in solitary after being "gang-validated," a label by the California Department of Corrections and Rehabilitation for proving someone is in a gang. Many say they are not nor have they ever been in a gang, and that CDCr (which many prisoners write with a lower case "r" to deride "the Orwellian use of the word rehabilitation," according to Claude Marks) uses the flimsiest of reasons to validate, as a means of control. Many of those who are put in solitary confinement indefinitely are politically active behind the walls, working to ensure their cries for justice are heard.

The demands of the hunger strikers hit at the heart of my brother's situation: abolishing the debriefing process which, as the strikers said, "is often demanded in return for better food or release from the SHU. Debriefing puts the safety of prisoners and their families at risk, because they are then viewed as 'snitches.'" Once you have been gang-validated and sent to the hole indefinitely, debriefing is your only way out. Prisoners also demanded major modifications to the gang status criteria, requiring real proof of gang affiliation from CDCr. In addition, the strikers wanted an end to group punishment, compliance with the U.S. Commission on Safety and Abuse in America's Prisons 2006 recommendations regarding an end to long-term solitary confinement, meals that met nutritional standards, and the end of denial of food as a method of control. They also demanded small things, as sometimes it is the smallest things that can change everything: Allow one photo per year. Allow a weekly phone call. *Allow us to be seen. Allow us to be heard.*

The striking prisoners suspended their strike (being clear that it was not finished and would not be finished until their demands were met and justice wrangled from the system) after California legislators expressed outrage and committed to hold public hearings.

This incredible feat of organizing required strength, courage, and enormous solidarity, and serves to inspire those of us on the outside. It highlights the fact that, far from being menaces and burdens, some of our best community organizers are locked down, and they have invaluable lessons to teach the movement outside. Kakamia felt the same way, and he also knew that those leading this movement—who had spent decades in solitary confinement, never touching anyone except a guard—were there because they refused to do what he had.

These are the contradictions that populate Kakamia's heart, because at the same time he knows he would not be alive if he had not debriefed. If he hadn't died outright, his soul would have continued its deterioration. He might physically be on this earth, but without the space created by the break with the gang, his spirit would have died a slow death years ago. He isn't proud of informing, but he is proud of surviving: "I made my choice. I live with it every day. But I'm here. I'm here every day."

His last fight was in 1994.

After getting to the new prison and settling in as much as he could, learning the different rhythms of a new institution, Kakamia tried to find other outlets to channel his energy. He had lifted weights before—if the prison he was at had weights and if they weren't controlled by a rival gang—but now he began spending hours working out his body, burning off the rage that still lived in him.

He worked in the kitchen, "cooking," if you can call it that, and it distracted him, and also made him popular since he could give out extra portions of food on the sly. He spent endless hours watching TV and the movies the prison let them have access to. Kakamia would watch anything that was on: any escape into another world outside of his own head. He couldn't escape into books; most of them were beyond his reading level. He felt embarrassed and frustrated when he picked up a book. It was like a locked vault he never had the combination to.

Kakamia did write well enough to send notes and cards, which he did copiously. Not to his family—that had stopped a long time ago—but to people he met through prisoner ads, dating sites, pen pal exchanges. He knew years stretched in front of him before he'd ever walk beyond these walls, but writing people out there and having relationships (mostly short-lived), made him feel almost normal.

He felt aimless. Of course he couldn't be with anyone he associated with before. He felt rudderless. Every day was like the next. Always so charismatic, he began to dull and lose his shine.

Then one day, Kakamia was in the dayroom, barely watching a college basketball game that was on. As he stared at the screen, his hand doodled on a scrap of paper he'd found on the table, almost on its own as his mind flew in a thousand different directions.

Kakamia was startled out of his reverie by an older inmate he knew of but had not engaged with before, who came up behind him. He leaned over Kakamia's shoulder and looked hard at the paper for a few heartbeats. Then the older man looked Kakamia in the eyes and said, "You got some serious talent, young brotha. Don't let that go to waste," before he walked away.

Kakamia blinked and stared after the man for a minute. Then he grabbed a full sheet of paper, and began drawing intently. Time flowed around him, people came and went, shows passed. He was aware of none of it. When he finally raised his head hours later, he took a step back to see what he had created. It was a lighthouse, shining a beacon across troubled waters, its glow cutting through the darkness.

When another prisoner offered to buy it from him later, Kakamia knew this was his path. He started taking art seriously. He created paintings and drawings, experimenting with as many different media and styles as he could. He did countless cards the other men bought: birthday and anniversary and Valentine's and Mother's Day. It sometimes felt like a production line in his cell. And of course he did tattoos—even though it was technically illegal, most of the guards turned a blind eye—translating his artistic talent to the flesh of those around him.

Kakamia would look forward to the prison art program all week, before it was cut along with almost all of the other programs. One of the paintings he created impressed his instructor so much, it ended up hanging in the prison visiting room. Kakamia and I took pictures in front of it every visit, while he was at that prison. Neither the painting nor he was free, but at least they both weren't so alone.

His art extended beyond prison walls as well. As I moved through the world, I always made sure Kakamia's art came along as well. When I edited a national hip hop magazine, both his art and his poetry appeared in it. Soon, it was featured in other magazines without any help from me, including his favorite magazine, *Juxtapoz*, which focused on graffiti and hip-hop-inspired art. I could hear the pride in his letter when he sent the clipping to me.

Artistic growth is not the only kind Kakamia has been concerned with. Over his years in prison, he tried many different religions. He was a devout Christian, a Muslim, a Five Percenter (a section of Islam born out of the Nation of Islam, popularized through hip hop). Like looking for the perfect dress, he has tried on a number that didn't fit quite right.

Then he found Buddhism. The stillness he found while on lithium returned while he was chanting. He started attending the Buddhist services the prison allowed once every two weeks. Being still and centered in a roomful of other men was something he hadn't experienced since he came to prison. It was always noise, movement, chaos. Especially after they converted the gym into a giant dormitory because of overcrowding. Kakamia was one of those moved in, who lived on bunk beds lined up like soldiers in a row. His bed ended one foot from where the next began. Living on top of so many, voices echoed constantly and there was no escape.

Because of Buddhism, Kakamia was able to control his bipolar disorder through chanting and meditation rather than through pills.

Finding calmness allowed Kakamia to face many fears, both internal and external. One day, he asked his cellie if he could borrow one of the books he was always reading. Kakamia struggled with it all that day, and the next, and the next, feeling so close to quitting each day. Then each day he felt a little less frustrated, until he reached the end, and finished the book. He finished reading his first book, sitting on the edge of his bunk in his prison cell.

He continued reading and practiced writing. He started out writing rhymes, hip hop lyrics, because it made sense to him and kept his mind engaged. Then one day he came to realize it had morphed into him writing poems. *Shit*, he thought to himself, *how did I become a poet?*

Despite being able to read and write at a college level now after years of struggle, Kakamia still didn't have a high school diploma. One of the few courses still functioning at the prison was the GED completion course. Everyone told him to do it. His counselor told him the parole board would not look favorably upon him if he didn't have it. Other prisoners told him he was too smart not to have it. His sister said he needed to take the test, to prove to himself that he could do it.

And yet, for years Kakamia did not take it. The old fears would rear up every time he thought about it. What if he failed? What if he wasn't smart enough? What if he was just as dumb as his teachers said he was, as everyone said he was? How could he live if he had worked so hard to become a new person, and it all crumbled before him?

Finally, he ran out of excuses. Kakamia didn't tell anyone outside when he went to take the GED test finally, though, just in case.

He could not remember a prouder day than the day he could call his sister and tell her he had passed finally.

Kakamia still feels the crushing rage, wanting to explode and take out his pain on another's body. But that is not who he is anymore; it is not the self he strives so hard to hold onto. He has grown beyond his prison numbers, and exists outside of bunks and bars. He has found a self that no guard can touch. He is able to move through the present—through all the disappointment, loss, pain and humiliation—because he knows that he now has a future. He has built a new community of chosen family that supports him, encourages him, and holds him accountable. He knows he is responsible to them, and he wears that responsibility like a medal of honor.

"I was raised in prison, but I was not raised by a prison. I have a family that loves me. I have a family that has stood by me. I am the man they have made me."

* * *

On a visit, Kakamia and I strolled to the vending machine to get some popcorn, one of the few things I can eat as a vegan in a visiting room. He was teasing me about eating grass like a rabbit, and I teased him back, saying if he didn't have all day to work out, he'd be so skinny, he could turn sideways and disappear.

Sitting at the table closest to that machine was a light-skinned Black man in a wheelchair and his wife, a full-bodied woman with beautiful dark flesh and a bright smile. After a few exchanges of pleasantries, she left to use the restroom.

Kakamia said, "Hey that's a great idea, I'm gonna go handle that too, while we wait for the popcorn. I'll be back. Don't go nowhere," he joked as he walked away.

"Your brother is a really beautiful person," the man in the wheelchair told me.

"Mmm hmmm," I responded distractedly, only half paying attention because I didn't want the popcorn to burn. There is nothing like having to smell burnt popcorn in an enclosed visiting room for five hours to make everyone even more on edge.

"You know I wasn't in this chair when I got here," the man tapped the handle. "I have this disease, and it's gotten worse since I've been here. Thanks to the joys of prison health care," he joked bitterly.

"I can only imagine how hard being in prison is period, let alone being in… your condition," I ended weakly.

"You ain't lying about that, now," he shook his head. "A lot of people just stopped talking to me, couldn't deal with it. I was having a lot of trouble getting used to this chair, getting my routine down, having to navigate everything in it.

"Your brother, who I met through a partner of mine, put in for a transfer to be my cellie. I never asked him for that. I wouldn't have asked him. That's a lot to ask someone.

"But he did it on his own. He helped me out. Just little stuff, getting my shirt on when it would get stuck on the hand rail, or in the evenings when I was getting tired and my arms were sore, pushing me back to the cell.

"Obviously he let me have the bottom bunk," he let out a short laugh.

"Your brother never said anything about it. Me being in the chair, I mean. Never acted like anything was different, was his same loud self with me. Just helped out when he saw I needed it, and when I didn't, he let me alone. And he did that for about six months, until there was a shake down on our unit because of some drug thing, and a bunch of people got transferred to other units, him included. But by then, I was used to it, and so were other folks, and things got a whole lot easier.

"But you don't know how much that meant to me, what your brother did. I don't know if I would have gotten through it without him there. It just reminded me that someone cared, when it felt like nobody, not even God, did, some days," he finished, staring deep into my eyes. I was a butterfly trapped under the glass of his stare, a breath held too long, a bruise, faded and sore, healing.

"Hey, miss me?" I turned to see Kakamia's lopsided grin.

I wrapped my arms around his long torso, and hugged him with all my strength, the smell of generic laundry detergent in my nose.

"Always," I murmured into his perfectly ironed blue prison shirt.

Walidah

IMAGINING HISTORY

I IMAGINE THAT THE FIRST TIME I WENT INTO PRISON, I WAS IN MY mother's womb. Her black eye was still fresh. My father's eyes were blackened by the shadows of the bars that stood between them. I imagine this because even though this is not what happened, this is what society says should happen.

My mother grew up in Iowa, sheltered by the smallness of the town and the minds living there. By the time she met my father in Mississippi, she already had my four white brother and sisters, all of them at least fifteen years older than me. My brother Carl was the youngest, and he was a teenager. My mother had weathered two marriages, the last one to a military man who had taken her all over the world and finally landed her in the south. It felt like home to her, with all the joy and horror that home connotes.

My father was born and raised in Mississippi, where the racial tension was hotter and heavier than the mosquito-laden summer air. I would have been born in Mississippi and not Iowa if not for that racial tension, which my mother fled.

Each of my parents had four almost-grown children by the time I was born. Thanks to my father, I also have a half-sister a few weeks older than me whom I have never met.

"Sure, it hurt me," my mother said. "It still hurts. But the way he grew up... he was already with a grown woman when he was thirteen.

Don't you see? He just needed love, and as much as I tried, what I gave him ended up not being enough, every time."

My mother and father met in rural Mississippi in the 1970s, which felt like the 1920s on so many levels. My mother saw my father at work; she was a teacher at a Head Start program, working with developmentally delayed and physically disabled children. He was a deliveryman, later to become a cross-country truck driver. My mother would get in early, before the students arrived, to start her paperwork. She looked for my father first thing every morning.

"He had long legs, and big hands, and a deep voice that just vibrated through you," she told me. "I had to ask him out."

After she heard my father sing and play guitar, it was all over. He had as much talent as his brother, who was a fairly well-known soul musician at the time. When I was a child, I would play my uncle's album on our living room turntable, totally unaware that the melodic voice that vibrated through my soul was related to me. Apparently, my father was even better. My daddy was an amazing musician going nowhere—a supernova always on the verge of imploding.

My mom would get off work at the child center on Friday, go home, shower off the smell of sticky fingers and chalk dust, get dressed up and walk through the door around dusk. In the south, dusk lasts for an eternity. She would head down to the small town tavern, where my father was as permanent a fixture as the bar stools.

My mother sashayed in wearing her prettiest blue dress, which reflected the blue in her eyes. My father would be parked in a corner, a regular, settled enough to put down roots, his long legs propped up on the table. I take after my father, mom says, because we were both "long, tall drinks of water."

The first few times, it caused a bit of a commotion; she was the only white person in the joint. But after a while, folks grew accustomed to her. My father was well-liked, so that helped. Sometimes a little too well-liked, as evinced by my half-sister born a few weeks before me.

Guitar in hand, the long fingers I also inherited plucking the strings absent mindedly, he carried on a conversation, took a drink from the ever-present glass in front of him and kissed my mom hello, all without missing a note.

They'd hang out till all hours of the morning, long after "respectable" establishments shut down. They'd drink and laugh, tell tall tales, sing along while my dad played the hits of the day. My mother cannot for the life of her carry a tune. But it didn't matter then. Everyone would join in, raucous and boisterous, drinks sopping over and spilling a little when they really got into it. I can imagine my mom's blonde hair cascading down her shoulders, her face flushed from the alcohol and the laughing, leaning on my dad's shoulder, completely off beat and out of key.

The only song they got quiet for was "Sitting on the Dock of the Bay." That was a solo, just my dad and his guitar. He'd drop his feet from the table, close his eyes, lift his head up and let the words slide out his mouth like rainwater. When he got to the middle, he'd really belt it out, shaking his head side to side, as if saying to the song, "Yeah, I know, I know it ain't right. I'm right there with you." And he was. My mom says it was the saddest thing she's ever seen in her life.

I think my mother might have been coming home from one of these late-night alcohol-saturated sessions, driving down the lonely, dusty highway, with thoughts of my father's smile and her comfortable bed and tomorrow's lunch intertwining in her head. She slammed on the brakes when the police car, parked blocking the street, came into view.

The sheriff, known to my mother and everyone else in a town that small, sauntered up to the car, resplendent in his *In the Heat of the Night* racist southern cop garb.

"Bit late to be out, isn't it?"

"What do you want, Vern?" (I imagine his name had to be Vern.) My mother's knuckles on the steering wheel, clenched white. Thoughts of Viola Liuzzo, white civil rights worker murdered by the Klan one state over in Alabama in 1965, flickered through her mind. 1977 was just a breath away from 1965 in the south.

"Just wanted to let you know sumthin, cause you seem like a nice woman, even though you do spend an awful lot of your time working with those retarded nigger babies."

His eyes flashed brighter than his badge in the headlights. "We know what you're doing late at night and who you're with. Consider this a warning."

He waited, a fat cat smile on his face. He waited for my mother to crumble before the combined Leviathan forces of Klan and cop.

He did not know my mother had survived a brutal abusive mother driven mad by schizophrenia and stunted dreams, that my mother had survived sexual assaults, intimate violence, and raising four children on nothing but a big bag of grits and determination. She might have swayed during those times, but she had never ever broken.

"Are you going to move your car?" my mother spit through her teeth, eyes staring straight ahead.

Vern blinked quickly, twice. "Beg pardon?" his surprise making him more polite than he intended.

"Are you going to move your car out my way so I can get home?" My mother finally turned her eyes toward him, her resolution like steel.

Vern toughened up as well. "I'll move it when you change your attitude, and your friends," he countered menacingly.

"Well, all right then." My mother, without taking her eyes off Vern, hit the reverse, skidding back 100 feet, and in one smooth motion, kicked it into drive, and plowed straight into the sheriff's car.

Vern ran over, screaming, "You crazy bitch!"

My mother replied, "You're damn right."

She drove off, one headlight busted out and the front end of her car accordioned in.

She told me that story when I was thirteen. I had asked her what it was like to live in the south and date a Black man. At the end, she laughed. "Don't you know, I saw Vern a few days later in the grocery store, and he tipped his hat, and said, 'How do?' just like always, and walked away. Think he was too embarrassed to tell anyone what happened that night."

I have thought of my mother's immense bravery many times since first hearing this story, and my heartbeats sounded with pride. I have also thought of her immense privilege, cloaked and choked in a white skin and a female gender. I do not know what that sheriff, or any white person, did to my father.

I do know they burned a cross in front of his mother's house, my grandmother. The flames illuminated their block of the Black section of town. It lit up the sky, white sheets billowing silent warnings from the dirt road. I do not know what the neighbors, or my aunt, or my grandmother thought. Did they plead with my father to stop messing around with that white woman before it got him killed, and just what was he tryna prove anyway?

If they did, I picture my father replying, simply, head and shoulders drooping slightly, "I love her, ma."

* * *

"Open up the door right now!"

The door shuddered again under the blows. My mother heard wood splinter somewhere.

My mother cradled her beginning-to-swell stomach and moved as far away from the front door as she could, which was not very far in the single wide trailer she shared with my fourteen-year-old brother and, sometimes, my father.

She worked to block out the waves of nausea only partially caused by being pregnant with me. My father had been gone for three weeks to god knows where. When she first told him she was pregnant, he seemed so excited. For two whole months, he was the dutiful husband, even though they were not common law yet. He took shorter hauls in his rig, gone for two days at the most. He brought home treats. He talked to her belly. To me.

"He tried so hard," my mother mused. "He really did, he did the best he knew how to do. By me and by you."

Then one day he disappeared. Mom asked around half-heartedly. It wasn't the first time, or even the fifteenth time. She had other concerns right now: taking care of her almost grown manchild at home, and the one growing in her belly.

"I had made the decision to have a baby, and I picked your father to be the one to give you to me. I knew me and your dad weren't going to last, but there was so much I loved about him. I guess I wanted to take some of the good parts with me after it was over."

Now he was back, drunk and angry. Angry at his out-of-control life. Angry he couldn't get a better job. Angry the only person who saw him as a man was my mother, her white privilege and white ignorance like a shawl draped over her shoulders. He could not even parent the four children he had—what right did he have bringing another child into the world? Especially a half-white child who would fit into no world?

* * *

The rage my father felt was not unique to him. Black rage, ignited like gasoline in the 1960s, lit this country aflame into the 1970s. It burned brightly, in homes, on the streets and behind prison walls. Countless brave souls took that rage, incubated and fed by centuries of white supremacist terror, and turned it against the structures of power, rather than against those closest to them. Even under the most repressive and brutal conditions, like at New York's Attica Prison in 1971, people made the decision to fight against oppression and demand justice.

"We demand, as human beings, the dignity and justice that is due to us by our right of birth. We do not know how the present system of brutality and dehumanization and injustice has been allowed to be perpetrated in this day of enlightenment, but we are the living proof of its existence and we cannot allow it to continue," from the Attica Manifesto.

In 1971, thirteen hundred Attica prisoners, of all races following Black leadership, rose up in the largest prison rebellion in U.S. history, in response to the murder of Black Panther Party prison leader George Jackson, who was gunned down by prison guards. Starting in the prison's D-yard, the prisoners took forty guards hostage and took over the prison, holding it for five days while demanding freedom.

The Attica prisoners issued twenty-eight demands, which, along with the history of the uprising, has been documented by Freedom Archives. These demands ranged from addressing living conditions, brutal racist violence by prison staff, creating a community review board for prisoners' grievances, and granting the right to unionize as workers.

The Attica Brothers demanded the truth be told about George Jackson, about all the hundreds of thousands of people locked behind bars at that time. They called for an end to overcrowding, and for a look at the racial disparity in incarceration rates. They wanted to be let out of their cells for more than six hours a day, and paid more than a dollar for a full day's work. They wanted education, real rehabilitation, and medical care that was not more fatal than the original disease or injury.

Give us more than one shower a week, they said, more than one roll of toilet paper a month (and too bad if it doesn't last). Give us letters from our loved ones that haven't been blacked out. Give us books that teach us our true history as oppressed peoples. Give us educational and vocational training that prepares us to do something other than return to this place after we are released.

Give us an end to the racist slurs and beatings by prison guards who referred to their billyclubs as "nigger sticks."

The rebellion at Attica went deeper even than these demands, though. Fundamentally, the prisoners challenged the foundations of this nation. Their cry was an end to racism, as well as an end to the brutality of incarceration. Indeed, the Attica brothers called for an end to prisons themselves, since those are the institutional foundations of the prison system. "We set forth demands that will bring closer to reality the demise of these prison institutions that serve no useful purpose to the people of America, but to those who would enslave and exploit the people of America."

Outside observers and journalists all reported that the guards taken as hostages were treated well, and that the community the prisoners created for those five days was in many ways a utopian one, based on communal support and respect. *New York Times* columnist Tom Wicker wrote as a citizen-observer allowed in: "The racial harmony that prevailed among the prisoners—it was absolutely astonishing… That prison yard was the first place I have ever seen where there was no racism."

The goal of Attica was freedom for everyone, as one of the Attica prisoners, Herbert X. Blyden, told those allowed in, "We are standing here for all the oppressed people of the world, and we are not going to give up or knuckle under, we are going to show the way! For we have the way!"

Despite this, then New York state governor Nelson Rockefeller refused to negotiate with the prisoners. Instead, he sent in five hundred state troopers who attacked the prison, firing more than two thousand rounds of ammunition in nine minutes. They wounded at least eighty-six, and killed forty-three people, including ten guards. Prison authorities lied and said the prisoners had slit the guards' throats, a fabrication mainstream media was only too happy to repeat, but autopsies showed they were murdered by that horrifically oxymoronic reality: friendly fire.

That was not the end of the punishment for those who dared to rebel at Attica. The leaders who survived were tortured and beaten for months, and shipped out to isolation cells where they were caged for decades.

This almost incomprehensible level of repression was not just about inhumanely punishing the Attica rebels; it was about sending a message to all others who would think of challenging existing power structures. No mercy would be shown in maintaining the existing order. Some heard this threat; they dropped their fists and backed away slowly, to return to the shadows and allow their rage to consume more socially acceptable targets.

Others chose to listen to the fearless, unwavering voices of the Attica prisoners' call, ghost-like, such as that of L.D. Barkley, a twenty-one-year-old Attica prisoner spokesperson murdered by state troopers in the retaking: "*We are men! We are not beasts and we do not intend to be beaten or driven as such. The entire prison populace—that means each and every one of us here—has set forth to change forever the ruthless brutalization and disregard for the lives of the prisoners here and throughout the United States. What has happened here is but the sound before the fury of those who are oppressed.*"

* * *

The call to be acknowledged as men can mean almost infinite things in this patriarchal society. The organizers at Attica used this call to put forth a united front—a unified call for self-determination and freedom. It is a call that echoed for decades, and continues to be heard today; the California prison hunger strike leaders understood their organization as part of a lineage of resistance stretching back to the Attica prisoners as well as George Jackson.

For others, often those who lack the feeling of collective power, who think themselves isolated and alone, the call for manhood often degenerates to the basest requirements of masculinity in this society.

"I know you got a man in there, so help me, god, if you don't open this fucking door!" The pounding of fists caused more splintering. My mom knew the door would not hold.

She rubbed her stomach where the not-yet-me lay nestled.

She grabbed the shotgun from behind the door.

"You need to get out of here," she said, voice hard with love. "Right now. Before you or I do something we'll regret."

The only response was a scream ripped from my father's lips, compressed centuries of rage, silence, and pain. The smell of lynchings. The scream blended with the door crashing in. My father's heavy stumbling boot falls, slurred by anger and alcohol.

The echo of the scream almost blocked out the sound of the gun firing, as my mother shot my father in the leg.

"It was you or him," my mother said sadly and resolutely. We sat on the floor of my bedroom. The walls were decorated with the passing pop stars only young teenagers know.

"Every woman should learn how to protect herself." My mother's litany echoed in my ears. That moment was the first time I really understood what she was preparing me for.

"When he forced the choice, he found out there never was one. Not for me."

* * *

My mother took me to visit Mississippi for a few days every summer after she left my father and we moved overseas. She took me back to the only place she called home: her best friend Miss Essie's house. At that time, the roads to Miss Essie's single level three-bedroom house, with the porch swing out front, were all dirt. I would walk with my friend Theresa, sun soaking into our brown limbs as dirt stuck to our sweaty legs.

We would walk the half-mile to Theresa's house, or up another half mile to the pristine white church, a shimmering mirage in the heat. They had summer picnics there for the young people; lemonade and sweet-ass iced tea was served in jelly jars and flowed like water.

Mississippi was the place I got darker, where my speech and my legs slowed down, where I never quite learned to play double dutch, but where I did learn to catch fireflies in those same jelly jars I drank iced tea out of during the day.

To me, Mississippi was all Black; the only white person I ever saw there was my mother.

My father's life is reported fragments. Out on his own by the age of twelve, he had no education and skin too Black to be beautiful in this country. He grew as wild as the tall grass Theresa and I crawled through.

My mother and I stopped going down south to see my father when I was eleven. "If he wants to see us, he can make some effort." I guess he never did, because I didn't see him again for fifteen years. I got one letter from him when I graduated high school at sixteen. "I am so proud of you," his handwriting so painstaking it hurt me to read. I crumpled the letter up, but couldn't bring myself to throw it away. Instead, I wrote a poem on the back.

At twenty-six years old, I decided it was time to meet this man whose absence had shaped so much of my life. My mother agreed to go with me, as buffer, therapist and safety, ready to pick up whatever pieces my father might carelessly scatter around.

We drove down the dusty roads of my Mississippi childhood with my mother in the passenger's seat, a mirror reversal of the many road trips we took when I was a child. It took ten hours, most of it full of my mother's stories of my father, which I had never heard before. She did this to prepare me and push me past the anger I felt, so I could see the man she had fallen in love with—who she was still in love with.

My mother and I slid into Miss Essie's driveway in front of the house, which looked exactly as I remembered it, except smaller. It was dark. Our headlights cut through foliage and shone on the newly paved roads. They bounced off a tall figure, slightly slouched, daddy long legs crossed easily at the ankles as he leaned against a porch post. Smoke snaked out from the silhouette.

"I think that's him," my mom squinted through the windshield and the years. "I think that's your daddy."

Already the shadow loped toward us, the cigarette hastily thrown in the grass. I slid out of the car. I stared at a man who might or might not have been my father. The same bushy hair in the one picture I have of him. Same heavy mustache. But the hair was mostly gray, not the defiant black I remembered. The eyes I spent many hours staring at in the photograph were covered by thick glasses. My mother always said he was tall, but I didn't imagine his legs would go on for so very long, his torso more of an afterthought.

I waited for some blood memory to activate, something in my DNA to tell me this man was part of me. Nothing. I surreptitiously stole a glance at my mother, who nodded.

He boomed, "Well, now, I would have known you anywhere. You look just like me. Doesn't she?" he shot at my mother, not waiting for a response.

"You remember me, don'tcha, gal?"

The only answer was yes, as he engulfed me in his arms.

* * *

My father drank from a beer wrapped in brown paper bag as we sat in the Mississippi heat. Staring at the scarred playground equipment, the beer belied the fact it was two in the afternoon.

He had asked me if it was all right if he stopped to get a beer along the way. "Just something to cool my mouth down; it's gonna be a hot one today." I did not want to embarrass him, or begrudge him whatever he needed to get through the inquisition to come. When we arrived at the convenience store, the clerk knew him by name. My father asked if I wanted anything. I knew he wanted to buy me something, wanted to be a provider. I got an orange juice, though I didn't think I could get anything past my constricted throat.

I asked my father about the Black Panthers, as we perched on the wall of the town park. During our first visit in a decade and a half, I asked him about the Black Panthers because they shaped so much of who I am—this daughter who was a stranger.

"Right on!" he shouted, a little too loudly, thanks to the beer. He raised his fist.

"I respected the hell outta them guys." (I did not correct him that more than half of Panther members were women.) "They didn't take nothing from nobody. I was all for them, and for the civil rights folks too.

"But you know, it's hard down here," he gestured around at this small Mississippi town. "I was all alone. What can one pea out by himself do? You know what I'm saying?"

"You know I do a lot of work with former Black Panthers, and some who have gone to prison?" I asked him.

His chest lifted with pride. He nodded for several shakes longer than necessary. "That's good, that's real good. That's some important work. I'm... I'm real proud of you."

These were words my childhood hungered to hear said to me, delivered to me now at twenty-six, after I had adopted new father figures, some of them former Panthers. These men taught me the ideology they learned from their days in the Party—that the real enemy was the white supremacist system, not all white people. If a white person was an oppressor, they were to be opposed. But if that white person believed in self-determination and freedom of oppressed people, then they were an ally.

The image of the black panther was chosen for the party because, as co-founder Bobby Seale said in the documentary *All Power to the People*, "If the panther can't go left and it can't go right, then it's coming out, straight through the aggressor, to freedom."

My father came straight out as well: into a bottle, strumming his guitar, swinging at the only white body close enough to hurt—the only white body close enough to love.

We perched on a high wall next to the picnic tables, worn with generations of names etched like Braille. A collection of motley-colored children played on the rusting monkey bars and the cracked slide. After several awkward starts and stops, I asked him. I asked him the question I had carried with me, the question every child should know the answer to.

"Did you... did you miss us? Did you love my mom, us?" I could not bring myself to say "me."

He didn't look at me, or even off into the distance. He stared at the beer can in his hand.

"I loved her. And you. I loved you both so much. Losing you both is the biggest regret of my life. I think about it every day. If I could go back..."

He broke off. Took a long pull from the can. He stared hard at me, with diamond cut eyes.

"Damn, you really do look just like me," he murmured.
And for that moment, I did.

* * *

I imagine myself nestled in my mother's womb, ear pressed to the wall of her stomach, with eyes that can see through the translucent skin of her belly.

She stands at iron bars. My father sits on a metal bunk, the stink from the bucket of shit next to him filling the cell. His is leg patched up at the hospital because my mother only meant to graze him. They stare on opposite sides of the bars, their separation now made tangible and real.

My dad's lips are chapped, his eyes blood-shot. Tears stand in them.

"I'm sorry." The words fall soft from his mouth.

"I know."

"I want to come home." His hands stretch outwards, grasping, then falling back limply next to him on the bunk.

"We'll see." One hand is on her stomach, the other on the bars, wanting both to break and strengthen them at the same time.

"Time's up," drawls the guard who suddenly appears at my mother's elbow. "You gonna have to leave now." His son was in her class two years ago, so he manages a brush of sympathy in his tone.

My mom gazes at my father for one, two moments longer. Then she turns and walks away. She doesn't look back. My mother never looks back.

My father memorizes her back as she goes.

Then his vision is obscured by the bulbous face of the guard.

"This is where you were always meant to be, boy, don't you know that?" the guard drawls. He barks out laughter and saunters away from my father's bowed head, now nestled in his long and silent hands.

* * *

These prison scenes are imagined, like so much of my father's life. I did not see him again after my visit to Mississippi. I received two brief letters, before the silence between us settled like a shroud.

I tried to put it out of my mind; I told myself I did my part. I reached out, went to see him, asked him the hard questions, got some even harder answers, and still extended love to him. The rest was up to him.

But there was always the me inside who waited, patiently and endlessly. I waited for a letter, a phone call, a second-hand message passed to me, any communication from him, however small.

Instead, a few days before New Year's, I got the message he was gone. Passed away. Six years since I had seen him. Six years of almost continual silence, and now the silence that would continue forever.

Then I found out he had been sick for over a year. And he had never reached out to me. What was I to make of that? My mother, forever picking up our broken pieces, told me it was because he felt he wasn't worthy of me, that he didn't have a right to ask me for anything, and that he had to lay in the bed he made.

That helped, and it didn't. How do you mourn someone who hurt you so deeply, someone you really don't know at all? These struggles continue. We have no cultural frameworks for how to deal with the death of an absentee parent, which is strange: there are so many missing fathers and yet we don't talk about how to grieve. How to grieve not only for this stranger who is father, but also for a lifetime of absence that now no longer has any chance of reconciliation?

The first few days after hearing my father had died, lines from Tupac Shakur's song "Dear Mama" played on endless repeat in my head: "No love from my daddy cause the coward wasn't there/ He passed away and I didn't cry, cause my anger/ Wouldn't let me feel for a stranger."

Anger is what we are left with. Anger is what we are told is an acceptable emotion towards fathers who weren't fathers.

But eventually I had to remember that all anger comes from pain. The larger the rage the deeper the hurt. I was allowed my anger. But I was more than just rage. To pretend otherwise would be to embody cowardice, scared of my own complexities and contradictions in the mirror. I also had to allow myself my sadness, as well as the love I had for my father, because it was out of that love that I could build a path forward.

The unanswered questions and unrealized dreams cut so deep, they leave me bleeding. The only poem I have ever written about my father is one I wrote in his voice, an attempt to gain the understanding I was denied:

> I felt the years pressing down on me
> And I didn't want
> To cry in front of my baby
> Not yet
> Anyway.
>
> I sat down
> When I got back to this one room
> I call all mine
> pulled out my guitar
> And played a song
> I wrote for her
> When she was seven
> And far away from me.
> She's never heard it.
>
> I wonder
> If she's ever gonna
> Put me
> In a poem?

And I work to find peace with the fragments of truth I have, and the imaginings I have created to fill the gaping holes in between.

GANGSTERS AND MARTYRS

LIKE MOST PEOPLE, I AM A MASS OF CONTRADICTIONS AND COMPLEX-
ities: colors that clash and fight for dominance. I'm an anarchist
who stridently follows the rules I agree with. I'm a writer who hates
the actual process of writing. I'm a poet with an ego both immense
and infinitely fragile. I'm a political organizer and activist who has
been obsessed, since I was a child, with mobsters, gangsters, and
"criminals."

I grew up on military bases overseas. My mother was a teacher
for the Department of Defense—not a soldier, though we sometimes
lived on base housing. We had access to the amenities offered military
personnel: the always understocked PX/BX, the only shopping outlet
on base; a movie theater that played one six-month-old film at a time;
and AFN, the Armed Forces Network. AFN was the only English-
language television station available. The military chose which shows
to import—obviously we got a lot of episodes of *M*A*S*H*. Since
they were the only game in town, we all grumbled about the lack of
selection, but watched anyway.

Sometimes on Sunday afternoons, they would show old gangster
movies, everything from James Cagney favorites to obscure 40s pro-
ductions with no-name talentless hoods in them. I would soak in the

overblown New York-drenched accents, the flat writing, and the dramatic climax where the gangster was killed and civility returned to a society now cleansed of a cancer.

The gangster always died. This was not a coincidence but a compromise on Hollywood's part, made to the conservative Catholic organization the Legion of Decency, which threatened to shut down all gangster movies from being produced. To assuage them, Hollywood agreed to create and follow a 1933 Production Code, popularly known as the Hays Code, after Will H. Hays, president of the Motion Picture Producers and Distributors of America at the time. In addition to regulating depictions of sex, drugs violence, and "moral meaning," according to the *New York Times*, the code mandated that the gangster had to lose.

PBS states, "The Code's preamble stated, 'crime will be shown to be wrong and that the criminal life will be loathed and that the law will at all times prevail.' Villains could not be protagonists, and at the end, they had to be dead or in jail." The foundation of the Code was to reinforce the dominant ideologies of the day, including white supremacy, patriarchy, and capitalism. The Code was designed to allow those in power to control and shape the imaginations of the public.

I always felt a deep sorrow when the gangster died. I connected more to his "make my own way out of no way" mentality than the "by the book" copthink. I never related to the hero, a struggling schmuck who didn't have enough money to marry his childhood sweetheart.

I dreamed of being a gangster's moll—the only position afforded women in the underworld. Molls weren't the stars of the show. In fact, they were little more than glorified props. But at least I would get to carry a gun—often hidden in my garter belt tucked snug next to my thigh—and pop my gum real loud. I carried this fantasy into real life every chance I got. I was a flapper girl at Halloween, the grinning plastic pumpkin head overflowing with candy behind me no match for the sinister gap toothed grin painted on my own face.

In fourth grade science class one day, my teacher, attempting to get us interested in the relationship between time and space, spoke of time travel. He asked us if we could go back to any time, when would we choose. My thin brown arm rocketed upward faster than any NASA shuttle launch.

Loudly, I pronounced, "I would go back to the 1920s and run liquor with other gangsters, and dance in illegal clubs in fancy clothes until the sun came up."

The skinny blonde kid with the twisted right front tooth who sat diagonally from me, Jeremy Somebody, snorted. "What? You can't be a gangster."

"Why not?" I retorted hotly. I had spent hours perfecting my "You dirty rat" inflection. I thought I sounded better even than the original.

"Cause you're Black. And you're a girl."

Jeremy triumphantly unfurled this point with a finality that rebuffed any response.

In truth, I had no response. I mean, he was right. White women were marginal enough in the gangster films I watched, and the only Black men I saw were waiters and chauffeurs. Black women? Other than a maid or two in the background, as far as these films were concerned, there were no such people.

It seemed like a decision had to be made between my dream and my waking life. So I forgot my dream of being someone's gun girl and focused on the immutable realities of being a young Black woman.

* * *

When I was thirteen, we moved from Germany to Springfield, Oregon. From a world of predominately Black and Latino (the military disproportionately recruits people of color; it stands to reason that their children, who I went to school on base with, would be too), to a world where I was a flygirl in the buttermilk, to reinterpret Black music journalist Greg Tate.

My mother's analysis of the middle ground I straddled as a Black mixed child was pretty simple: "When someone asks if you're Black or white, you tell them proudly, 'I'm brown.'" I was a new concoction unto myself. Meant to provide me a safe haven and new terrain, it just ended up making me feel isolated and alone.

This was only a novel racial concept to me. Black mixed-race people were certainly not new to the United States. White slave owners frequently increased their wealth by making the enslaved Black women as "productive" (reproductive) as possible, using the brutal means of intimidation, sexual assault, and rape.

Because of this country's vicious legacy of racist chattel slavery, unless someone just got off a plane from Africa (and maybe not even then), Black folks are going to have some white up in them (and the reverse is true for many white people as well, whether they want to admit it or not).

The concept of the "tragic mulatto," the sad little mixed and mixed-up Black girl, is not a new idea either. Perhaps memories can be held in blood vessels, passed down in DNA. They are most certainly transmitted through popular culture and, whenever we talk about Black women who are in any way shown as human beings, the tragic mulatto surfaces. Donald Bogle wrote in *Toms, Coons, Mulattoes, Mammies and Bucks: An Interpretive History of Blacks in American Films*, "Usually the mulatto is made likable—even sympathetic (because of her white blood, no doubt)—and the audience believes that the girls' life could have been productive and happy had she not been a 'victim of divided racial inheritance.'"

I could have easily fallen victim to tragic mulatto syndrome if it were not for the prisoners who entered my teenage years. From my mother's boyfriend to Kakamia, they drew me a map through my convoluted bloodline until I stepped onto the western shores of Africa. Kakamia repped for his African history hard as a Puerto Rican. Puerto Ricans, he said, are both the most African and most mixed peoples in the new world. To paraphrase Nuyorican poet Pedro Pietri, "My mother is white, my father is Black. That must make me Puerto Rican."

"You know how many Black folks are mixed?" my mother's boyfriend asked me in a letter once. "Sheeiiit, we all might as well start checking 'other' right now then."

* * *

There were a total of seven Black people in my high school of over a thousand. Some, like Floyd with his skateboard cool and laid back attitude, hung out with the group of slackers, punks, metal heads, and weirdos I ran with. There was Angela, a star athlete. Her lean frame ate up the track like a prairie fire. Rather than feeling pride in her accomplishments, she made me feel even chunkier and clumsier than I was. Others, like Troy, were part of the Blacks and Browns, Black and Latino hip hop kids, classified by the school as a gang because they wore baggy jeans and hard faces, and because they chose not to associate too closely with white students.

I had lived in a racial borderland, shielded to a large degree by my mother and her white privilege. I was more easily accepted by white people because of her, and because of my "appropriate" manners, my "articulate" speech, my lighter skin, and my less nappy hair. "Oh you speak so well!" has plagued me my whole life, as has the Black counterpart of "How come you sound like a white girl?" It stands not as a challenge, but a test: will you abandon those darker who grew out of scorched earth, with no white mothershade to mitigate? Or, to put it more plainly, when the shit goes down, whose side are you gonna be on?

It was not until I moved to Springfield that I began to understand what Blackness was, what Blackness meant in America. Pickup trucks with gun racks adorned with the confederate flag started to wake me from my deep race sleep.

I worked on the high school newspaper. One April Fool's edition was full of fake stories advocated sowing the U.S./Mexico border with landmines, which was an actual proposal from a U.S. congressman at the time.

April Fools.

White male students, all baseball caps and tobacco can rings in their back pockets, carried copies of the issue. They read aloud from it over greasy school cafeteria lunches. Others snickered and exchanged glances any time a Latino student walked by.

When two white students pushed a Mexican girl down the stairs, her books spilled all over the stairwell as her tears spilled all over her cheeks. They shouted at her, their voices echoing all the way down, "Go back to where you came from!"

I knew the line had been drawn for me.

I found guidance in the most unlikely of places. Mrs. Borrevick wore bright lipstick drawn around her actual lips to make her mouth appear bigger. She didn't have to do the same with her heart. She was the guidance counselor who took in the misfits and rejects. Mrs. Borrevick became my Advance Placement History Independent Study teacher after I quit AP History on the first day. I opened the textbook, saw five pages of glossy photos labeled "Before Columbus" out of the five-hundred page book. I slammed it shut and announced I was dropping out of school. Mrs. Borrevick handed me Howard Zinn's radical history of this country, *A People's History of the United States*.

"Get to work."

I asked about an internship. I wanted to be a historian. I thought I could work at the pitifully small local museum that shared the same building as the library.

"Oh you don't want to do that," she said dismissively. "I can't imagine you being happy locked away with dusty memorabilia from the pioneer days. You should give these people a call instead." She slid me a card with the number to something called Clergy and Laity Concerned.

"What's that?" I asked suspiciously, thinking she was trying to recruit me for some Christian youth group.

"Just check it out," she said, shooing me out the door and waving another student in.

I had to take the bus from Springfield to the transit center in Eugene, the larger town over the bridge. Then I caught another bus to the Whiteaker neighborhood. My skin shivered slightly. Never go to the Whiteaker neighborhood, they said—especially after dark. I was too young politically to know "bad" and "unsafe" parts of town meant "brown."

Clergy and Laity Concerned's Eugene office was in a creaky old building with pipes that rattled when you did the dishes in the faded kitchen. On the frayed worn couches near the bay window, I first heard the words "communism" and "socialism" as more than a dangerous evil sent to devour. I typed stories for the newsletter into an antiquated box of a Mac. Talk of the Zapatistas, U.S. political prisoners, Sandinistas, Central America, Cuba, apartheid, Assata Shakur, and the Black Panther Party all swirled around me. I didn't know what the hell these people were talking about. But I was beginning to get the feeling there was a whole world out there I knew absolutely nothing about.

I was damn sure going to find out, though.

One day, I timidly asked Jon if he could recommend something for me to read. A young white indie rocker with cardigan sweaters and converse sneakers, he looked more at home in a 50s car hop poster than organizing in support of farmworkers.

He reached up without hesitation and handed me a small black book. A dreadlocked man stared solemnly out of the cover.

"I think you might find some good stuff in here."

I started Mumia Abu-Jamal's *Live From Death Row* on the long bus ride home. I stayed up until three in the morning, neglecting schoolwork and my favorite show on TV, to finish.

Mumia: an award-winning independent journalist in Philadelphia and former president of the Black Journalists' Association, became a resident on Pennsylvania's death row for thirty years. His reporting helped lay the foundation for Philadelphia police being one of the only police departments ever indicted by the U.S. Department of Justice for brutality and corruption. He was convicted of the murder of a white police officer in 1981. Millions around the world believe him to be innocent.

Many more believe Mumia did not have a fair trial. The stenographer heard the blatantly racist judge say he was going to help "fry the nigger." The prosecutor repeatedly violated Mumia's constitutional rights. The incompetent defense attorney was later disbarred. There were no resources for research or experts. Mumia was physically bound and gagged when he tried to assist in his own defense, and was found guilty of murder. He was sentenced to the death penalty. Entire books have been written by and about Mumia.

Let me state clearly, I believe Mumia is innocent.

But I have come to feel that doesn't really matter in the final equation. Over the years, "guilt" and "innocence" have become cloudy terms.

As discussed earlier, it's not what you do but who you are that lands you in prison. As Michelle Alexander notes, "Although the majority of illegal drug users and dealers nationwide are white, three-fourths of all people imprisoned for drug offenses have been Black or Latino." With endless statistics like these that show the chasm between who "does the crime" and who "does the time," it is very clear that it is identities and not actions that are criminalized.

"Every crime that I do is petty/ every criminal is rich already," sang
rap group The Coup. Mumia led me to other political prisoners, older
ones. Some have been incarcerated for more than forty years, casualties
of America's war on revolution, waged in the 1960s and 1970s. Overwhelmingly Black and brown, along with some white allies, most are
veterans of the Black Panther Party, the Black Liberation Movement, the
Puerto Rican Independence Movement, the American Indian Movement, and the white anti-imperialist struggle. They organized protests,
wrote articles, cleaned up streets, fed children, taught people to read,
engaged in civil disobedience, observed the police in their community—legal and armed—operated free health clinics, provided security for
prominent movement figures, went to every political trial happening,
took over the Statue of Liberty and Alcatraz Prison. They were part of a
global struggle to recreate a more just world. Some of these people have
become my mentors, my support system, and my family.

Many of these political prisoners were framed, like Geronimo ji
Jaga Pratt, Black Panther leader, framed for the murder and robbery
of a white couple on a tennis court. He served twenty-seven years in
prison, even though the FBI had wiretaps that prove he was at a Panther Central Committee meeting hundreds of miles away when the
murder occurred.

There are some of these political prisoners, though, who do not
deny the "crimes" of which they are convicted. Their language sub-
verts the images we are given. Bank expropriation (read: robbery).
Retaliatory strikes (read: shooting police who brutalized communities). One person's terrorist is another community's freedom fighter.
As Kuwasi Balagoon, Black Liberation Army member and prisoner of
war, said in his trial statement where he was convicted of expropriat-
ing funds (robbing a Brinks truck): "Expropriation raids are a method
used in every revolution by those who have got to get resources from
the haves to carry on armed struggle. When George Washington and
company crossed the Delaware, it was to raid the British, to take money, supplies and arms…"

George Washington is an American hero, but he was a terrorist to
the British.

Like Balagoon, folks locked down who hold this framework do
not call themselves political prisoners. They call themselves prisoners

of war, because they believe that the United States has declared war on their communities. They feel they should not be tried as criminals, but as soldiers captured during battle. They claim their actions not as crimes, but acts of warfare, of armed resistance. Any occupied country or nation has the right to fight back for freedom, by whatever means are necessary. They believe in the words of United Nations Resolution 3246, passed in 1974, which "reaffirms the legitimacy of the peoples' struggle for liberation from colonial and foreign domination and alien subjugation by all available means, including armed struggle."

They were not the only ones who felt that way. When Black Liberation Army member Assata Shakur escaped from prison in the early 1980s, signs sprouted like dandelions across the Black community: "Assata welcome here." The same happened for Angela Davis when she was placed on America's Most Wanted list and forced underground; she was accused of owning the guns used in a failed 1970 attempt by seventeen-year-old Jonathan Jackson to negotiate freedom for prisoners (including Panther prison leader George Jackson) by taking a courtroom hostage.

So I believe Mumia is not guilty of the crimes for which he was convicted. And I also admire the ways he stands in solidarity with those incarcerated for practicing their right to self-defense, here and around the world. This was one of the many lessons about the complexities of life I learned as his writing leaped off the page at me.

Mumia's words in *Live from Death Row* sparked a path that led me to the gates of countless prisons, from the SHU in California to Texas's death row. They connected me with others who refuse to let their voices be buried under concrete and bars, who organize concerts, events, newsletters, and campaigns from rooms the size of my bathroom. Others, like Mumia, wrote only with the ink refill inside of a pen; the pen casing confiscated because "it could be a weapon." That is how Mumia brought the book that captivated me to life, hid it away until it could escape free, like an enslaved Black person heading towards the North Star.

So many times in my life, Mumia has acted as my North Star. Through *Live From Death Row* and researching more about his life and work, I learned what integrity looks like when it carries the weight of death on its back. In his essay, "L.A. Outlaw," Mumia challenged the legal right for the police in Rodney King's beating to be retried. At first I was horrified when I read it: why would Mumia be siding with these racist, brutal cops? It was a mistake that they hadn't been found guilty, and now we were supposed to give up the scraps thrown to Black communities after their deferred dreams exploded? It must have been on my fourth reading of this essay (so short—less than three pages—like the majority of his essays) that I came to realize what he meant when he wrote this: "To be silent while the state violates its own alleged constitutional law to prosecute someone we hate is but to invite silence when the state violates its own laws to prosecute the state's enemies and opponents. This we cannot do. We must deny the state that power."

There is a strategic mind here—if they come for you at night, they'll come for me in the morning. But there is also a mind fixed on integrity. We must not let the state have the power to change our principles, our values. We cannot allow them to break us and reshape us as they attempt to do inside and out of prisons every day, and as they have attempted to do to Mumia for thirty-five years. He has refused both their stick and their carrot: the insidious psychological games designed to compromise your character, your very soul.

This was never clearer than when ABC's *20/20* filmed a segment on Mumia's case in 2000. The level of national exposure could have greatly helped Mumia's struggle for justice. Even if the piece had been biased, having even the briefest clips of Mumia speaking would be certain to stay with those who heard his brilliance, his clarity, his insights. However, because there was a strike happening at ABC during that time period, Mumia refused the interview, saying he would rather die than cross a picket line. From most, this would be hyperbole. From Mumia, who has come within hours of having the state take his last breath, it is a declaration of the highest form of integrity.

Mumia's words in *Live from Death Row* sparked a path that led me to the gates of countless prisons. His words are elegant, poetic, searing. Undeniable. He wrote life on death row real, vignettes about the people around him, the supposed scum of the earth. He wrote them human: beautifully flawed and tragically human.

Mumia wrote of his youngest daughter Tiny's first visit to death row. She became infuriated by the glass barrier between all Pennsylvania death row inmates and their visitors. She did not understand why Mumia had not been allowed to touch his wife or his children for over thirty years—why he had grandchildren he had never touched.

Sadness and shock shifted into fury as her petite fingers curled into tight fists, which banged and pummeled the Plexiglass barrier, which shuddered and shimmied but didn't shatter. "Break it! Break it!" she screamed… "Why *can't* I hug him? Why *can't* we kiss? Why *can't* I sit on his lap? *Why can't we touch?* Why not?"

Mumia illuminates why prisons exist, who benefits from them, who is getting rich on the trading of flesh, and whose flesh is traded to create dollars—poor and Black and brown. Illiterate. Those with mental health issues.

His book was not about himself. He was eyes, ears, mouth, and heart recording. He showed me the web of oppression threaded through my life, ensnaring me.

And Mumia showed me how to begin to hack away at those threads.

* * *

The flyer said to gather at the entrance to the University of Oregon. Unfamiliar with activist time, I showed up twenty minutes early. A group of patchwork-pants-wearing, patchouli-downed white kids with dreadlocks sat in a circle with replicated African drums, happily banging away, completely off rhythm. Frat boys in polo shirts with upturned collars stared at every passing woman's ass. I sat on the low wall awkwardly. Maybe no one was coming. Maybe they already left. How would I know who they were if they did show up? My palms started to sweat.

Then ten young white people, some in all black with patches on their ripped hoodies, approached me. They carried signs reading "Free Mumia!" and "Free All Political Prisoners."

A woman with a smile wide as the skateboard she carried asked, "Are you here for the Mumia protest?"

I nodded my head so quickly I injured my neck.

"Great," she handed me a sign. "We're almost ready to start."

In ten more minutes, the group of forty or so folks began to stride down the street, passing shops and bars. The sound of chanting and banging drums erupted. Slogans brand new to my ears rumbled from voices all around me. Traffic stopped for us and waited as we marched through the street.

Since that day I have marched in crowds numbering tens of thousands, knowing we were marching at the same moment as millions around the world. But I never felt as inspired as that first protest, where I learned a collective of people are strong. Powerful. Unstoppable.

Someone jabbed play on a boombox. Mumia's rich voice, honey and steel, burst forth. It rained down on the boutiques and pizza shops. On me. It was the first time I heard his voice speaking hidden and forgotten stories, smuggled out from the watchful eyes of the guards.

Mumia said the name Rabbani. Rabbani, a fifteen-year-old manchild was sentenced as an adult and got fifteen to thirty for robbery: one to two of his lives.

> His first six or seven years in this manmade hell found him constantly locked in battles with guards, and he logged more years in "the hole" than he did in general population status. He grew into manhood in shackles, and every time I saw him, he seemed bigger in size but more bitter in spirit. I was always struck by the innate brilliance of the young man—a brilliance immersed in a bitterness so acidic that it seemed capable of dissolving iron. For almost fifteen years, this brilliance had been caged in cubes of time and steel.

Snapshots of prison life: Mumia pulled back the curtain, to reveal the machinations behind. This was not an isolated mistake or a glitch in the program. It wasn't even a system-wide failure. It was the system of incarceration and criminalization working perfectly, exactly as intended. Rabbani's experiences were the norm, not the exception.

> [Rabbani] has been "corrected" in precisely the same way that hundreds of thousands of others have been, that is to

say, warehoused in a vat that sears the very soul. He has never held a woman as a mate or lover; he has never held a newborn baby in his palm, its heart athump with new life; he hasn't seen the sun rise, nor the moon glow, in almost fifteen years. For a robbery, "armed" with a pellet gun, at fifteen years of age.

Did he say Rabbani? Or did he say Kakamia?

I knew then why Mumia's voice was more dangerous than a gun. You could not listen without being moved. You could not listen without wanting to fight. For Mumia. For Rabbani. For all the Mumias and all the Rabbanis.

"Live from death row, this is Mumia Abu-Jamal." The sound of bars slamming echoed from the speakers.

I hoisted my "Free Mumia NOW" sign high and joined the rumbling voices around me.

"Brick by brick, wall by wall we're going to free Mumia Abu-Jamal!"

That day I was sure we could, led by Mumia's voice, full of "musings, memories, prophesies."

I have since learned the bricks of prison walls are much stronger than I imagined and incredibly resistant to dismantling. But I also have the example given to me by Mumia, that the resilience of hope and determination is a wildflower growing through concrete. And given long enough and with enough pressure, those flowers' roots will break apart concrete, to continue growing free and unfettered.

* * *

The Human Rights Coalition (HRC), now a statewide Pennsylvania organization of prisoners' families I helped found, was the brainchild of political prisoner Russell "Maroon" Shoatz. The goal was to put families at the center of the work being done to challenge a bloated prison system that devoured their loved ones, and spit them back out more battered than they went in.

HRC has an advisory council made up of organizers in prison. One of my duties was communicating with council members. Hasan Shakur was one.

He and I quickly grew close. His wide-eyed innocence was not
what I expected to find on Texas's death row; though in his twenties,
he had the face of a fifteen-year-old. His was a textbook case of Black
underresourced and overexploited life: family ripped asunder, with
little to no education, slanging and banging and hardening his face
to survive. He lived on Texas's death row for nine years, dressed in
the baptismal white of that death house. He was reborn there, not
through heavenly hands but through nightsticks and pepper spray.
Not baptized gently in a lazy stream—his head was pushed into toi-
lets. His balls were crushed under boots. Hasan Shakur, born out of
Derrick Frazier, not through water but through a hail of bullets and
billy clubs. Child of George Jackson and Angela Davis, Mumia and all
political prisoners. Grandchild of Nat Turner. Great-great-grandson
of Seminoles and maroon colonies and quilombos. He took this heritage as seriously as the heart attack induced by the poison ultimately
shoved into his veins by the state of Texas.

Hasan consumed any knowledge he could get his hands on: history, politics, economics. He shared that knowledge with everyone
around him, including me. He helped HRC focus not just on reform-
ing the prison system, but on becoming abolitionists in the tradition
of slavery abolitionists, based on the idea that the entire prison institution is rooted in inequality and the exploitation of bodies for the
will and profit of others. Prison abolition is grounded in the idea that
the system cannot be reformed. It must be dismantled.

With Hasan's support, I began learning about alternatives to incarceration and police. Hasan spoke about communities keeping each other safe, not relying on police, who patrol as if they were in Baghdad or
Fallujah. I later learned more about organizations like Safe OUTside the
System (SOS), started by young LGBTQ folks of color in Brooklyn to
address street harassment and violence they experienced. Instead of focusing on asking for more police patrols, which these youth understood
actually made them less safe because of the continual persecution they
suffered at the hands of the police, SOS made the community responsible for everyone's safety. After multiple years of community dialogues,
every public institution, from the corner store to the church to the laun-
dromat, identified as a space where LGBTQ folks—and everyone else
who experiences violence or threats—could go. Organizing by and for

those who are most marginalized in the community made the entire community safer, stronger, and more whole.

I learned about decriminalization of crimes like drugs as a major alternative to incarceration, by using the lens of health crisis instead of war, and using money to create programs to treat addiction. This also meant recognizing that the number-one way to reduce all crime is addressing the social inequalities in society. What would it look like to use the tens of billions spent on the prison system differently: for living wage jobs, for public education, for health care, for quality affordable housing, and more? What if we actually used that money to build up communities, rather than give the police tanks and body armor to fight a war on communities of color?

Alternatives to incarceration need to focus on more than restorative justice; we want transformative justice, because we don't want to restore what was unequal before, but to transform it into something new. We want alternatives that recognize the humanity of everyone involved. Instead of locking someone up, they'll stay in the community to make right, and to be part of a healing process for the individuals and the larger community. These are responses like the one I saw in a video for the Community Conferencing Center in Baltimore, where a woman's car was stolen by two young men who were caught. Instead of sending them to prison—which did nothing for her or the community—they had a mediation where she shared how their actions affected her and they shared what they were thinking and what led them to the act. At the end, the youths apologized and a repayment schedule was set up. The mediation had been so successful at defusing anger that when one of the young men confessed he was unemployed, the woman, whose car he stole, gave him a lead for a job.

For me, the ethos and the heart of alternatives to incarceration and police is encapsulated in this story: My friend's family owns an Ethiopian-Eritrean restaurant. One day, his father saw the tattoo on my back, which is a huge oak tree, bare branches stretching for my shoulders. He said, "Is that a wanza tree?" I said no, that I didn't know what a wanza tree was. He replied, "It was the center of life back home in villages. All major events happened under it—celebrations, weddings. And when someone did something wrong, the entire village would gather under the wanza tree. They would form a circle and place the person who did harm in the middle. Then they would go around the circle, and each community member would tell a story about the person who did harm when they were at their very best. At the end, the village would give the person a choice: do you want to be the person we know you are, who helps people, or do you want to be this person who hurts the community?"

The door that led to thinking about alternatives to incarceration and police was just one of the many Hasan showed me. Hasan opened up doors with infinite numbers of paths beyond.

Hasan was the hardest worker I ever met. He founded organizations, sat on boards, and planned antiviolence concerts in the community. He put out a newsletter a hell of a lot more regularly than many groups on the outside. He helped numerous organizations with strategic planning. He pushed everyone around him mercilessly. And he did all this from a cell the size of a bathroom, with the held breath of murder's stench on it.

"Wa, when are you gonna get me that report I asked for last week?" his letter would start off abruptly. Sans salutation. No time for nicety. "Did you get feedback from my last proposal to the group yet? Break it down for me, cuz."

Sometimes I snapped at him. I complained there were only so many hours in the day. I had other responsibilities.

"Wa Wa, I'm a workhorse and I'm going to push everyone around me. If I see someone leaning back, Ima crack that whip."

If Hasan expected the best around him, he expected the impossible from himself. And he delivered it consistently, sacrificing sleep and health.

The first time I got to see him in person was also the last. The death warrant had been signed. Death hung over his head. And yet he was still Hasan, planning and organizing in case the unspeakable happened. He instructed that Haramia, another prisoner on Texas's death row, was to take his place on the HRC's advisory council. Haramia was ready, and would contribute much, as organizer and poet.

I nodded, struggling to hold back tears.

To lighten the mood, Hasan joked, saying I should be proud of him—he got six hours of sleep the night before, double his usual dose.

"Yeah but how many did you get the night before?" I asked, cracking a smile.

Hasan had been issued a death warrant before, in April 2006. Three days after his twenty-ninth birthday. Across the country, allies of Hasan's and opponents of the death penalty organized. And we won that day—a stay was given. Facts needed to be reviewed. There was more to be discussed.

Hasan was convicted of killing a white woman and her son in Refugio, Texas. There was no physical evidence. The only evidence against him was a forced confession. He was intimidated, interrogated for hours, promised a thirty-year deal in return. Hasan was denied a lawyer for the entirety of his questioning. In the videotaped interrogation, the officer informed nineteen-year-old Hasan of his right to an attorney.

"If I could afford one, I would," was the reply.

The officer began to question Hasan, despite this obvious expressed desire for a lawyer: unconstitutional.

"The videotaped 'confession' became the prosecution's smoking gun," wrote the National Campaign to End the Death Penalty. "With no physical evidence linking Frazier to the scene of the crime, the district attorney relied on the coerced confession to convince a nearly all-white jury that this young Black defendant was, in fact, guilty of killing a white mother and child." Members of the jury had contact with the victims' family during the trial.

Hasan's lawyer did not mount a defense to show any mitigating circumstances. There was no mention of fact that he'd dropped out of school in seventh grade, or of his abusive father and his beloved drug-addicted mother, who had died of an overdose by Hasan's fifteenth birthday. The defense attorney was placed on probation by the state bar soon after Hasan's conviction.

All of this evidence led to a stay. So when another execution date was set for August 31, 2006, a few months later, his friends and supporters banked on another stay. Hadn't we, after all, shown more than a case for reasonable doubt? Wouldn't the system have to do what was right? I naively believed all we had to do was show Hasan to be unjustly imprisoned. The magic key maybe wouldn't set him free, like in the movies, but it would at least keep him alive. There were too many eyes watching, and too much doubt, I was sure.

When the day arrived, I waited outside of Huntsville Prison, where state executions in Texas take place. "One execution is one too many," read the sign in my sweaty hands. Minutes ticked by, each dying a little death, and my hope dying right alongside them.

Hasan's wife Debbie came out of the death house, tears streaming down her face. A friend held her to keep her walking.

My belief in any justice from the prison system died that day alongside Hasan. We failed him. I failed him. I had forgotten one of Hasan's favorite quotes, by Frederick Douglass, formerly enslaved visionary, "Power concedes nothing without demand—it never has and it never will."

I stood outside the death house, soul numb. Hasan's last words to me sounded in my ears: "Whether they murder me or not on Friday, I'm telling you, watch what Ima do; the ancestors are gonna be proud." I knew they were so proud of him. And I also knew that to honor them, I would have to work harder, to try to fill just a tiny piece of the gaping void left by Hasan's absence.

So when I learned that the words Hasan uttered, as they strapped him down to the gurney and prepared the poison that would take his life, were words of encouragement for those of us still struggling for justice, I was not surprised.

"Tell my people we must continue on. Do not give up the fight. Do not give up hope. We can make it happen."

Until the very last second, Hasan was preparing us for the struggles that lay ahead.

* * *

A year later, while I was still carrying Hasan's loss around my neck, a death warrant was issued for Haramia KiNassor, legal name Kenneth Foster Jr., who took Hasan's place on the HRC advisory council. My innards twisted inside my gut. Not again. Never again. We had learned a brutal lesson with Hasan. We could not expect justice. We had to demand it. We would rip it from this fundamentally unjust system.

The organizing for Haramia was truly incredible. His supporters were tireless. There was international media coverage, celebrity support, tens of thousands of petitions, and multiple protests across the country. The victim's best friend says he didn't believe Haramia should die for what happened. Haramia had been sentenced under the Texas Law of Parties, by which a person can be tried for murder in the first, even if they did not commit the crime. They can be sentenced to die if the court finds that a "responsible" person could have deduced a murder might take place. Haramia had been involved in a series of store robberies with two friends. He had no gun. He drove the car. As they headed home, one friend told him to stop. A girl he knew was talking to some guy. Minutes passed. The door was flung open, a gun was drawn. Shots. His friend screamed to *drive, drive now!* The man's body crumpled on the street. Haramia was convicted and sentenced to death, even though no one—not police, not prosecutor, not judge or jury—ever argued for a second that he killed anyone.

Even under these circumstances, Texas gave him a death date. The days peeled away as it drew closer. His supporters worked feverishly, as if possessed. They called in every favor, hounded every media source, worked every angle.

Then what so many said was impossible happened.

* * *

"What?!" I screamed in disbelief. The crushing heat of an August Texas day—almost exactly a year since Hasan's execution—was made worse by the fact all five of us were standing in a concrete parking lot. Heat radiated up, distorting Huntsville Prison in front of us.

"The governor commuted his sentence!" Haramia's campaign organizer smiled brighter than the sun beating down on us.

"It's the first time Perry ever did it! The Board of Pardons voted 6:1 for clemency—they haven't voted to stop an execution in twenty-five years. We did it! We won!"

Silence. Incredulousness. Too scared to believe, to hope.

Then the explosion—yelling, hugging, crying.

Tasha, Haramia's wife, and I ran up the steps into the prison. Two hours before, I walked through those doors, sure this would be my last visit with Haramia. He had stayed strong, like Hasan. Both had rapid-fire ideas, ways to keep the organizing against the death penalty and prison injustice going. Whether or not they lived through the night was not their biggest concern.

"Regardless of what happens today, you all have to keep up the struggle. I know this is bigger than one day." Seriousness was etched on Haramia's face as he spoke, echoes of Hasan's last words on his lips

Tasha and I rushed into the prison, which is normally such a tedious and difficult procedure, but there are different rules in the death house. And, with the news of the commutation spreading, the guards did nothing to stop us as we ran up to Haramia's father and screamed the unbelievable news. He let out a whoop in the middle of the prison. He raced back to the death row visiting section. Thick glass separated visitors from the inmates, and a crackling phone connected the two sides. Haramia was talking with his grandfather, his longest and strongest supporter. When Haramia's father told him about the commutation, he simply smiled serenely.

"I prayed on it. I knew it would come."

Haramia's grandfather had never lost the faith.

* * *

They commuted Haramia's sentence to life in prison. On an L.A. radio show later that day, I spoke of this victory. A woman called in: "But he's still in prison, for life. Isn't that a death sentence too? How can you call this a win?"

I paused. "We won a battle in the larger war. We know that tomorrow we have to get up to continue. Tonight we celebrate. We celebrate that tomorrow, Haramia will see another dawn. Today... Today was a good day."

We took over the prison yard, the supporters. Sprawled out on the grass. Screamed the good news into cell phones. Fell into each other's arms, laughing. Unable to give words to my feelings, I somersaulted across the prison lawn. It was the first time I ever felt truly joyous in a prison yard, without a sense of dread and sadness nestled underneath.

It was the only time I saw guards do absolutely nothing as we broke every prison conduct rule, written and unwritten. They knew we won that day.

I couldn't help but feel Hasan's presence. Smiling his child-like grin. Whispering softly, "Yeah, Wa Wa, enjoy it now. Tomorrow we got a lot more work to do."

BLEEDING OUT IN A PRISON VISITING ROOM

My memories of my prison interviews with Jimmy McElroy, aka Mac, are stark in my head: the way light played across his rough features, the smell of Lysol, the squeak of cheap guard boots, the ringing clang of scraped blue metal bars.

Eerily interspliced between gory tales of mob hits would sit the mundane and the cherished: stories of Mac's children, his girlfriend, his plans when he got out, everyday incidents with my brother, questions about my life.

"Hey," Mac interrupted himself, "how is that young man of yours? What's his name? You told me last time but I forgot. You two doing okay? He treating you right?"

The last question had more weight, a gravity born of an earlier conversation. Mac had said my boyfriend "better treat you right or the Westies will pay him a visit!"

Mac's question during this visit hit me like a punch to the gut. I slapped as neutral a smile on my face as I could.

"Oh Dovid. He's fine, we're good, he's treating me right."

He wasn't, we weren't, and again he wasn't. We had, in fact, broken up right before I got to the prison. I was too needy, and he was too lazy. I was too demanding, and he was too selfish. He wanted to be with me but wanted none of the work that entailed. I made what should be fun nothing but tedious work. The arguments went around and around and increased in frequency, pitch, and desperation.

In reality, we moved too quickly in our relationship. We were more interested in being in love than in seeing who was directly in front of our faces. Dovid was infatuated with a big-haired, fiery Black woman poet who didn't take any shit, and who looked six-feet-tall on stage. I fell in love with a politically aware, sensitive white Jewish man who was an amazing father, who dedicated his life to struggles against racism and imperialism.

Unfortunately for both of us, neither of those people existed. Or more truthfully, they did not exist in their purest forms. I might be a poetry Amazon on stage, but I also suffered from deep depression with the state of the world, my life, and myself. He might work against racism, but that didn't mean he didn't carry his own issues with him into our relationship, tracking them around like mud on a clean carpet.

I had met his parents—his father was a brutal tyrant in the house growing up, and an angel in the street. I could see how Dovid lived in fear of becoming like that. His own son, Zakai, seven when we first started dating, was always at the forefront of his mind.

The first time I met Zakai was at a concert I planned. I had picked my afro out to its full glory. I was surprised and happy when I turned to see Dovid there. I was already infatuated with him, well before our first date. He introduced me to Zakai, whose face was inscrutable, as only a seven-year-old can get away with.

I shook his hand, and said, "It's really nice to meet you. I heard from your dad that you love Spiderman. Next to Wolverine from the *X-Men*, he's my favorite super hero."

A lie. Spiderman was a boring character to me when I started reading comics at Zakai's age, and I promptly shunned him. It is a lie, however, I will never regret. Zakai's face cracked into the wide missing-tooth grin I grew to love. As I turned away, he yelled out, "I like your hair."

It was the beginnings of a family I had wanted my entire life. I was not ready to let that go without a fight—and Dovid and I had many of those.

So I left Philadelphia for a two-month trip to Mexico, a trip I had spent years planning. I saved up my vacation days and squirreled away money. I went to learn from an indigenous rebel group there, the Zapatistas, who rose up against the Mexican authority to demand their independence and autonomy. They set up liberated communities all over the state of Chiapas, dreaming new ways of living and being into existence. There are hundreds of thousands who proudly call themselves Zapatistas.

Setting out on this trip of a lifetime, which changed me more than any one thing in my life, all I could think about was losing Dovid and Zakai. Losing this family. We were already coming apart at the seams when I left, though neither of us wanted to admit it. I was worried we would completely unravel in my absence.

Many prisoners recreate family, building to make up for what they never had and for what they lost. I understand this longing. My mother was an incredible woman who raised me well and lovingly. I still longed to be part of a unit, more than just a solitary pair. This was something denied me by the everyday prisons of racism, poverty, masculinity, and low self-esteem that trapped my father. I used to think I could love away all of the intangible prisons that keep people separated.

* * *

All of my memories of my interviews with Mac are stark, except one: the visit with him two weeks after I had an abortion. I remember almost nothing from the time that does not have to do with the abortion. It devoured everything.

The visit I don't remember happened in June 2006. It would have been sunny and warm. I know this because it is California. I know I rented a car at the Oakland airport (which is cheaper to fly to from Philly than SFO). Perhaps it was the time they gave me the PT Cruiser, or the Grand Am. I only know it was not the time they gave me the SUV. I begged them not to give me such a big car. I had gotten my license, belatedly at twenty-four, less than a year before. This proved to be prophetic. I brought the car back three days later with a dent gouged into the entire passenger-side door. That was when I learned: always get the insurance.

I know which hotel I checked into, because I have only ever stayed at one. Once I find a clean hotel in a town, I keep going back, unwilling to push my luck. From past experience, I know that I must have unpacked, read through some of my notes, set my alarm for 6:20 AM, and fallen asleep to the late night sounds of cable television.

I would have risen with the alarm, showered again, dressed. Double-checked I was not wearing anything my visit would be denied for (underwire bra, see-through clothing, open-toed shoes, skirts too short, sleeveless shirts, hoodies, coats with linings).

On one trip to California, the airline put my luggage on a flight arriving hours after me. They promised it would be there that night. I was wearing a tank top, a puffy vest, tight jeans, and flip-flops. Not a single item would pass prison regulations. I waited all night. At 5 AM, I ran to Walmart. Every small prison town has a Walmart somewhere nearby. In my mind, Walmarts are inextricable from prisons. I bought the first outfit that looked like it would fit me. I ended up wearing a t-shirt with "I Don't Do Drama" emblazoned on the front, a black skirt so big it swept the floor, and awkward boots.

On the trip I don't remember, I would have gotten in my car and driven the fifteen minutes on winding, one-lane roads to the prison, parked, lined up, and been admitted and processed. I would have gone into the visiting room and sat at my assigned table, waiting for Mac to come out. I would have had extra sanitary napkins in my pocket. Even though I can't remember it, the guards would have hassled me at the front gate about it.

I had extra pads because I was bleeding heavily. The abortion had been three weeks before my visit. I was not supposed to fly. I had had a medical abortion, taking a pill that induces a miscarriage, rather than a surgical removal. Flying at high altitudes could put pressure on my uterus and cause serious bleeding. It could put my life at risk, the doctor said.

He was right. On the flight back from the west coast, my bleeding became so heavy that I went through a pad an hour. Then a pad every half hour. The doctor had clearly told me if I went through more than a pad every two hours, I was to go directly to an emergency room.

I crouched in the cramped airplane bathroom, staring down into the toilet bowl where my blood dripped, a faucet not turned completely off. I went to stand up. Pinwheels of light exploded in my head. I opened my eyes to find my head resting on the sink, a knot where it hit when I passed out. I passed out three more times on the taxi ride to my house.

I had gotten pregnant after I came back from Mexico. Dovid and I had not taken that time apart as a break. We wrote love letters every other day, and paid for exorbitant international calls once a week. By the time I returned, we had both forgotten what we should have remembered.

Our "honeymoon" lasted a month. Nothing had been solved. We took it out on each other. One day we fought—as most other days. Our frustration was a screaming teapot boiling over. Energy was transmuted, passion transferred. We fell into each other's arms. We clawed at each other, then fell into one another on my hideously orange couch. He moved inside of me. We moved as one.

His dick slipped out of my vagina behind me. There were no words between us. Then I felt its pressure on my asshole. In my asshole. Barreling in. Rearranging.

We had had anal sex before. He always asked. Used lube. Moved slowly.

This was a package crammed into an overfull mailbox at Christmas.

I heard myself say no. Again. And again. I was suspended in time. My mind was hazy. An eternity, a minute—which was it, or was it both? He got off me, seeing I was upset. He did not understand—*Are you still mad from before?* He kissed me. He said he would call later after picking up his son. I did not know what had happened. I pulled a blanket off the back of the couch and wound it around my nakedness. I began to cry. To sob. To howl.

I called him, tears splattered in my voice. I told him it wasn't right. Something wrong had happened. Something had been stolen. Broken. He did not understand.

"Did you—do you—are you saying… I… raped you?"

No. Yes. Was it or wasn't it? How to give words to a violation gone in a breath? An assault, unintended or not?

I knew it was not right. He agreed. He knew it was not right. "What do you want me to do?" an endless refrain. What did I want him to do? I turned like a sheet in the wind. I did not know what would make it better. I only knew it was not right. I did not think of calling the police for so many reasons. I did not believe in calling the police; I felt it only made a bad situation worse. In this situation, it was also a Black woman's word versus a white man's. This was Philly. This was America. There would be no "proof," no rape kit testing positive.

Even more than all of this was the forensic evidence of my love for him. I did not want him thrown away. I could not imagine a guilty verdict in any court in this country, where women—even those who are the "right" kind of survivors, who fight off strangers that attacked them and did violence—are put on trial, dragged through the mud and made to prove they were not "asking for it." Even if I would have been certain of conviction, I did not want Dovid broken. I only wanted to be made whole again. I did not realize how important the feeling of being safe in the arms of the person you love was until it disintegrated. I wanted safe back. I did not have answers about how to do that. I wanted to stay and find the answers. I did not want to walk away carrying the pieces of me cupped in my hands. I needed to know how to fix this.

I searched for answers in the exact wrong places. I went through his computer, through his journal. Was I looking for clues to understand this? Clues to hold against him?

I found an entry. Undated. The entry said it was not the first time. Another assault. Another violation. He did not know. He did not know at the time. She told him later. He did not know if he could believe. He trusted her word. He was a feminist man. But what did that make him in his own eyes?

I was wounded. I was angry. I was also unsure. I was angry he had not told me this before—angry I was not the first. He had asked himself all these questions before. And here he was again.

And yet when I read his description of what happened with this other woman, I saw it through his eyes. It did not bear the color of rape or the shape of assault. It was not what we are told rape is. It was wrong. But how much wrong could she claim?

How much wrong could I claim?

I told him what I had read. He was angry. He, too, felt violated. I thought his violation of me gave me immunity. We yelled and yelled ourselves hoarse. I threw things: keys, plates, a framed picture of us.

I left. I cried. I looked at myself. I did not know who I had become. We did not talk.

Days later, I met him in the park by my house. We sat on opposite ends of the bench.

"This is my list of things for you to do. This is what you have to do to make this right," I said.

He nodded as I read through the list so quickly my words slurred together. *You have to tell people what happened you have to reach out to a local anti-assault organization to get help we can't see each other you have to tell me when you are going to be at an event I want to see your son like we said whatever happens between us I want to make a schedule to pick him up I will wait outside.*

He nodded through the entire list. He said yes. He said this makes sense. He said this is reasonable. He said I want to make this right. He said I am so sorry. He said you are right. He said I love you.

We both got up to leave. He walked me up the hill to my front gate. This is the last time I will see him like this, I thought. I felt panicked. Things were not fixed. I did not want things to be accountable right then. I just wanted to forget. I wanted to pretend.

He asked if he could give me a hug. In his arms, I only remembered hours of being there, of telling life stories, of laughing uncontrollably—of being safe.

"Will you come upstairs?" I asked.

He hesitated. I held my breath. I did not know which answer I wanted more from him.

"Yes…. Yes, of course I will."

And that was the day I got pregnant.

We continued together, not knowing of the pregnancy, our relationship in stasis, our hearts in crisis. I did not want to let go. Swimming in a sea of pain, I clung to him. I wanted him to make it right. Neither of us knew what that meant.

I knew I was being torn apart by staying together. I knew space was the healthy thing, for both of us, the only path to growth.

I wanted him to be accountable. I told him he had to tell his friends what happened. I reached out to my friends, asked them to speak with him. Accountable was the word. I had heard it so much in radical activist communities—this is what we did. We did not call the police.

We did not rip our communities apart. We held accountable those who had done serious harm. I did not know exactly what it meant. I wanted him to tell enough people, as if the telling could make our community fix the situation. I wanted a community accountability process, though I did not know exactly what that meant. I wanted him to go through the list and check it off. Most of all, at the end, I wanted to be healed. More than healed, I wanted all of this erased.

In a vegetarian Chinese restaurant in Center City, I sat across from Em, one of the friends I asked to speak to Dovid. I knew Em had done this process before. I was relieved when Em said they would be involved. I was off the hook. Someone else would know what to do. Someone else would make it right.

"I talked with him." They took a bite of fried veggie dumplings. "He is back and forth. He says he did something wrong, but he doesn't want to be called an assaulter. He doesn't want to think about it as assault."

I nodded. I knew this. I knew Em was one who believed me, supported me.

"He also said it could not be that bad, as you and him were still together and seeing each other all the time." Em's face was unreadable. I read into it disappointment.

My face grew hot. I knew I could not let go of him. I did not think I could find the words to explain the convolution of my situation—of my heart, my head. I wanted to be with him. I wanted him to be accountable. I also wanted him to be punished. I wanted to punish him. I wanted him to heal me. I wanted it fixed. I wanted everything, including him, to go away.

I evaded. "He's trying to minimize what happened. He's trying not to have to admit what he did." True.

"I mean of course I see him," I continued. "I go to pick up Zakai, and I see him. And I met to talk to him about this. And we're working on a film project together." True. And not true. None of these reasons explained me lying in his arms, in his bed, closing my eyes as he entered me, trying not to think about before—only thinking about before.

Em didn't believe me. I was trying desperately to believe myself.

I did not tell any of my friends how much time we were spending together. I thought if I did, they would think I was lying. Lying about the jagged edges of me. Lying about the assault. That it was not as serious as I said. It did not shine the bruised colors we are told are violation anyway. I thought they would deny my pain, leave me alone with it while telling me it was nothing.

Dovid told a woman who was his friend what had happened. I pressed him afterwards, asked what she said in response. He hesitated. "She said it didn't sound like that big of a deal to her. She said stuff like that happens all the time. She said you're being dramatic."

It rang in my head. It haunted me. Another woman, this woman who knew me, said it was not real. It haunted me because there was a part of me that agreed. This is not how it happens, the something inside me whispered. There was no dark alley; there was no knife. There was no stranger. There were no hours of pain and devastation.

My friend Bayla, the keeper of my heart and my secrets since the age of fifteen, said this was not true. She is a teacher of self-defense, she worked at an abortion clinic. She saw women every day surviving violations, of all kinds, taking back control of their bodies.

Assault happens on a spectrum, Bayla said. Assault can be done in the blink of an eye. Women make different decisions after. None of those decisions are wrong. This was not the first time this happened, she assured me. This is actually how it happens most of the time.

You are not alone.

As a feminist organizer, I knew this. I knew this about others. But I did not know it about me. It has taken years to know this about me: to allow myself to see the complexities of the situation; to see myself as a survivor and to lay claim to that word; to forgive myself for what I felt was weakness—the weakness of staying. Staying past the point of trying to fix it. asha bandele wrote in *The Prisoner's Wife*, "And now, today, I know myself well enough to understand that there is a part of me who always wants to make what is ugly somehow beautiful."

I stayed to make our relationship beautiful. To see him as beautiful. Most of all, to see myself as beautiful.

It has taken me years to see Dovid as more than a villain—more than someone who hurt me, violated me, and left without piecing me back together.

The truth is not simple.

Yet I needed to find the space to claim what I had gone through. I needed to be able to name it, because to name something is to know it.

It was not until I reread bandele's memoir about meeting, falling in love with, and marrying a man in prison that I found a framework to allow my heart to rest. In *The Prisoner's Wife*, bandele realizes she had been assaulted and sexually abused when she was younger; she had repressed those memories, packed them away like clothes outgrown in the attic. She had turned off the lights and shut the door.

I read and reread bandele's exploration of herself as a wounded woman, as a strong woman. I heard faint knocking: something in my attic, tapping at the door. I did not know I had packed away childhood pains, violations so old they had yellowed and faded. Probing hands before my mouth knew it had the right to no. Eyes of authority that froze me, told me to lie still.

bandele and I unlocked our attic doors. Her book taught me that assault is a prison as well. Assault is about power, and about taking what is not given. This is power that continues after the actual act is finished, reasserted with every memory. There is a reason rape is a tactic in warfare. It is a threat.

There is a reason Dovid could not name what he did as assault. He did not want to see himself as someone who took without permission. He thought if he admitted this, it would erase his other identities. He would become nothing more than that. And I would become nothing more than victim. We were both denied healing. Only stolen power was left.

Prison is power: control of the individual, community, people, nation. It is a taking from our community and our spirits that which is not given. It is a threat to all of us.

I lost control of my body. It was a colonization of my flesh. In prison, people are nothing but bodies. My brother becomes nothing but a body. He is told when his body must get up, when his body will feed, when his body will exercise, and when his body will lie down.

And what of the bodies that live at the crossroads? What of those that have had so many foreign flags planted in their soil that they have lost count? The population of women in prison is mushrooming: up 646 percent in the last thirty years, says the Sentencing Project. Black women are the largest growing group of faces in the shadow of bars.

So many of them dwelled in prisons before they ever set foot in one.

Fifty percent of women in prison have extensive histories with sexual abuse before the walls. These are the stories on the other end of the spectrum, where no one would deny these violent, brutal violations as rape. They made me feel my violations were as miniscule or nonexistent in comparison.

And once they get to the gates, the violations do not stop. They increase. All people—men, women, trans—are assaulted. They are assaulted not just by other prisoners, but often by guards, especially women and trans prisoners. They are assaulted by authority—by the state.

In her book about women prisoners, *Resistance Behind Bars*, Victoria Law writes of "Gina," a prisoner at Oregon's Coffee Creek Correctional Facility. Gina worked in the kitchen. One day, the food coordinator ordered her to "drop her pants and bend over so that he could have sex with her. Scared, Gina complied." The assaults continued every day. Gina did not say no. She did not feel she had the power to say no. Months away from her release date, a bad write-up could push it back so far she would not be able to see it. She could not say no.

Even more so than the assaults enacted sometimes by other prisoners and often by guards, Angela Davis tells us in her book *Are Prisons Obsolete?* that prisons themselves function as daily assault. "[This] exposes an everyday routine in women's prisons that verges on sexual assault as much as it is taken for granted." The very mechanisms prisons use to maintain power and control can be defined as sexual assault. Davis cites the example of the Brisbane-based organization Sisters Inside, who did an action at a national conference of corrections officers, where activists re-enacted a routine prison strip search on stage. The audience, who do this every day for their living, was utterly repulsed. "they must have realized... that 'without the uniform, without the power of the state, [the strip search] would be sexual assault.'"

This is how the system maintains itself.

Assault is a prison where the physical act may only last one minute. Or an hour. Or many hours. Then you are to forget. If you cannot forget, you are to be silent. Admitting to being a survivor brings shame not on the perpetrator but the perpetrated.

In our society, those who assault are invisible. Men (and those of all genders unfortunately) on the street drift past. I wonder if they have scarred someone: slipped it in while someone was sleeping, pushed to turn a no to a yes, or took silence to be a yes. The first time I had sex was like this: with my first boyfriend, six years older than me. I had panted no for months, in response to his frenzied hands and even more frenzied "please." That night I strung nos like pearls on a necklace—so many I became scared they would form a wall between us. So I did not say yes, I just stopped saying no. For him, that was enough. It hurt. I felt tingles of pleasure. I did not know what I was supposed to feel.

This is a typical story. I have told many women this. So many nod their heads in recognition. I loved him. He was good to me, for a time. This is how those things happen sometimes, unfortunately.

My first boyfriend left the next morning. We did not talk about the sex. He kissed me. He said see you tonight. I cleaned the stained sheets. Scrubbed them to remove the blood and the semen.

This is not a "real assault." I would never call it rape. I did not know what to call it. We do not have words for this in our society. It is not the stories I have heard from every single woman I love in my life: stories not of silence but sobs and pleas to stop, for mercy. I know every time they hear someone make a joke about rape, see a movie with a gratuitous assault scene, hear how someone got "raped" at their job because they had so many taxes taken out, they are right back in the prison of sexual assault—bodies not their own, memories invaded.

I feel this too. I wonder sometimes whether I have the right to feel that pain, and to carry around that wound. Did I endure enough to claim this as mine? I cannot stand prison rape jokes, so acceptable in almost every social context. "Don't drop the soap." They remind me of the women I love, of myself face-down on an orange couch, and of the horrors Kakamia has suffered that I do not even know about, that he will never tell me.

I have to turn off pop culture in my head. I have to push away the jokes that trivialize this pain and the frames that question whose fault it is. Most of all, I have to battle the feeling of being weak, for my decisions and for my indecision. None of us—not a one—is weak. We are stronger than anyone could imagine. As asha bandele wrote, she fought not to "be defined by my experiences. I would be defined by what I chose to do with my experiences, if I was open and willing, and uncompromising and honest."

What I have decided to do with my experiences is attempt to wedge open our understanding of assault, to see the ways that people (often women and trans folks) are violated every day in a male-dominated society, and that a single assault does not happen in isolation. It is not confined in that alleyway. It did not originate in that bed. It is the thousand acts every day, which many (often cisgender men) are not even aware of. It is this sea we have all learned to swim in. It is the polluted air we have learned to suck in. We do not even recognize it is there.

This is the definition of a rape culture, where those who are valued less by patriarchy—women and trans folks—are disposable tools to be used and to reinforce power. It serves to maintain the hierarchy that is the foundation of our society, where white supremacy, patriarchy, capitalism, imperialism are inextricably intertwined. In that way, every assault is state-sanctioned.

A joint statement by two abolition organizations, INCITE and Critical Resistance, spells this out clearly, calling for movements to "develop an analysis and strategies to end violence that do not isolate individual acts of violence (either committed by the state or individuals) from their larger contexts. These strategies must address how entire communities of all genders are affected in multiple ways by both state violence and interpersonal gender violence."

The fact that so much of what I have been taught tells me that this is not mine to claim because I should have figured out a way to fix this—that if I had just been stronger I wouldn't feel this way—is one of the mechanisms that keeps this system functioning. Claiming my experience, calling it wrong, a violation, is not only my right; it is a liberatory act.

I find more comfort and strength in the words of Indian independence leader Mahatma Gandhi when I think of my assault than in most of the books on assault I have read. When asked by Black radical intellectual W.E.B. Du Bois for a message to the "twelve million people who are the grandchildren of slaves," Gandhi replied, "Let not the twelve million Negroes be ashamed of the fact that they are the grandchildren of slaves. There is no dishonour in being slaves. There is dishonour in being slave-owners."

The shame of any violation, personal or historical, lies with those who committed the violation, not with those who survived to heal and rebuild. And just like during slavery, every individual abuse, violation, and brutalization served to uphold, reinforce, and strengthen the larger systems of oppression.

This is the analysis needed, I believe—the framing to understand painful experience.

But the question remains: then what? In this society where all of us are taught that any bodies other than cisgender men are virtually worthless, how do we respond when someone's actions reinforce that?

I have worked to use this experience to reinforce for myself the belief that people cannot be thrown away like used tissues. I was so angry at Dovid for so long. I was angry at myself. I tried to throw us both away.

But I believe in transformation, and therefore, for me, I have to believe in both of our abilities to change. This is where my beliefs become the most difficult to live, in my own skin. I do not believe prisons make us safer. I do not believe prison helps anyone come out better than they went in (if they come out better, they do so in spite of prison, not because of it).

I absolutely believe communities need to hold people who do harm accountable, while still holding them as humans who can change. Redemption cannot be unattainable if we are all to remain human.

We did try. I have to remember Dovid did try, while still holding him accountable for the original harm and the ways and times he failed to try.

He agreed he wanted to help. He wanted support. He wanted to be accountable to something other than him—at least at times.

We turned to two linked organizations in Philadelphia, one a group for survivors of assault, the other a group of mostly cisgender men working to hold perpetrators accountable, to make communities safer, and to not throw anyone away.

This is one of the hardest things to imagine when you think of a world without prisons. "What will we do with the rapists?" It is a valid question. And part of me wants to say no, not them. They don't deserve redemption. They can rot.

But I cannot allow myself to believe this, because we would be throwing away so much of our community. The vast majority of assaults happen by someone the survivor knows. These people are in our communities, at our jobs, or sitting next to us in the pew at church. Our parents. Our partners. Ours. Redefining assault, claiming every violation that has happened to us for what it is, would implicate so many. They are absolutely culpable, and behavior has to be addressed and changed—but are they all irredeemable?

Dehumanizing those who do harm dehumanizes all of us, especially marginalized and oppressed communities. Communities Against Rape and Abuse (CARA) wrote, "Dehumanizing the aggressor undermines the process of accountability for the whole community. If we separate ourselves from the offenders by stigmatizing them then we fail to see how we contributed to conditions that allow violence to happen."

And I absolutely must be clear that I do not speak for or to survivors of assault. I do not speak for them, because survivors are not monolithic. I also would not presume to speak to survivors in a way that scolds or dictates responses. There is no "right" way to feel in any assault, and I certainly cannot begin to imagine my own feelings if my situation had been different, if I had felt cold steel at my throat, felt blows on my body, or feared this pain every night.

Often the responsibility for maintaining perceived political integrity is shifted to the survivor in radical circles. What we do in response to trauma is scrutinized. Did you call the cops or not? Did you file a restraining order or not? Did you try to take it to court and get a conviction or not? For people who do not believe that police make us safer, we often end up policing other people's survival strategies, rather than focusing on the gaps in the larger movements. We, as a movement, have not developed organized mechanisms to address harm done in communities outside of the criminal legal system. We have not prioritized keeping people, especially those most vulnerable in our communities, safe from harm, from gendered violence. It is so much easier for us to look at and confront state violence, rather than the ways we individually replicate that violence in our relationships.

While we all want our actions and our principles to be in alignment, we cannot abandon our collective responsibility and leave the onus on the shoulders of those who have survived, and are surviving harm.

Too often we are used as tool against one another, held up as the example of how we "should" feel, what we "should" do. I do not know what we should do, beyond starting with questions, not answers. We need questions that make us examine the deepest parts of our beliefs and ourselves.

* * *

Dovid reached out to the group in Philly working to hold perpetrators accountable. I was glad. Someone else would figure this out. Someone else knew what to do. It was no longer my burden.

But I did not join the survivors' group. I was not ready to call myself a survivor, again didn't know if I deserved it, had suffered enough to have "earned" it. I was also not ready to sit in a room of mostly white cisgender women, because that's what they were. That's who society so often tells us survivors are. In that space, my Black radical womanness would be bright as a bullseye.

I was not ready to let the larger community know what I "let" happen to me. I was not even sure what to call it. I knew I did not want to walk into a political event, into a room full of knowing eyes.

And I was not ready to disengage from Dovid, to sit alone with myself. I was not ready to open the attic door.

It is so much easier to imagine a new world than to go about the painful work of constructing it out of our bones and hearts. I believed and still believe in community accountability processes for people who do harm to a community. I still believe it was right for me to try to address this in a way that honored my principles.

But theory is not practice. Practice is messy, like sheets stained with blood and semen and no answers to contradictory questions. These organizations understood this situation. They knew there was a spectrum of assault. They did not think I was overreacting. They had a strong analysis about holding perpetrators accountable. They truly wanted to support me as the survivor.

But then human realities take over. I wanted confidentiality. Dovid told the organizer he was working with my name. This was a no-no, but the organizer had not told Dovid that before they started talking. A small oversight. A pebble in the ocean, but it created a tsunami in my life.

They created an accountability plan together: counseling; ongoing sessions between Dovid, the organizer, and people in our community; and telling those we knew jointly about the violation, without minimizing it. No more "she's overreacting" ringing in my ears. The plan was good. The plan might have worked. I had input into it. It satisfied my need for accountability. I was on a merry-go-round of emotions. On the days I was being the best me, I wanted Dovid to change and to rectify. I wanted both of us to move forward better people than we were at that moment. On my worst days, I wanted him shunned, punished, and ostracized. I wanted him to hurt for a long time. The accountability plan reminded me of my best self's intentions, when I could not see through the pain. Looking back now, I do not blame myself, as I did at the time, for perceived weakness. I see what I was going through was absolutely and completely understandable and natural: a multitude of feelings, needs, and desires that raced through my injured heart. All of them were true; there were no lies. This was me, in many ways, at my most human. Transformative justice organizer Kiyomi Fujikawa talks about the ways we don't allow for humanity in accountability processes. We often expect people to be their best selves a hundred percent of the time under the worst possible conditions. That is not transformative, that is not sustainable and it absolutely does not set people up to be able to complete this process.

And this is why I needed a community around me to hold the course towards a shared vision of accountability when the tumultuous seas inside me cast me about—a community to remind me of the visions of justice I held sacred, when I, in my pain, was not able to see them.

But then the organizer working with Dovid on the accountability plan left for three months. No prior warning. No backup point of contact. In fact, no one from the organization returned Dovid's calls. The plan crumbled, a sandcastle in high tide.

In the meantime, I had found out I was pregnant. And when I realized it happened that first night of weakness, I was filled with shame. I felt I was being punished for not being stronger, for not adhering to the boundaries I set.

This was not my first abortion. I had had a surgical procedure previously. It was immensely painful: the sound of suction, a white doctor who looked through me while patting my leg, saying patron-izingly, "Good girl."

Despite the conditions surrounding it, I knew that first abortion had been the right decision. While my partner at the time was very sweet, neither of us was prepared on any level to be a parent.

But this time it was different. I was older, financially stable with a regular job. And my heart yearned to have that child, lick the sweet of a little brown sugar to camouflage the taste of blood I was having to swallow, to paraphrase the poet Staceyann Chin. If I couldn't have the family I had dreamed of with Dovid, perhaps this would be the beginning of my replacement.

But when my friend Bayla asked the hardest question I've ever had to answer—"Do you think this would be healthy for you, for a child?" —I had to answer no. I knew what was necessary.

It has taken years for me to work through my feelings around the abortion, which are so intimately connected to the assault. Though I have done work around reproductive justice for over a decade, I did not often speak about my assault or my abortions, the two most gen-dered, personal-as-political issues I carry with me. They are the locales where I struggle to see the larger systems of oppression at work. This is how the state invisibilizes its role in inequalities: we (especially those who are gender oppressed in this society) are encouraged to think of it as our "personal" concern, and often a personal failing or stain that is ours alone to carry. In my work organizing against prisons, against militarism, against police violence, and for political prisoners, the role of the state in perpetuating and maintaining oppression is clearer— though of course the blame for mass incarceration is shifted to indi-viduals, pathologizing people and communities.

Part of what allowed me to begin to viscerally explore, claim, and connect my assault and abortions to broader issues of justice was the abolitionist framing offered by many women and trans folks of color: "By constantly shifting the center to communities that face intersect-ing forms of oppression, we gain a more comprehensive view on the strategies needed to end all forms of violence," says the introduction to INCITE's *Color of Violence* anthology. "[We] better understand how various forms of intersecting oppressions contribute to the creation of a violent world, and... devise the strategies necessary to end violence."

By shifting the way we organize and the way we envision the world from separate social issues to seeing them all woven together, and by centering folks like LGBTQ folks of color, we see the ways these systems are interlocking and interdependent. If our movements and our communities are not addressing the very real ways oppression is enacted upon individuals' bodies, we can never hope to fundamentally transform the current system.

* * *

Months later, Dovid and I no longer spoke. He moved to New York. I had begun moving forward. There was a miscommunication in the survivor's group. I was contacted by an organizer with them. She had heard I wanted to join them, and that I had reached out. I reared back. This was my biggest fear. Who else had they told? Who else would look at me with knowing eyes? With pity, disgust, disbelief, anger, judgment? I felt naked in a hailstorm.

I called and emailed them, enraged, taking this as the opportunity to vent my pain at the failed accountability process. My pain at myself for staying, for not being the woman I thought I should be. I felt this validated my fears that my situation was not real, that I did not deserve support, and that I would not get support.

No one from the organization called back.

This is not the only way this process can go. I have heard many stories of healing, of closure, of communities and individuals made whole again. I have had the opportunity to work with organizations like CARA and others who show how the process should truly be undertaken. I have seen communities taking responsibility for supporting survivors while creating avenues to hold perpetrators accountable.

However, it is incredibly important to recognize there are no magic solutions. There are no perfect endings in something like this. And I think our expectations in this quick-fix, solution-oriented society are to blame. While I have seen processes where people have been held accountable, I have not seen processes where anyone could be described as "happy" at the conclusion of it. I have seen individuals and communities achieve closure, which is something wholly different. I originally thought that how you judged a successful accountability process was if everyone was healed at the end of it. But I now believe that is not something that happens in the process. A "successful" accountability process is one in which the person who has done harm takes responsibility, makes amends as possible, and sets the foundation for life-long changes in their behavior, mentality, and actions. A "successful" accountability process is one where the person who has been harmed feels they are able to move forward from this—that enough poison has been sucked out so that they can heal—eventually. It is not the "happy ending" we have all been taught to expect. It is not, in reality, even an ending, for the successful completion of whatever requirements made for the person who has done harm is just the beginning; everyone involved, including the community, will have to revisit this. Rather than a neat, linear progession towards healing, at best, it is a spiral. We continue moving upwards, but we will revisit the same place over and over again, hopefully each time moving a little closer to healing and closure.

Fujikawa, on a panel at the 2015 INCITE Color of Violence conference, talked about the disconnect between our ideas of community accountability processes, and the lived reality:

> I feel like we have sort of pitched this image of community accountability and transformative justice as this really sparkling package that you're supposed to check out… [We tell survivors], "Well, we have this awesome thing called community accountability and it's going to be great!" And then survivors open up that box and it is not as pretty as they thought it was going to be. And we're doing a disservice to survivors by doing that.

And none of this is to be taken as an excuse for doing nothing or for abandoning those who are most vulnerable and marginalized, within already-oppressed communities, to deal with the replication of state violence enacted through familiar, intimate hands.

* * *

My visit with my brother on the day I was bleeding out in a prison visiting room was hours long, but it lasts ten minutes in my memory.

Before the visit, I did not tell Kakamia of the tumultuous waters Dovid and I navigated. I did not tell him my boat capsized, that there were days I did not think my head would break water, or that there were days I wished it wouldn't.

When I see incarcerated loved ones, I imagine the horrors they live every day. It is not just brutality and violence—those are extreme daily manifestations. I imagine it is the loss that must weigh the most. It is a loss of freedom: taking a walk when you want, going to the store to pick up food and cooking a meal, calling up a friend, going over to your grandmother's for an unexpected visit.

I want to bring light and fresh air with me when I come into a visiting room, or when my mail gets dropped on their bunk. I want, most of all, to bring a piece of hope with me—to stem any extra pain with my hands.

They've seen enough ugliness for one day.

But Kakamia knows me too well. Though we do not share the same blood, we share the same face. He reads my expressions as he does his own.

"What's wrong?" he asked, after an hour of our visit.

I don't remember what I said. I know it did not satisfy him. In the end, I told him.

I remember his eyes on my face, his hands on mine, his voice.

"Why? Why?"

I thought he was asking why I got the abortion. I hung my head.

He lifted my chin. "Why didn't you tell me? That's what big brothers are for. Why didn't you tell me?"

He wrapped me up tight in his arms, knowing why all too well, loving and hating me for trying to protect him, knowing he couldn't protect me.

I don't know if he knew how much him holding me in his arms and rocking me meant to me.

I felt the safest I had felt in so long; my brother's arms pushed back the bars of all prisons, even if just for a moment.

* * *

Any movements for justice where we do not see the ways that larger societal oppression is replicated by individuals we know and even sometimes love—where we do not create mechanisms to address serious harm that is done within our communities—achieves no real justice at all. Instead, we just reproduce the brutality of the larger system.

This offers us frameworks and no clear answers. Because even if the accountability process happens, even if the perpetrator is held accountable and meets every requirement, completing the entire plan, then what? This is the question that plagues communities of justice who go this route. How do we accept perpetrators of assault back into our communities? And yet that is the very purpose of the entire accountability process: to heal the individuals, to heal the community—to make whole. Often, this is the hardest part. How can people in our communities—especially other survivors—feel safe around people like this? I have seen too many processes crumble here, where the perpetrator who has completed everything is shunned, often through social media, where the ability to have nuanced, heart-centered conversations is reduced to an infinitesimal possibility. We become caught. How do those of us who are marginalized—women, trans folks, queer folks, youth, people of color and most especially those who sit at the intersections of identity and oppression—balance our desire to keep safe, honored, and centered with our belief in systems outside of police, outside of prisons, outside of destroying those who have hurt and harmed?

I do not have any answers to offer. I wish I did. I only know that we must ask these questions, and not settle for easy, simplistic answers. We must not forget, ever. We must not hide from intimate violence, close our eyes and just hope it will go away. And we must hold fast to transformation. We have to believe transformation is possible, or our accountability processes, and our larger visions of a new world, are doomed before they begin.

I have been indelibly changed by my assault, and by the response of my community afterwards. I am less idealistic. I am less trusting. But I believe more firmly than ever in the ability to redeem and to change—to fundamentally transform. I believe that through my own process, it has happened for me. I truly hope it has happened for

Dovid as well. And I want with all my heart to be part of a community able to embody this transformation. Most of all, I know if I want a world free of sexual assault, outside of the criminal justice system—if I want a community built infused with determination, dedication, forethought, accountability, understanding, and care—no one will build it for me. I have to submerge myself in the messy, sometimes painful, and hopefully beautiful process, trusting the waves of love will bring me back to shore.

Mac

CONCEPTION

MAC'S GREAT-GRANDFATHER WAS ONE OF THE ONE AND A HALF MIL-lion people who fled the Potato Famine in mid-1800s Ireland, a colony of Great Britain, devastated by a pathogen. It attacked the only crop Ireland had been engineered to produce: the potato. It not only wiped out the food source for the vast majority of the country; it wiped out their main economic export, completely destabilizing the economic system and plunging millions into starvation and death. The devastation lasted long after the famine ended and drastically shifted the course of countless lives, including Mac's.

Like many others, Mac's great-grandfather disembarked from the overcrowded boat hoping to make a new life for himself in the United States. What he found was dangerous, back-breaking factory work—when he could get it. There were too many mouths to feed, and too little food to go around. He found a home of sorts in Hell's Kitchen, the beginnings of an Irish ghetto offering remembrances of a home most would never see again.

Located on the west side of Manhattan along the Hudson River all the way over to 8th Ave, from 34th St up to 59th, flanked by Times Square and the waterfront, Hell's Kitchen was mostly a shantytown when Mac's great-grandfather came there. Delicate, dilapidated frames were weighed down by the despair of dockworkers and railroad hands.

The origins of the neighborhood's name are lost to time. Rumor grew into legend swaddled in myth. Dutch Fred, "The Cop," was the most famous of these origin stories. The veteran police officer is said to have walked with his rookie partner down West 39th Street, near 10th Avenue past a small riot in process. The rookie, new to the environs, was horrified by the occurrence.

"This place is hell itself," he bemoaned.

Fred flippantly replied, "Hell's a mild climate. This is Hell's Kitchen."

After the Civil War, the community increased dramatically. Tenements were erected that drew immigrants to the area, where they were crammed together. Living in poverty, facing few job prospects and signs that read "No Dogs, Blacks, or Irish Allowed," many in Hell's Kitchen turned to gangs for survival. According to the *New York Irish*, Hell's Kitchen soon became known as the "most dangerous area on the American Continent."

During the late-nineteenth century into the early-twentieth century, Hell's Kitchen was under the control of a gang called the Gophers, estimated to number around five hundred. They hid out in basements, says the *New York Times*, and focused on robbing freight cars. They were known to be extremely violent, not only bashing heads of rival gangs, but of police as well.

It was in the blazing inferno of ethnic pride and clashes that Mac's progenitor set down roots that determined the course of the rest of his and his family's lives.

It certainly affected Mac's father. He was a truck driver for notorious Irish bootlegger Owney "The Killer" Madden (who created and owned the famous Cotton Club) during the Prohibition days, which started in 1920 after the passage of the 18th Amendment banning the "manufacture, sale or transportation of intoxicating liquors." Madden and a multiethnic syndicate of mostly Italian (with a smattering of Jewish and Irish) gangsters ran a factory and distribution network for their illegal alcohol. The Combine, as the factory was known, at one time was the largest producer of liquor on the eastern seaboard.

Rory Dubhdara wrote, "American gangsters like John Dillinger remain household names and telling signs of a bankrupt society that continually sees crime as the only alternative to a grim life of hopelessness and perdition. For many, robbing a bank or some other 'get rich quick' scheme may seem to be the only viable solution to the despair of poverty."

When prohibition was repealed in 1933, the decriminalization of alcohol rendered that avenue of escape largely closed to gangsters. Though there were still counties and municipalities that continued the ban of alcohol even after the 18th Amendment was repealed, the demand for bootleg alcohol dropped dramatically. Some of the Combine, like Owney Madden, left town to expand operations in other cities—Hot Springs, Arkansas in Madden's case. Most simply "diversified their portfolio" and looked to other operations like gambling, drugs, extortion, prostitution. Mac's father moved on to other more legitimate, and much less lucrative, forms of employment.

Mac paints a 1940 and 1950s childhood in Hell's Kitchen straight off a movie set. Full of James Cagney swagger: a "you'll never take me, dirty copper" mentality, which would undoubtedly meet a "Top of the World, Ma!" ending. My television generation mind sees an old black and white film. Tough hoods with cigarette packs rolled into their sleeves, leaning against Cadillacs. Cigarettes hanging dangerously cool from their lips. Kids with striped shirts and dirty faces played baseball in between passing cars, sandwiched between tenement buildings. Imaginings of a bygone era.

* * *

Saturday bled into Sunday as five in the morning rolled around. Three young friends sprawled on a Hell's Kitchen tenement rooftop, drunk off Guinness and youth. Mac leaned against the pigeon coop, his head pleasantly spinning. He heard the pigeons cooing soothingly in their cages, the rustle of their feathers like a gentle hand on his neck.

Up here, he could almost forget about the poor grades on his math test last week. He'd had to hide it from his father. He wasn't scared of him; after all, Mac had been boxing since he was nine. He'd won the Sugar Ray Robinson Award. He'd spent hours at the punching bag, hardening his fifteen-year-old lithe frame into muscle. He knew he could take his father, worn down by life, poverty, and alcohol.

He didn't want it to come to that, he thought as he looked down at his misshapen knuckles, his calloused palms. He loved the old man. But Mac knew he wanted more than that life, working so hard. Breaking your back and at the end of the day, you still don't have enough to feed your kids.

No, that wasn't the life for Mac. He wanted more. He just didn't know how to get it. School obviously wasn't the way. Not with his eighth grade teacher's words still ringing in his ears like a cross-hook combo to the head: "I would strongly encourage you to give up any thoughts you have of college, James; it's just not practical for someone of your abilities. Especially not for interior design, which requires much training and is really, after all, not a very suitable occupation for a young man anyway. Why don't you find a job where you can work with your hands, and put your strength to your advantage?"

He squeezed his hands into fists until the knuckles whitened. Yeah, he thought, except there are no jobs around to be had. That's why he had dropped out after ninth grade—that and he still wasn't reading too good.

That's what you get for going to PS 17. Since he was in elementary school, his report card had never been stellar: mediocre to failing grades, comments about the fighting, his "overly aggressive behavior," his lack of focus. "Occasionally resents group control. Occasionally evades responsibility." On and on. It was enough to make him feel like he was nothing at all.

That's okay, though. A smile flickered across his smooth cheeks. He and Jackie and Jimmy Coonan had thought of a way to make some real money, working with their hands. All they needed to do is get a couple of guns, hold up some stores real quick, and get the cash. No problems. No one gets hurt.

Jimmy C. and Mac had already done it once. A few months back, a bookie in the neighborhood came to them with a proposal. He had a problem: some deadbeat who didn't want to pay what he owed. He offered the two fifty dollars to rough him up. They couldn't believe their ears. Fifty dollars for a half-hour's worth of work? In 1959, that was a lot of money.

Mac had put to work what his brothers Billy and Mickey taught him in the ring at the Boys Athletic League where they were instructors.

Both of his brothers were champions; both had won titles in the military. They saw his talent, nurtured and encouraged it with gloves and pads. They both told him he could go pro, and encouraged him to, in fact. Especially this past year, when they saw him growing wild like ivy in the streets.

But Mac didn't see that as a way out of poverty either, unless he got real, real lucky. They were so poor when he started boxing that he had to borrow shoes and the right shorts just to be able to get in the ring. And even after he began winning, he still had to deliver meat for the butcher to be able to bring anything to help out at home.

Mac's brothers were tough. Real tough. But they weren't like Mac. They weren't ready to do what Mac was planning.

Up here, with the cool summer breeze, the lingering smell of the day's heat playing on his face, it seemed easy to him. So easy, he couldn't understand why everyone wasn't doing it.

Mac threw his head back and laughed, feeling the weight lifting just a little off his chest. He opened his eyes. He saw Jimmy Coonan slow dancing with his beer bottle around the roof, his older brother Jackie good-naturedly ribbing him.

"Is that really how you'd dance with a girl? Man, no wonder you spend your time in the corner when we go out!"

Jackie turned to Mac. "C'mon, get up and show him how it's done. Can't you see my little brother needs some dance lessons, fast! How is he ever going to get a girl with moves like that?"

Mac demurred, mostly because he wanted the older Coonan to tell him again what a good dancer he is. He knew he could move, but it was still nice to hear. His older sister and her friend had taught him, radio blasting when their parents weren't home. Mac went out all the time, though not much in the neighborhood lately. He had started sneaking into clubs in the Puerto Rican neighborhood, where he'd learned to dance meringue, the cha cha, and samba. He learned it all just by watching other people move like blood through veins to the heartbeat rhythms. He could salsa with the best of them. It was funny, actually, because his blond hair curled as it grew out until he had a mini afro. With the hair and the moves, he was mistaken for Puerto Rican all the time.

Some of the Irish kids from the neighborhood said it with derision. "You look like a fucking Puerto Rican shaking your ass like that. Why don't you get a haircut?"

Mac didn't care. He knew he looked good. And the girls knew it too. He, Jimmy C., and Jackie would go over to Jersey to the school dances there, the ones Jackie had been teasing Jimmy C. about minutes before.

Jimmy C. would just hole up in the corner, taking swigs from the bottle he had snuck in his pocket and eyeing people until he got drunk enough and started a fight. They'd all jump in, giving licks and taking them too. They'd recount the whole story on the train back home later that night: "Did you see that big one come at me from behind? I just sensed he was there, and spun around so he ran straight into my fist. Yeah, he gave me this black eye to remember him by."

But before the inevitable brawl, Mac would spend every minute dancing with one girl after another. They all wanted to be his partner. The guys from the school would line the wall, grumbling about city rats coming in and taking their girls. When the fight finally broke out, they often made sure Mac took an extra couple of lumps. Of course, with his boxing training, he most often gave better than he got.

If nothing else in his life was going well, at least his love life was smooth. Sometimes a little too smooth: it was hard keeping up with the different girlfriends he had. He'd always had more female friends than male; he wasn't sure why. He tried to be respectful with women: nice, honest. Not too honest, but honest at least about his feelings— enough for them to know he was for real. He'd always pay for dinner, even if it was his last buck. He didn't think a woman should have to pay even her half. Jimmy C. and Jackie laughed at him a lot, called him old-time, because he tipped his hat and opened doors. But he always had more girlfriends than both of them put together. So in the end, he got the last laugh.

"You gotta show him how to do that one move again, Mac, show 'em!" Jackie implored.

"All right, all right," Mac finally conceded, his ego appeased. "But I'm going to need a beat to dance to."

Jackie, chuckling, staggered to his feet, and started to tap a beat on the metal fire escape that pulsed throughout the neighborhood like a heartbeat. Mac closed his eyes. He let the beat swell inside him, filling out until it was a twelve-piece orchestra playing just for him. His body began to move on its own accord. Sway and dip. Turn and glide around the rooftop, deftly avoiding clotheslines and air shafts like they were other couples on a crowded dance floor.

Jimmy C. clapped his hands adding to the percussion, then lifted his blonde head to the inky darkness singed bright at the edges, and began to sing. His voice billowed out, beautiful on the wind. It wrapped around a tune sung by a local group Nicky and the Citations. It was playing on everyone's radio that summer: "When you're not by my side/ The world's in two, and I'm a fool/ When you're not in my sight/ Then everything just fades from view/ The mystery of love belongs to you/ The mystery of love belongs to you."

Mac raised his voice too and stumbled over to throw his arm around his best friend's shoulder. They worked out the harmonies as they went, Jimmy C. taking the accent voice, Mac taking the lead. Mac's voice was strong, sensual, and rough—spun out silk threads fluttering like the laundry on the line next to them.

Mac never felt better than when a song was coming out of his mouth. He thought back to singing in the choir at St. Albert's Church, where he had his confirmation, and where he was an altar boy.

He thought of his doo-wop group. They hadn't come up with a name. But you don't really need one when you're just singing weekends at the beer rackets. Despite the locale, he and the two young Black men also in the group had been really good. Mac knew it in his soul.

He had hoped they would get signed to a label and make it big, their voices coming out of jukeboxes and radios across the country. Then other people would stand on rooftops belting out his music. His voice would help kids just like him escape everything, if only for the length of a chorus.

It would never happen. Mac would drift away from his group, out of frustration and hopelessness. There was no future in that—just like school, regular work, and everything else he tried. He felt trapped when he was inside his cramped apartment with his five other siblings. His mother worked so hard. He had felt that way tonight. He had run out into the streets, heading down the block to Jimmy and Jackie's. The brothers felt just as trapped, despite being middle class.

Their family, elevated by their father's job as an accountant, lived in more spacious quarters than Mac's.

How much money their families made didn't affect their friendship. They grew up on the same streets and had known the same people all their lives. They were friends before they knew of differences. They were bonded by restlessness and a desire to break out of the boundaries of Hell's Kitchen, to leave a mark so bright and so red it would take an eternity before they were forgotten.

Yeah, Mac thought as he looked at Jimmy C. and Jackie, they were going to do something real great, the three of them. They're going to be something. Mac was going to be somebody.

The three sang the night into the dawn.

* * *

This then, was part of the incubation of the Westies, the notorious incarnation of the Irish Mob that outraged a country and terrified a city. The Westies were deeply and inextricably rooted in the neighborhood they were born out of, their history of oppression, and the legacy of violence they continued.

To Mac, Hell's Kitchen was more than his home: it was an amusement park; it was a maze he maneuvered in the dark; it was a meeting place for friends. It was a training ground where he flexed his muscles until he was ready to take on the mantle of mobster.

In our first interview I asked how Mac came to be part of the Westies. He waved his hand dismissively.

"I grew up in the mob. I was born into it."

The mob was his legacy: a bastard birthright, left to him by generations before.

Born into poverty, Mac, his family, the majority of the working-class Irish in Hell's Kitchen lived in the borderland of survival. From the moment the Irish stepped off boats in teeming numbers to escape famine and disease, they were pressed from all sides to fit into the shape America desired or imagined: cop, menial laborer, barkeep, domestic, vagrant, or corpse. A few were able to rise above the stink and sweat by hard work—along with a few kickbacks from Irish politicians and businessmen who tended to take care of their own.

A lot more chose to make it by whatever means necessary. Mac and the rest of the Westies were just the latest, some say the last, incarnation of the Irish American gangster.

T.J. English wrote in *Paddy Whacked: The History of the Irish American Gangster*: "The American mobster as we perceive him today—violent, impulsive, disreputable, often irredeemable—is tethered to the earliest days of the Irish immigrant experience, when the Mob was born out of starvation, disease, desperation and bigotry."

When most people think of organized crime, they think of the Mafia. There were many significant differences between the operations. As opposed to the Italian Mafia, with its rigidly set rituals, codes, and inductions, the Westies formed naturally, organically and inevitably. However, they were both born out of similar historical circumstances.

The Italian Mafia, or La Cosa Nostra (This Thing of Ours), did not begin on American shores. Instead, it came over with the tens of thousands of poor Italian immigrants, many from Sicily. It originally began in the 1800s as a means of supplementing the woefully undermanned police forces on the island, and to protect communities from bandits and address land grievances from the growing numbers of landowners.

In 1864, a high-ranking military official was the first to speak of the Mafia, calling them a "sect of thieves." This sect of thieves had gained overwhelming support from the local populace. Rome's attempts to crush them only drove the people deeper into the Mafia's folds. The sect made "affiliates every day of the brightest young people coming from the rural class, of the guardians of the fields in the Palermitan countryside, and of the large number of smugglers; a sect which gives and receives protection to and from certain men who make a living on traffic and internal commerce. It is a sect with little or no fear of public bodies, because its members believe that they can easily elude this," according to *Mafia Brotherhoods*. The soldier detailed the secret signals to recognize each other, according to *History of the Mafia*, and had a code of loyalty and non-interaction with the police known as *umirtà* (humility).

Compared to La Cosa Nostra, the Westies were almost completely structureless. Jimmy Coonan was the boss, but that's because everyone made him the boss. The small handful who had been around since childhood formed the inner circle. But that was the extent of their organization.

This is why Mac scoffed at the idea of the Irish Mob presented in the film *State of Grace*, loosely based on his gang. In the film, an Irish cop who grew up in the neighborhood infiltrates the gangsters. Mac said the movie is simply Hollywood doing what it does. Trying to turn Irish kids into a syndicate more in the vein of La Cosa Nostra.

"It wasn't like that at all. We were all from the same neighborhood, we all grew up together. We were friends. We weren't those Italian guys, made men or whatever. We were there cause we wanted to be there with one another. No one could have infiltrated that. No one infiltrated Hell's Kitchen."

There were three in the beginning. Others would soon come: a rise to power, fame and most definitely infamy. But it began with three.

Jimmy Coonan became the feared and brutal leader of the Westies. He was the one who hatched the plot that wrested power from Mickey Spillane, the benevolent godfather of the Irish, and rocketed the three into history. "He was smart. Real smart. And dangerous. Real dangerous," Mac says.

His brother Jackie was, by all accounts, a crazy loose cannon even by the Hell's Kitchen standards. "Jackie? Jackie was intelligent. But nuts!"

And Mac. "Me? I was never too smart. But I had common sense."

It was hard to imagine the diamond tipped glares I had seen in mug shots of the three melting into the smiling eight-year-olds they used to be, with rumpled clothes and even more rumpled hair, chasing after a loose ball rolling towards the gutter. When Mac told me they played Ghost Tag, a cross between Tag and Boogeyman played after dark, I pictured Jackie Coonan volunteering to be it, a lopsided leer stretching across his face as thirty kids ran through the darkened streets and alleys echoing with muffled laughter stifled by sleeves.

Some of the ways they found to entertain themselves were not so picturesque. Mac's favorite game when he was eleven: get a dummy, hide behind a parked car, wait for someone to drive by. Then scream out and throw the dummy in front of the car, as if a person had fallen into the road. Some drivers would be able to skid to a halt or swerve dangerously close to other cars, almost causing an accident.

Others hit the dummy. The driver would jump out, hysterical and frightened they had killed someone. The kids rolled in the bushes with laughter.

One time, however, it was Mac who was surprised: "We did it, I was around twelve, we threw the dummy out—only to find out the person in the car was my father…We stopped doing it after that."

Mac's father always had a big car, a Buick or a Cadillac. His cars always had a rumble seat. Mac loved riding in the seat with his father, the wind whipping through the open windows, the sun shining down. It brought a rare feeling of escape from Hell's Kitchen's omnipresent gaze.

The escape never lasted long. It seemed to always stall in the middle of 10th Ave, where Mac's father often left it after the occasional drinking spree. Because his father was in no shape and having no inclination to move the car to the side of the road, Mac would organize his siblings to push the car out of harm's way.

"My father was not an alcoholic," Mac corrected. "Once in a while he came home drunk. He was tough."

* * *

The youngster Mac and the Coonan brothers did more than just play games and pranks. They also stole together. But they weren't the only ones, according to Mac.

During that time, the neighborhood was full of factories filling the dietary needs of New York City: milk, bread, candy. Mac and his friends stole from them all. Slipped in at night under fences. Distracted a driver while the others grabbed what they could out of the back.

Mac's mother, in addition to taking care of six children, worked at a candy store. Mac would walk in with a few friends and pepper his mother with inane questions.

"Hey mom what's for dinner tonight?" Mac's crystal blue eyes were wide and innocent.

His mother turned away from refilling the peppermint twists with exasperation. "What do you think? I have the bag of french fries I bought. That has to be enough until your father's paycheck next week. You know that."

Out of the corner of his eye, Mac saw his friends, just out of his mother's gaze, grabbing handfuls of lemon drops and chocolate squares, shoving them into their pockets.

"Oh, okay, that's what I thought. I just wanted to make sure. Okay, thanks, mom, see you later tonight!" he tossed over his shoulder as he and his friends sprinted through the door.

"Don't be late getting home tonight again, or I'll tell your father!"

"Okay, mom," he yelled back, turning the corner of his street. He hoped he caught up with his youthful cronies before all the good candy was gone. He didn't want to get stuck with a gumball and nothing else.

"Hey Jimmy!" a voice called from above.

He skidded to a halt, looking up. The neighbor from the next building over was leaning out of the top floor of the building. She lived with her daughter, her daughter's husband, and their four kids in an apartment smaller than Mac's family's place. Her white hair was always in immaculate condition. On Easter, she sometimes gave Mac and his siblings pennies.

"Yeah?" he answered.

"Run up to the store for me and buy three potatoes, will ya? I'm making a stew for tonight," she called down, tossing a handful of coins wrapped in an old handkerchief.

Inwardly Mac moaned. He'd never get any of the candy; there wouldn't even be a gumball left by the time he got done running the two blocks to the store and back.

But he liked the neighbor. She was always nice to him. Besides, if he said no, she might come down and smack him for it. If not, she'd definitely tell his mother, who played cards with her every week. He would be sure to get hit for disrespecting his elder. He didn't mind so much if it was his mom punishing him. She usually only hit with her hand. Mac could hardly feel it, since he started boxing at the boys' club last year. But if she told his dad? Forget about it. His favorite instrument was the belt.

Mac remembered one time a month or so ago he had gotten in trouble for something. He'd hidden the belt so his parents couldn't find it. They searched the entire house, not knowing that Mac had put it in the rooftop pigeon coop. He outsmarted himself that time, though. His mom had started hitting him with a broom in lieu of the belt. He had run down the five flights of the building like a shot, two stairs at a time, just to get away, which of course only made it worse when he finally came back home.

Mac sighed. "Yeah, sure, I'll be right back with the potatoes," he called up to the neighbor.

He mentally released the taste of ill-gotten candy in his mouth.

Retelling some of these stories, Mac shook his head. "We were poor, see, but we didn't know it when we were kids. We were happy. We knew there was never enough to eat though, even with mom working such long hours. That's how I learned to cook. I'm a good cook now, ask anybody! I can cook with almost no ingredients."

Even though Hell's Kitchen was predominately Irish, other ethnicities were present: Puerto Ricans, Italians, Yugoslavians. Several families of "the Yugos" lived on 48th St. Like many of the immigrant residents, they made their own goods, to make a quarter stretch. Some of the Yugoslavian families grew grape vines in their backyard, and made their own wine. Mac and his friends delighted in climbing over the fences and grabbing grapes right before they got ripe every season. Running through the yards lined up, they would grab grapes as they went.

"It's funny," he shook his head slightly. "Today, they'd be shooting at us, saying we're thieves. It wasn't like that then."

The kids also tried to find other, more legitimate ways to help their families make ends meet, and to have money for the movies, pocket change for candy and baseball cards. Hell's Kitchen borders the waterfront. In the 1940s, the Port of New York was the most lucrative commercial port in the world. The kids used to make extra money shining imported cars as they came off the boats. When they grew up, the Westies used the waterfront for stealing goods, sometimes cars like the ones they used to shine. They also used the docks as a way to provide associates, girlfriends, and friends paper jobs, where they only had to show up once a week: to collect their paychecks.

Back when they were still shining cars and playing Ghost Tag, Mac was tough. He was not, however, the toughest kid in his family. Ten-year-old Mac, blonde hair sticking up in different directions, missing a front tooth, followed behind his older sister.

"The Boss. She was The Boss."

Mac's older sister was the leader of a group of young kids called the Black Hawks. She ran the fundraising operations, which turned out to be very lucrative, for her. She intimidated all of the other kids into giving her the money they made. They gave it, too. Everyone knew you didn't mess with The Boss.

As they grew older, the kids had to choose their different gang affiliations. For the girls in the neighborhood, there were a couple choices: the Dizzettes or Satan's Debs. Mac's older sister chose the Dizzettes. In a couple years, she was running it just as she had run the Black Hawks. For the boys of the Black Hawks, and Mac in particular, there was no contest of what gang they would join up with: The Junior Satans. You could tell a Junior Satan by their skateboards: emblazoned with a black box, with a devil's head etched in it.

"These were bad guys. That's who we wanted to be," Mac intoned.

Later on, young towheaded boys with smudged cheeks and scabbed up knees would watch Mac, Jimmy, and Jackie Coonan ride around in sleek cars with sleek clothes and chic women. They had become those guys kids wanted to be when they grew up.

It wasn't all stealing and running wild in the streets, though. Mac remembers fun ways of bonding with his family and getting some added income. They'd go down to Broadway during Thanksgiving and Christmas, when the streets of downtown Manhattan would be packed with tourists and shoppers. Mac's family would set up shop on a corner. His sister hummed a few notes, then they all joining in singing carols. A cup sat out in front of them for donations.

* * *

With such vibrant memories of family, Mac thought his parents' relationship a strong one, so it came as a complete shock when they separated when he was fourteen—the same year he and Jimmy Coonan first got paid to beat someone up. Mac said he never truly understood why his parents separated and why they did not reconcile.

It wasn't until later in his life that Mac (as well as his mother) found out that, in addition to the six children his father had with his mother, he had three others by two different women.

Mac's answer was a simple one. "Well, see, my father was a bootlegger."

Even with all of his other endeavors, Mac's father still came by to see Mac and his siblings every day. He strictly enforced the eight o'clock curfew whether he was in the house or not. And every week, he would have Sunday dinner with his children and former wife.

One of his father's mistresses even worked at the school Mac attended. She would tell his father when Mac was in trouble.

"I used to think he had a sixth sense, because he always used to know when I did something bad."

So Mac came by his own womanizing honestly. Portrayed in T.J. English's book *The Westies* as a sort of Hell's Kitchen Romeo, Mac has four children, by two different women. "Evenly divided, two and two." One was not his biological child, and yet Mac claimed him as his own.

In his vocabulary, there exist multiple categories for women you are with: wives, mistresses, and girlfriends, all distinct types of relationships.

Most times, he had one of each.

Mac met his first wife when they were still kids. He was hungry for something more, something better. He was a lean, muscled seventeen-year-old who loved to dance, drink, laugh, and do whatever was needed to make money. She was a bubbly, bright-eyed girl of fourteen.

"From the minute I saw her, we were together. She was my best friend. She was my angel."

Mac swore he didn't cheat on his first wife for the majority of their relationship. Even then, he felt it wasn't his fault.

His cousin Tommy was a hitman with the Westies. Tommy's work is most remembered in the killing of union leader John Riley. Tommy himself was killed in a shoot out with police. He left his distraught wife (who conveniently already had the last name McElroy from her late husband) with a young child, whom Mac would come to consider his son.

The code of the gangster says you take care of any member's family if they are killed in the line of duty. Plus, this was family. So how could Mac not go over every so often and check in on Tommy's wife? It was natural for Mac to sit with his cousin's widow. Each visit was a little bit longer—holding her hand for support, giving her a long hug, rubbing her shoulder.

It went from there.

This double life meant a great deal of love and support for Mac, who stayed close with both women. He even spoke to his first wife and her new husband ("a nice guy") on the phone from time to time while incarcerated.

Having two families, one in New Jersey and one in west Manhattan, had its disadvantages—say, around Christmas.

* * *

Mac was awakened by a small body plowing into him. His eyes slowly registered his youngest daughter jumping up and down on him, shrieking, "Merry Christmas, Daddy, Merry Christmas! Are you up? Can we open presents now?!"

Mac's face cracked with a smile. He stole a glance at the clock on the wall. 5:50 AM. He would have to rush if he was going to get everything in today.

"Yes, sweetie, you can open presents, just as soon as daddy gets back."

His wife rolled over and snuggled into the crook of his arm. "Where are you going so early?"

He kissed her cheek, then stood up, grabbing his pants slung over the chair. "You know I always go out to get donuts on Christmas morning. It just wouldn't be Christmas without it for me."

His wife rolled over and burrowed back into her pillow, savoring a few more minutes until both her children attacked the bed again. "I just don't know why you have to go to Jersey to get them every year. They have donuts at the shop on the corner."

"Yeah, but you know, baby, I need my special donuts from Jersey, gotta have them." He leaned in and kissed her lightly on the lips. "I'll be back so fast, you won't even know I was gone. I love you."

Driving in his car through the Lincoln Tunnel, he thanked God nobody was up this early on Christmas morning. He made it to his mistress' door in twenty-five minutes.

He used his key and let himself in. Two small bodies immediately smothered him. "Daddy, we're so glad you're here; now we can open presents. We've been waiting!"

He kissed them both on the head. "Sorry to keep you waiting. Yeah, go ahead and open presents."

He dropped into a seat. His mistress came over to him, brushed her lips against his. "Thought you might not be able to make it. I was worried."

He slipped his arm around her waist. "You know I'd never disappoint you, baby."

He innocuously dropped two hundred dollar bills on the table.

She smiled down at him, and walked back in the kitchen to finish making the eggs and bacon she had just put on.

"Don't forget the donuts," she called over her shoulder. "I picked them up right before you got here."

* * *

Though I deplore men cheating on women, I did have to admit to being impressed not only by Mac's ingenuity but his commitment. My own father couldn't show up for one family Christmas, let alone two.

Apparently Mac's charm was enough to carry him through. His wife, his mistress, and numerous girlfriends spoke highly of him during various trials. Some of them wrote him throughout his incarceration. He wrote a poem, "Heavenly Delight, for _____." He originally wrote it for his wife, though he also sent it to at least five other women, with their name inserted into the title. He told each the poem was written special for them.

"What can I say?" Mac spread his hands. "I love women. I think all women are beautiful. I love getting to see the beauty within them."

My face must have read as disapproving as my thoughts, because he chuckled. "I know I'm terrible. All those girls knew me very well. They probably all thought I'm full of shit anyway."

He went on to tell the story of setting up a date with his girlfriend (separate from both his wife and his mistress) at the Skyline Motel Bar, a notorious Westies hangout. He was sitting at the bar sipping his drink when a fourth woman he had been seeing came in. She sat down and joined him. Soon enough Mac's mistress came in, and then the real show started. "I try not to curse in front of ladies, but these girls called me every name in the book!"

One thing Mac said he never did was lie to any of his girlfriends. "They both knew I was married and had a mistress. You know what, they are still my friends."

Mac paused during the interview. "I don't know if you can love more than one person at a time, but I did."

He stopped again.

"I think I did," he murmured, more to himself than to me.

Apparently multiple women were capable of loving the same man, even when they found out about the others. When interviewed after his arrest, his wife, mistress, and at least one of his girlfriends all described Mac as loving, caring, and attentive. In addition to the four children he claimed between the first two women, one of his girlfriends had a daughter as well. The girl's father was a drug addict, and Mac's presence in the home had been a calming influence.

This is ironic, as all three women said Mac's only downfall was the drugs he started doing after the Westies' "business" began to really take off. All of them left him ultimately because of the drugs. His wife got tired of driving the streets with Mac's older sister, scared she would find him dead in a gutter, or not knowing where he was sleeping at night for months at a time.

The drug use didn't start all at once. They all agreed Mac took care of himself, even to excess. When he would go to the bar where his girlfriend worked, he would order fruit drinks instead of alcohol: that's how much of a health nut he was.

But memories begin to pile up, teetering as they grew. One day they became an avalanche and Mac was trapped underneath. Rather than fighting to get free, however, Mac sank deeper—into drugs and the Westies.

* * *

Hell's Kitchen, the incubator for the Westies, suffered from many problems, and racism and racial tension numbered among them. In a city like New York where neighborhoods jostle one another for space, working-class immigrants and folks of color are often pitted against one another. The history of Hell's Kitchen bears this out: people lined up based on skin color and ethnicity.

Mac was a product of his environment. He got into fights for territory with other Irish boys against Puerto Ricans. But by the time he had pull in the Westies, Mac wasn't interested in hearing it.

"I would say to the guys who didn't want them [Puerto Ricans] there, 'Leave them alone, they're trying to make it without connections.'"

The beginnings of these tensions were highlighted in a 1959 news story. On August 30, a back and forth war between the Puerto Rican Vampires from the upper West Side, and the Irish Norsemen from Hell's Kitchen, ended in tragedy when members of the Vampires attacked a group of white, unaffiliated teenagers. The Vampires sought vengeance for the beating of a friend at the hands of the Irish gang.

Sixteen-year-old Salvador Agron stabbed two of the young men to death. He was wearing a black cape with a red lining. The media called it the "Capeman" killings. Agron was sentenced to die in the electric chair, the youngest person ever given the death penalty in New York state.

The Capeman story became a flashpoint for the shifting racial demographics, tensions, and prejudice brewing not only in the city but in the nation. Eric C. Schneider writes in *Vampires, Dragons and Egyptian Kings: Youth Gangs in Postwar New York*:

> The letters [to newspapers and officials by white residents] reflected all the stereotypes of Puerto Ricans and African Americans and linked crime, welfare and social change to the arrival of the migrants. The reaction was that of a people challenged in their dominance, forced to accommodate newcomers who rejected New York's color line and who pushed their way into new neighborhoods and the city's public spaces. In the discourse of the streets, African Americans and Puerto Ricans were nearly always the aggressors.

The Capeman incident took place at a playground between 45th and 46th streets, just around the corner from Mickey Spillane's White House Bar. This history of racial fault lines is not new. The 1863 Draft Riots featured in the film *The Gangs of New York* were fueled by racism. Poor whites in the north were disillusioned with the Civil War. There was a draft for conscription. But if you were rich, you could pay someone to take your place. So, as is usually the case, it was the poor fighting on the frontlines. White workers felt the Civil War was a fight for Black people. When the Emancipation Proclamation came out ending slavery in Confederate states, they felt betrayed by Lincoln. They were convinced that after they fought and died for Black people, those same Black folks would move north and take their jobs. Echoes of this anti-immigrant sentiment are heard in this country today.

* * *

That racialized tension and animosity ran through the entire history of New York and in this nation. Like in so many other places, these tensions have been handled not through reconciliation, but through gentrification.

Hell's Kitchen—this bastion of working-class Irish-American culture and the place that shaped Mac and the Westies and so many others, for good or for ill—no longer exists, not as the location hotter than Hell itself. Part of Hell's Kitchen was devastated by the construction of the Lincoln Tunnel in the 1950s. By the 1960s, when the Westies became a real force to be reckoned with, Hell's Kitchen was watching its most reliable source of employment—the port—die before its eyes, as alternative forms of shipping and transport became available. The neighborhood was dying right alongside it.

During the 1970s and especially the 1980s, the face of Hell's Kitchen, the West Side of Manhattan, and the city as a whole was changing rapidly. A push from developers to get ahead of property that was now a hot commodity forced out the traditional residents. Working class Irish, Italians, and Puerto Ricans were replaced by white, upper class professionals. At the end of the day, these were forces even the Westies couldn't stop.

The neighborhood lost pieces of its history—like the Market Diner, a regular Westies hang out also frequented by Frank Sinatra, Bette Midler, and Geraldo Rivera. It was a community icon. In fact, it was charmed. Eighty-four-year-old Saul Zelin, whose family owned the diner, said, "Fortunately we were very lucky—we had no murders, and that was quite a thing for that area under those circumstances," according to an article by Tina Kelley.

But in 2006, the Market Diner closed. "Losing Market Diner is losing what are the last vestiges of Hell's Kitchen, as it existed in the 60s, 70s and on into the 80s," said T.J. English in the article. "There are very few places of that era left. This is one less place for older people in the neighborhood to hang out, to have some familiar link to the history of the neighborhood."

Mac sent me Kelley's *New York Times* article about Market Diner closing.

"We used to hang out there," he scrawled in the margins. "Now it's gone."

True to their fighting Irish spirit, the denizens of Hell's Kitchen did not go quietly. The case of the Windermere apartment complex shows that. Built in 1881, it stands as the second-oldest apartment complex in Manhattan. According to a report by the Land Preservation Commission, in the 1980s, the owners began a campaign of harassment to get the tenants to leave because of the intense gentrification of the neighborhood. Court papers show that rooms were ransacked, doors were ripped out, and sex workers moved in. They even sent death threats to the tenants to get them to leave. Alan B. Weissman, the Windermere's landlord, was listed in the *Village Voice's* annual "The Dirty Dozen: New York's Worst Landlords" list as the second worst for 1985. Eventually the building's agent, manager and superintendent were convicted of harassment.

The Commission granted the Windermere landmark status in 2005, but it wasn't enough to save the building. The majority of tenants had moved out by that point. The remaining seven tenants hung on until the Fire Department deemed the property unlivable in 2007. When the New York Supreme Court ruled that Japan-based Toa Construction Company had to repair the building, they decided to cut losses and sell. Because of zoning laws, the Windermere still has to include affordable housing, but the new developer has said he will make the building over into a boutique hotel, focused on attracting European tourists.

Hell's Kitchen has been reborn, christened Clinton and sometimes Midtown West. It has been rebuilt: boutiques instead of delis, and high-rise condos instead of tenements. Sidewalk cafes line the street where Mac played kick the can. In fact, according to a 2014 Manhattan Rental Market Report, prices have increased so rapidly that rents in the former Hell's Kitchen surpass those in the rest of Manhattan.

What the entire force of the NYPD, FBI, and Attorney General Rudolph Giuliani couldn't accomplish was finally accomplished by eager real estate agents, gentrification, inflation, and Mayor Giuliani: the end of Hell's Kitchen.

Mac had been off the streets of his home for more than twenty years when I talked to him about it. He knew of the changes through stories from family and old friends, and from pictures and news articles. He took the information that he had no home to go home to with stoicism and resignation.

"You know, back in the day, everyone helped each other. They respected each other. Not like now. Hell's Kitchen has changed."

THE GESTATION OF VIOLENCE

"The underworld has become a metaphor for American capitalism. Anyone who has tried to get ahead and make a living in the United States, from the lowest street vendor to the most powerful corporate CEO, recognizes the brutal, dog-eat-dog reality of the American Dream. Some fantasize about taking matters into their own hands. In defiance of the laws and mores of polite society, the gangster does just that."

—T.J. English,
Paddy Whacked: The History of the Irish American Gangster

In 1970s, Ford Motor Company rushed to get its Pinto car on the roads. This was in spite of the fact that the company knew the car had an unprotected gas tank that would explode if the car was hit, even at five miles an hour. According to author David Simon in his book *Tony Soprano's America: The Criminal Side of the American Dream*, Ford executives had full knowledge of this defect. In fact, internal memos showed they had done the cost-benefit analysis of recalling and replacing all of the gas tanks, or paying out settlements for wrongful death suits.

The memo clearly demonstrated that it would be more profitable to let people die or be seriously injured than to insert an $11 rubber bladder inside the gas tank. The result: Ford let the unsafe Pinto roll off the assembly line and hundreds of people were killed or maimed.

Under pressure, Ford issued a recall in 1978. No one went to jail for the severe injuries suffered by people as young as thirteen. No one went to jail for the deaths that ensued. This was not called murder in the first, even with evidence of premeditation.

We like to think punishment is universal: we are all held to the same set of laws and credos, and when we do wrong, we all face the same punishment. But murder is called by a different name when it is committed in a suit, in a board room, at the Stock Exchange, when it speaks proper English, when it has a university degree, when it is state-sanctioned, when it is wrapped in an American flag, and when it does not get its hands dirty. Lynda Milito, wife of Gambino *capo* Louie Milito, wrote in her book *Mafia Wife*, "For what those CEO types did, the government should tie one of those yellow plastic crime-scene tapes around the entire United States of America. The only difference between them and organized crime is they took more money from more people in a shorter time than all the Mafia crime families combined took in the past fifty years."

* * *

The term "The Westies" was invented by police. It was primarily used by law enforcement during the group's existence. In fact, if you search newspapers like the *New York Times* for the Westies, before 1986 (the year of their arrests), all you'll find is dog sale ads and the results for Best in Show.

To folks in the know, especially in the neighborhood, Mac and his associates were just the Hell's Kitchen Irish Mob or Coonan's Crew.

"We never called ourselves the Westies," Mac scoffed. "We didn't call ourselves anything. We were just some guys who grew up together, who helped one another out. We weren't organized or anything."

"I remember the first time I heard that term, I was reading the newspaper and I saw Joe Coffey, you know the cop who was supposedly so big and caught us, and Joe was saying, 'Oh the Westies, the Westies,' and I was like, 'Who's he talking about?' It was only later that I found out they meant us. Me."

Mac chuckled. "He got his ten seconds of fame in front of the cameras. And it stuck."

Everything started in the 1960s. Jimmy Coonan, just a teenager, watched as his father was kidnapped by Irish boss Mickey Spillane. Spillane ran Hell's Kitchen in those days. His father was held for ransom at Spillane's White House Bar. Kidnapping was not an unknown occurrence at that time. It was more reliable than going to the bank for a loan. A mobster strapped for cash finds someone in the neighborhood with a little extra (or friends who had the funds), and snatches him. He gets the money, releases the guy, and everything is forgotten. No cops, no paperwork, no mess. This is what happened with the elder Coonan, give or take a little pistol-whipping for good measure. He was more than ready to forgive and forget. He was ready to get back to life as usual.

His son, however, was not.

Jimmy C. brazenly let the whole neighborhood know he was gunning for Spillane. He gathered people, mostly younger gangsters, disgruntled by not getting enough play from Spillane's empire. These were guys looking to catch a lift going straight to the top.

Mac felt divided loyalties during this period. He had been tight with Jimmy C. since they were kids. But Mac had also worked for Spillane as a bartender at the White House Bar since he was eighteen. He mostly worked after four in the morning, when all the other bars in New York closed for the night; that's when the White House became an illegal, after-hours spot, and when the real money was made. Though Mac was robbing Spillane hand over fist, the old man didn't mind; there was enough money to go around.

Mac needed money. For Jimmy C., it started off as revenge. Then it became about power, about protecting his assets. For Mac, it was about having enough money in the bank to never hear rumbling stomachs again. Each move up the criminal ladder was driven by ghosts of the past. Petty thief to burglary to armed robbery to hitman: each was a step away from old specters and into the arms of new ones.

Mac lost track of the number of times Jimmy C. tried to off Spillane, referred to by the *New York Times* as "one of the last of the old fashioned gangsters, handing out turkey at Thanksgiving and paying visits to the elderly." Mac remembered the night Jimmy C. was waiting outside the bar. When Coonan saw Spillane, he let loose with the machine gun. He fired hundreds of rounds at Spillane and, incidentally, into the White House Bar where Mac was cleaning up. Spillane miraculously survived that time.

Eventually, though, everyone's luck runs out. May 13, 1977, Spillane was gunned down in front of his home by Gambino crew boss Roy DeMeo and members of his "Murder Machine," as his crew was known, as an "early birthday present" to Jimmy Coonan.

When the Westies began working with the Gambino family, they were "assigned" to DeMeo's crew. Like consultants hired to work with a specific department in a company, the Westies coordinated their assignments through DeMeo, the *capo* of the Murder Machine crew. He in turn coordinated with the larger Gambino hierarchy.

The Mafia higher-ups must have thought it fitting to pair up the Westies, considered to be the most terrifying thing ever to come out of Hell's Kitchen, with DeMeo's crew. Gene Mustain and Jerry Capeci quote FBI Special Agent Arthur Ruffels as saying of DeMeo and his gang, "They were the scariest people we've ever seen. Just in Roy's crew there were five people you would have to call serial killers." Murder Machine was said to have killed over two hundred people in the time they operated.

One of them was Spillane.

The night of Spillane's murder, Jimmy Coonan stopped by The White House Bar while Mac was working. Mac had known his friend for a very long time. He didn't have to guess what had happened that night.

Mac walked to where Coonan was after handing a customer their drink.

"So what," Mac asked quietly, "you're the boss now?"

Coonan replied simply, "Yeah. Yeah, I'm the new boss."

And he was. Coonan planned ahead; he had already recruited Spillane associates like muscle Eddie Cummiskey and loanshark Tony

Lucich, who had previously hired Coonan to be his muscle, to his side. Others in Spillane's crew saw which way the wind was blowing. They either got outta Dodge or got behind Coonan.

Hell's Kitchen was a small place. Word traveled fast. There was a new force to be reckoned with. "Justice" came hard and swift, armed with butcher knives and spattered in blood.

* * *

Now that Jimmy Coonan was boss of Hell's Kitchen, he intended to remain so. More than that, he wanted to have a crew so outrageous, so terrifying, that no one would ever forget them. Jimmy made sure the Westies had hands in many different rackets: kidnapping, theft, loan-sharking, extortion, drug dealing, gambling, fraud, and counterfeiting.

But the thing that they became infamous for was murder. The Westies practiced a specifically horrific brand of it, almost guaranteed to ensure the individual seemingly disappeared, without a trace.

It went like this: Shoot the guy. Make sure everyone in the crew put a bullet in him, if possible, so all were accomplices: it reduced people's inclination to rat, knowing they were facing murder one as well.

Then lay down the plastic, roll the body on it, strip it naked. Have an assortment of knives at the ready: butcher knife, an eighteen-inch steak knife with a serrated edge, a small fillet knife. As T.J. English reported in *The Westies*, Coonan told Billy Beattie in his tutorial that the fillet knife was needed "to take off tattoos, birthmarks, anything's gonna make it possible to identify the body."

The next step in what they called the Houdini: start to cut. Sever the limbs, head, hands, and feet. With a couple guys who knew what they were doing, it took less than an hour. Billy Beattie was repulsed by this part of the job: "I'll kill anybody, but I'm not into cutting them up," he said later at trial. Mac was definitely of the same mind, and while he certainly participated in the murders, he is not known to have engaged in the dismemberment.

Last step: get rid of the body. They often used Jimmy Coonan's red van to transport the dismembered parts to dump, often in the Hudson River. Jimmy C. jokingly called it "The Meat Wagon," which disturbed even Mac. Even so, Mac often served as driver for The Meat Wagon on these missions, and helped with the gruesome task of disposal.

This almost assured that the fate of the murdered person would never be known. No one could be certain if they were killed, whatever their suspicions, and police would be unable to investigate the case as a homicide. As Jimmy C. told Billy Beattie, "No *corpus delecti*, no investigation."

Mac and the others learned to do the "Houdini," from Jimmy C. He in turn learned it from Eddie "the Butcher" Cummiskey, an older gangster who had been trained as a butcher during one of his frequent prison stays, hence the nickname. Roy DeMeo's crew engaged in the same disposal method, but put their own spin on it: before they chopped up the body, they would drain the blood in the shower.

Jimmy C. also added his own twist to their Houdini: he kept the hands of the victim in his freezer. Far from being a gruesome fetish, it served a diabolical purpose: you could use the severed hands to plant fingerprints at a crime scene, thus sending the police on a chase for a person who was floating in pieces in the Hudson River.

Mac knew it was diabolically brilliant, but never felt comfortable with it, or any other part of the Houdini. He usually snorted a couple lines or downed a row of shots before job assignments that required it. Even though he knew these guys they were taking out had signed up for this life, it didn't make him sleep any easier at night.

* * *

Finally, all of Jimmy C.'s hard work paid off.

He didn't plan on just running Hell's Kitchen; he wanted to step onto the bigger New York underworld stage. And while he was more than capable of employing brutality, he didn't want to be like the turn-of-the-century Gopher gang, bashing heads for fun and engaging in mostly-petty raids on freight trains. Instead, he looked to gangsters of the past like Owney Madden for the multi-ethnic alliances he forged in order to create one of the most successful and powerful illegal organizations: The Combine.

To do so, he had to get in good with the Italian Mafia. But first, he had to get their attention. Jimmy C. told Billy Beattie that he had some people he wanted to impress, and that "the more bodies he had, the better he looked."

Here the day finally was—one of the first times that the Mafia partnered in a real way with a non-Italian organization; however, many others, including Mac, used the words co-opted, took over, leashed.

It was February 1978 when the inner circle of the Westies assembled in Mickey Featherstone's living room. It was the three, of course: Mac, Jimmy C., and Jackie. In addition, their numbers had swelled to include Mickey, Richie Ryan, and Billy Beattie, three other neighborhood kids Mac had known his whole life.

They gathered to hear about Jimmy C. and Mickey's sit down with Big Paulie the day before. Paul Castellano. The head of the Gambino family, the most influential of the five Italian Mafia crime syndicates. The names of these families—Lucchesse, Genovese, Bonanno, Colombo, and Gambino—were legendary, though they didn't particularly impress Mac.

Paul Castellano took over from his uncle, Carlo Gambino, for whom the family was named (and supposedly, on whom Marlon Brando's character in *The Godfather* was based), when Gambino died of a heart attack in 1976. That left Big Paulie the head of all the crime families: the *capo di tutti capi*, the boss of all bosses. Not someone to leave hanging when you are called to his table.

So Jimmy C. and Mickey went to Tommaso's, the notorious Mafia hangout, in Bay Ridge, Brooklyn. The upper echelon of the Italian Mafia was in attendance. Mac knew what the meeting was about. Ruby Stein's body had been found. Well, at least part of it. His bloated torso washed up on the shore of Brooklyn's Rockaway Beach. That made a lot of people very unhappy for a variety of reasons.

It made Big Paulie unhappy because Stein was one of the most successful loansharks in New York City. Stein gave Castellano a piece of the action he collected. It made Jimmy C. unhappy because he'd been the one to organize Stein's murder. Danny Grillo, one of Roy DeMeo's associates, asked the Westies for a favor. Grillo was in debt to Stein for over $150,000. There was no way he was going to be able to pay that back. Would the Westies be able to make Stein disappear?

It seemed only fair, given the gift of Spillane's death from DeMeo's crew, which had catapulted Coonan to Irish boss of the city. Plus, Jimmy C. also owed Stein, to the tune of fifty thousand dollars. He was more than happy to see that debt disappear as well.

It made Mac unhappy because now they were stuck dealing with the Italians (for whom he had little respect), and because the Westies had made a huge blunder in disposing of the body.

They had lured Stein into their trap like many before him. That was the easiest part in this case: Stein knew all of the Westies and trusted them. So of course he came to the club Jimmy C. owned, the 596 Club.

With Stein, though, things hadn't gone according to plan. Mac found out from Jimmy C. that the medical examiner had been able to identify Stein's torso: a heart operation scar clear as a business card across his chest. They had forgotten to cut open the torso and puncture the stomach and lungs. If you don't, they fill with air. The torso will float and eventually wash up on shore. Instead of the Houdini, it was like delivering the murdered body directly to the cops' front door.

Big Paulie had heard rumors, and wanted to see the Westies in person, to decide their fate. Jimmy C. and Mickey took the meeting, but told Mac and the others to be on alert, armed with machine guns and hand grenades.

If Mac and the others hadn't heard from Jimmy C. in two hours, their orders were to rush to the Gambino club, right next to the restaurant, where many of the Mafioso hung out, and kill everybody.

* * *

Despite the initial tension of the entire crew when Ruby Stein made his miraculous return, Mac remembered Jimmy C. exuberant when he came back from the meeting with Big Paulie. There had been questions about Stein, but both Jimmy C. and Mickey stuck to their story of not knowin' nuthin' about nuthin'. They weren't scared of the Italians, they bragged many times in the retelling.

Big Paulie moved to what was for him the more important conversation: bringing these wild Irish boys under control. Big Paulie saw they were a crew to be reckoned with, but they needed to be shown how business was properly handled. These Irish boys were too crazy, acting like this was the Wild West.

Big Paulie told them, "Stop acting like cowboys, acting wild."

Then Paulie offered Jimmy C. and the other Westies the opportunity of a lifetime, as it were: make a lot of money working for the Mafia.

"You're going to be with us now," Big Paulie said.

There were rules though: While the Westies had permission from the Gambino family to use the Gambino name and to run things on the West Side, they had to give the family ten percent of all profits, and be available for hits that needed a disappearing act.

Oh and one more thing… "If anyone is going to get killed," Paulie stared straight at Jimmy C., "you have to clear it with us."

Mac watched as Jimmy C. swelled with pride and power as he told the crew what happened. The look of disgust on Mickey's face more closely mirrored Mac's feelings. But Mac said nothing during the telling and retellings of the story that would change the course of his life and ensure the Westies a place in crime infamy. They had all named Jimmy C. their leader, and this was where he was leading them. While Mac loved and respected Jimmy C. like a brother, he wasn't so sure about these Italians, who smiled to your face while they got ready to whack you. It was dirty. You didn't kill friends—at least not for money. It was all about money for these Italians, and though they talked big about honor, in the end, they didn't have any.

Mac pushed away the gnawing questions of their own honor. He had to cling to the fact that he never hurt anyone who didn't put themselves in that position. If you want to make money, you have to play the game. Sometimes the chamber comes up empty and you win. But you know some day that chamber is going to be loaded. That day will come for everyone. And so Mac snorted his way into blocking out the sound of the bullets he had fired, blocking out the clicking in the back of his head, counting down to the bullet with his name on it.

Mac sighed. The two Jimmys were a long way from scheming and planning on the rooftops when they were children. He worried they might be in over their heads. Since his great grandfather arrived, and on through Spillane's reign, the Irish mob was known for fighting, corruption, stealing, sure—but not as contract killers.

Mac just wished they could go back to when it was simple, when he didn't wake up screaming from nightmares, reaching for the coke-coated mirror next to his bed.

* * *

One of the Westies' biggest money-making endeavors was the *USS Intrepid*, an aircraft carrier that had served in WWII and Vietnam and was permanently docked at Pier 86. In 1982, it was opened as a museum. The Westies took it over almost immediately. They gave jobs there as rewards for loyalty, for doing "the right thing." That was the case with Bobby Huggard, the main witness in a murder trial against the Westies and against Mac. He perjured himself on the stand. He was the main reason Jimmy C. wasn't doing twenty to life. His reward was $227 a week for absolutely nothing, courtesy of the *Intrepid* Air-Sea-Space Museum.

The piers weren't the only place where the Westies held sway. They got control of Teamsters Local 817, the theatrical truckers' union. 817 was responsible for transporting props and film equipment to various movie locations around the city. A lot of filming for movies happened right in Hell's Kitchen. For the Westies, it was like Santa brought his sack of goodies right to their door.

Mac worked at 817 as a scenery driver. He worked on a large number of films shot in New York in the 1980s, including *The Warriors*, *The Wiz*, *Endless Love*, *Funny Girl*, and *9½ Weeks*, to name a few. He wasn't the first in his family to work for the union. His grandfather also worked for the Teamsters, driving a horse and buggy.

Obviously by the time Mac came around, they were using trucks instead of horses, but according to him, the stink of the industry hadn't changed. Contrary to the myths of how glamorous being in the movie industry is, Mac said it was long hours, hard work, and short on fun. It was not, however, short on perks.

In addition to his healthy paycheck, he would help himself to pieces of furniture from different sets he was working on. "I had a roll up desk for my daughter from *Days Of Our Lives*." He also helped his son start his own thriving extralegal enterprise when he gave the boy advance copies of that soap opera's scripts. Mac's son would sell them to neighborhood girls for fifty cents.

Another perk was getting to meet a number of stars, often at a softball game the union put on every Thursday. Mac played against Danny Aiello, Willem DaFoe, Bette Midler, and Liza Minnelli. He showed off his famed dance moves to Gilda Radner at the wrap party for *Hanky Panky*. From telling Sylvester Stallone where to pick up women to selling cast members from *The Wonder Years* cocaine with Jackie Coonan, Mac was able to open up celebs to a side of New York they might not have seen otherwise.

Of all the celebrities he met, Mac's favorite was Mickey Rourke, whom he met on the set of *9 ½ Weeks*. Rourke became a good friend not just of Mac's, but of all the Westies. After the massive arrests in 1986 that would put many of them behind bars for decades, Rourke came to the courtroom to show his support.

"I remember I gave him a picture of me and Kevin [Kelley, Westies member] at Wildewood, an amusement park in Jersey, dressed up like we were in the old west with guns. He loved it," Mac reminisced.

* * *

Despite his interactions with movie stars, Mac's life wasn't always champagne and caviar. Many believe the life of a mobster is one of leisure. Movies portray gangsters sitting around in smoky rooms, plotting, playing cards, drinking, or else out on a hit. The reality of the day-to-day life for all but the dons and underbosses—the upper echelon of organized-crime figures—was much more mundane. The majority, like Mac, held steady regular jobs at points in their underworld careers. They ran scams and schemes, sold drugs on the side, and took "jobs" as they came up, but their stable income was often their daily employment.

This is not unique to the Mafia and its affiliates. The same has been noted as true for gangs and street-level drug dealers. While we are presented with the image of the drug kingpin, with his Cayman Islands bank accounts and French Riviera villas, the vast majority of those involved in the distribution of drugs are low-level subsistence dealers.

As Marc Mauer wrote in *Race to Incarcerate*, "As is true nationally, the *Time* analysis revealed that many of the African Americans charged in federal court [for drug trafficking] were not... drug king-pins, but rather low-level dealers or accomplices in the drug trade."

This street-level dealing leaves marginalized populations—too often working-class Black and brown communities—much more vulnerable to increased policing. Mauer quotes Delaware Prosecutor Charles Butler as saying, "Sure, it's true we prosecute a high percentage of minorities for drugs. The simple fact is, if you have a population, minority or not, that is conducting most of their illegal business on the street, those cases are easy pickings for police." Blacks are no more likely to be drug users than whites. According to the Sentencing Project, Black people comprise twelve percent of the U.S. population and 14 percent of regular drug users. However, they account for over one-third of all drug-related arrests and almost sixty percent of those held in state prison for drug charges.

They are also the human wreckage of a system that began to eat more of its poor, especially if they were of color, in the 1970s. New York, like all major cities, was devastated by the departure of industrial jobs overseas. But hardest hit were Black and Latino communities. Unemployment for young Black men was as high as 60–80 percent in some neighborhoods of the city. It was not that people did not want to work; it was that there were no jobs to be had. It was into this devastated landscape that politicians like Nixon and New York's Democractic Senator Daniel Patrick Moynihan introduced the concept of "benign neglect." As Jeff Chang described the idea in *Can't Stop Won't Stop: The History of the Hip Hop Generation*, "benign neglect became the rally cry to justify reductions in social services to the inner cities, further fuel for the backlash against racial justice and social equity." The result was almost unimaginable: post-apocalyptic landscape, burned-out buildings, and burned-out futures. "City politicians applied a mathematics of destruction to justify the removal of no less than seven fire companies from the Bronx after 1968... Less than a decade later, the South Bronx had lost 43,000 housing units, the equivalent of four square blocks a week."

While not as heavily affected as the South Bronx, these conditions exacerbated the already gripping poverty felt in Hell's Kitchen. It birthed extreme nihilism, both in the Westies and in what would become the hip-hop generation. After the promise of the 1960s, this was the first generation to face a worse economic situation than their parents before them. After the marches, the protests, the beatings, the sit-ins and the legislation, material conditions were actually worse for marginalized communities.

* * *

In 1982, Jimmy Coonan was on one of his semi-regular prison stays on gun possession charges. Thomas "Tommy" O'Donnell, head of 817, saw an opportunity to get rid of what he thought of as "the traditional gangster element" that had tainted the union's history for so long.

Rather than going to external authorities, according to T.J. English, "O'Donnell turned to what he believed to be a *rival* gangster element, the Italians, and took out a contract on Jimmy Coonan." By going to the Gambinos and contracting a hit, O'Donnell moved himself from civilian to someone in the life: a moving target.

O'Donnell didn't know about the sit-down with Big Paulie four years before. The Italians went straight to the Westies with the information. The Westies, in the form of Mac and Kevin Kelly, went straight to O'Donnell.

Mac told O'Donnell the Westies were taking over, then proceeded to pistol whip him and the vice president of the union. They wanted union cards whenever they asked for them. Having a union card or "book" meant that you didn't have to wait in line to possibly be picked for work that day on a job site. You were guaranteed work.

O'Donnell told Mac there weren't enough union books for that.

"Oh yeah? Well then, we're gonna kill one union member a week till there's enough openings for our people."

The books miraculously appeared.

Though O'Donnell wasn't a mobster, Mac felt that when he chose to enter into that world, he did so knowing the consequences. "He wanted to play tough, wanted to play gangster. A lot of guys did. But they didn't want to deal with what happens next," Mac mused.

* * *

Just because Mac usually had a regular job did not deter him from engaging in the ugliest side of Westies business. When on the job, Mac sometimes used his background in movies to avoid prosecution, often creating elaborate disguises he wore when he was out on "a piece of work" (what the Italians called a contract murder). He dressed up as a bag woman, a junkie (not the furthest stretch for some of the Westies), and used the fact that his hair was naturally curly enough to pass as Puerto Rican on jobs.

The disguises started with Jackie Coonan and Mac applying to be police officers. Mac took the test but realized it wasn't for him. Jackie, however, was really excited about the idea. He passed everything with 100 percent, both the written examination and the physical. The police, however, were reluctant to let Jackie in, based, they said, on his "character."

"Jackie was crazy, I'm telling you, he was the craziest one of all of us," Mac told me. "I actually think you would have really liked Jackie. He was the anarchist in the group, the political one. He was always talking about the [Vietnam] war when it was happening, all that. He was at Attica in 1971, really involved with that. He was always fighting against the system. He was real smart too. But like I said, crazy."

Not being real police officers, however, did not deter Mac and Jackie from dressing as cops. They used the disguise at first to rob prostitutes of their nightly earnings by threatening to arrest the women if they didn't cough up the dough. Of course, the reason it worked so well, Mac said, is they weren't the only ones doing it; real cops did the same thing regularly.

To some, Mac robbing female sex workers might stand in sharp contrast to the fact Mac repeatedly apologized for cursing in front of me during our interviews, afraid he had offended my "womanly" sensibilities. But the roots of chivalry grow out of patriarchy, as Abigail Collazo shows in her essay, "Chivalry Must Die: On Women's Expectations and Men's Obligations": "chivalry is about viewing women as fragile, delicate creatures who need special protection, special consideration, and special treatment."

Anyone who knows me knows I have the mouth of a sailor—in fact, once I became more comfortable with Mac during interviews, I definitely dropped a few f-bombs myself. But that did not deter Mac from continuing to apologize for his "profanity."

Collazo says it is necessary to see that chivalry "actually… is *patriarchy*… asserting its power." It's important to see these connections because chivalry is based on the patriarchal hierarchy of "good" and "bad" women. There are some women who are delicate flowers that must be protected. Those are the women who confine themselves to their "appropriate" place in the gender binary. They are juxtaposed with "bad" women, who challenge the idea that a woman should follow society's strict rules (and double standards) about what she can and cannot do with her body. Those women not only do not deserve chivalry; they deserve any kind of societal punishment meted out against them. This is often tied to class as well: I, with my college degree and my journalistic background, am placed higher on the patriarchal chivalry hierarchy than working-class women who are engaging in sex work, many of them for survival.

* * *

Not every hit went as planned. The Westies were not always the criminal masterminds they were made out to be in the media. This truth is borne out in one of the hits that Mac was contracted on by the Gambino family, targeting a drug dealer who was selling drugs to children.

All of the Five Families had official policies against dealing in drugs or pornography. They were from the old days. Part of it was moral. The Mafia thrived on the idea of being protection for the Italian community, a community cut off from accessing resources and services reserved for Anglo Saxon, non-immigrant Americans. The Mafia purported to fill that void for the community, so dealing in things like drugs, which hurt innocents in the community, was forbidden.

It was also a decision made for practical reasons. Drug trafficking involved much more danger. Because it involved smuggling across state and even international lines, it became a federal crime and carried stiffer penalties and because of that, the police were sometimes less likely to look the other way for the right price.

The ban on drugs wasn't what it used to be by the time the Westies came on the scene, however. Big Paulie, ever the businessman, turned a blind eye to any associates bringing in profits from narcotics. He didn't want to know where the money came from. He just wanted the steady flow to continue.

Even under the new lax policy on drugs, however, some things were not to be tolerated—not by the Italians, or the Westies. The Westies thought of themselves as desperadoes protecting Hell's Kitchen, getting what was owed to them and the Irish community after so many years. Selling drugs to kids was not part of their image.

"The old people in the neighborhood, they loved us. I remember I used to go play bingo with my mom and her friends. They welcomed us because they knew the Westies weren't big time drug dealers," Mac remembered.

He is quite clear that the Westies were involved with drugs, but from the other side: "We did the drugs; we didn't sell them."

And while one of the charges leveled against all of them, especially Mac, during the trial was that they were drug dealers, Mac's final word on the subject makes it clear why he took the job, no problem: "I would never sell drugs to kids."

Instead of a photograph, the Gambinos handed Mac a police sketch of the man selling, and told Mac where the guy worked. When Mac arrived, in disguise as a junkie, he saw that it was a huge office building. Hundreds of employees streamed in and out.

Mac waited for hours, pretending to nod out across the street. He wasn't sure what he was supposed to do; he could just leave and let them know he needed a real photo of the guy. That was probably the smartest course of action.

Ah, but what the hell, he was here, he was in costume, and hey, that guy right there looked like the sketch! Mac ran over, grabbed the man by the back of the neck and threw him in the alley he had already scoped out to do the job.

Mac pulled his gun out. Put the cold steel right up against the guy's forehead. Pulled the trigger quickly, and... "I swear to God, the bullet bounced off his head! Seriously, right off his forehead! It was 'cause I was using the wrong bullets for the gun and 'cause of the angle it was at."

The comedy of homicidal errors doesn't end there, because after Mac repositioned the gun at the man's neck, he pulled the trigger again and… the gun jammed. Mac stared at the gun in his hand, and so did his intended victim. Mac was at a loss about next steps.

Figuring he had to at least do something to fulfill this contract, Mac gripped the gun by the barrel and started hitting the guy with the butt of the gun. The man would fall down, and Mac would drag him back up again.

He chuckled retelling me the story, saying, "It must have looked so funny to the folks walking by, 'cause they just see this guy falling down, getting back up, falling down, getting back up."

Who said mobsters didn't have a sense of humor? The punchline is Mac was hanging out months later in a well-known Mafia club, playing cards with one guy he met there, having a great conversation. The mafioso who originally gave Mac the contract came in and motioned for Mac to come to his table.

"What?" Mac asked the mafioso, itching to get back and finish the game.

"You West Side boys really are crazy, you know!"

"What do you mean?"

The Italian gestured back to the table. "I mean, you sit and play cards with the guy I hired you to whack four months ago like it was nothing. You got some balls on you, kid; you shoulda been an Italian."

Mac whipped his head to stare hard at the guy. In all honesty, he hadn't really taken a good look at the guy once he picked him out of the crowd at the office building. And the last he had seen of the guy, his face was a bloodied mess.

"Well, whattdaya know about that… So, you want I should take care of him?" Mac asked casually.

The Italian waved him off. "No, don't worry about it, Jimmy. After the beating you gave him, he was in the hospital for weeks. After he got out, he never sold a single crumb of that junk to any of the kids. Forget it, today's his lucky day."

Mac was relieved not to have to get himself and the club messy with the blood. He was also proud of himself for picking the right guy out of a crowd with only the sketch to go by.

"It just goes to show you, sometimes you gotta take a chance."

* * *

There is not a lot of overlap between radical political movements and organized crime. In the 1970s and 1980s, the Westies and groups like the Black Liberation Army (BLA) had at least two things in common: they were not fond of cops or drug dealers. Both were, in fact, part of a larger debate around policing and drugs happening in New York and nationally.

The Black Liberation Army was a radical, armed Black liberation formation, with units across the country. Their analysis saw the Black community in the United States as an occupied colony, one that had the right to fight for its independence in the same way Third World countries around the world were overthrowing colonial powers. Many of their members were former Black Panther Party members.

The Black Panther Party was an organization that began in Oakland in 1966. The goal was to address the repressive conditions in Black communities across this country. The Party issued their Ten Point Program, which highlighted the changes they wanted: Point Seven, an immediate end to police brutality, was the point the Panthers started with. They began nightly patrols—the prototype to what is called "copwatch" today—in which Panther members would go to where police were stopping individuals or making arrests. The Panthers would observe the arrest or the stop, sometimes sharing information about the individual's rights. The Panthers did all this while carrying guns, which, it must be noted, was perfectly legal at the time: in California it was legal for citizens to observe the police carrying out their duties as long as they maintained a reasonable distance, and it was legal for citizens to carry firearms openly.

The Panther Party grew into a national organization in a matter of two years, catapulted by the bold stances they took against police brutality, by their revolutionary analysis that demanded self-determination for all oppressed peoples, and by their survival-pending-revolution programs. The most famous of these programs was the free breakfast program, which fed tens of thousands of children across the country every day for years. In fact, according to the documentary *All Power to the People*, in 1969 the California Treasurer admitted that the Black Panther Party fed more children than the United States government, which is why this nation soon saw the advent of federally funded free and reduced-fee lunch programs across this country.

Though the Black Panther Party was a legal organization, they were attacked viciously and continually by law enforcement agencies at city, state, national, and international levels.

But this level of attack was not reserved solely for the Panthers. According to Akinyele Omowale Umoja in *Liberation, Imagination and The Black Panther Party*, between 1971 and 1973, almost a thousand Black people were killed by American police across the country. Unfortunately, it must be noted, these numbers have not changed much to this day. Umoja's piece, aptly titled "Repression Breeds Resistance: The Black Liberation Army and the Radical Legacy of the Black Panther Party," explains that these horrific numbers led the BLA to launch a "defensive/offensive" campaign against police. "BLA members saw themselves coming to the defense of an oppressed and colonized people that were victims of a genocidal war. American police were seen as the occupation army of the colonized Black nation and the primary agents of Black genocide."

Organized crime, including the Westies, also had a very harsh outlook on the police and their role in making sure "business opportunities" stayed in the hands of the wealthy few. Mobs usually left police alone, however, unless they were on the take. Killing cops brought down more heat than almost anything else, including drug dealing, which the BLA soon found out.

Obviously, the Westies did not have the same radical analysis of the political situation in the U.S. as the BLA. In fact, Mac rejected the Irish Republic Army's (IRA) armed efforts to address the colonial status of Ireland.

"Those guys were the worst. Going around, planting bombs. Hurting kids. They wanted to work with us, reached out to us sometime. We told them to get the fuck outta here."

Not all factions of the Irish-American underworld had the same response, however. Whitey Bulger, head of the Boston Irish Mob (and long-time FBI informant) was a "chest-beating IRA sympathizer" according to Dick Lehr and Gerard O'Neil. He played a key role in gathering together over 150 firearms and seventy rounds of ammunition to support the Irish independence cause, though that might have had more to do with economic gain than political ideology.

Nonetheless, the Westies, the Mafia, and the BLA agreed (at least in theory for the first two) that drugs were a scourge destroying communities.

The BLA recognized the means of political control that the criminalization of drugs has historically made possible. As Noam Chomsky wrote in Herivel and Wright's *Prison Nation*,

> In the United States the drug war is basically a technique for controlling dangerous populations internal to the country and doesn't have much to do with drugs. That's always been true. It goes back to England in the nineteenth century when they made gin illegal and kept whiskey legal. There was a simple class reason for it. Gin was the drink of the working class and whiskey was the drink of the upper class. This is a way of controlling the working class people.

In this context, the BLA saw the introduction of massive amounts of extremely addictive drugs like crack cocaine in the 1980s as a specific attempt to stifle liberation organizing.

Despite their acknowledgement of the larger political and economic conditions of Black communities across the nation, which left many feeling they had no other options than to get involved in the drug trade, the BLA's response to dealing with it was swift and sometimes brutal. The BLA brokered no excuses on selling what they considered to be genocide to the community. According to Umoja,

> In New York, the BLA initiated a campaign called "Deal with the Dealer" to make it "difficult" and "unhealthy" for drug peddlers to traffic in Black communities. BLA units would identify the "hangouts" of prominent drug merchants and drug-processing facilities and raid them. In some cases, drug dealers were physically attacked and even killed.

Fate sometimes hands us the strangest of bedfellows.

* * *

Like many crime organizations, by the mid-1980s, the Irish mob had begun to eat itself from the inside. There was mistrust, internecine violence, and the ultimate betrayal, worse than killing someone: turning state's evidence against your crew. The Westies began to see their own codes shredded. Though they weren't La Cosa Nostra with its blood oaths, omerta, and codes of honor, Mac said they also weren't animals—at least, not all of them.

Richie Ryan, however, was another story. Mac and Ryan were out on a hit for the Italians, which felt to Mac like all they did: work for the Italians.

They walked up the stairs of a nondescript building, following the information they'd been given. The guy would be inside a room, waiting for a meeting he'd been told he had to attend. Mac and Ryan would kick in the door, and that would be the last meeting he'd ever have.

Suddenly, they heard a noise behind them. They both whirled around, guns drawn, only to find a young boy, around seven years old. He had dropped a toy car.

Mac laughed a little and lowered his gun. The laughter died in his throat when he saw Ryan's weapon still firmly trained on the kid.

"C'mon, Richie, what are you doing?"

Ryan didn't answer. The little boy started to cry.

Mac whipped out his own gun and trained it on Ryan.

"Go ahead, Richie, do it. Do it and I'll blow your fucking head off. Do it."

Ryan stared at Mac for a moment, then dropped his gun.

"Shit, Mac, you take stuff too seriously."

Richie Ryan later became infamous in the neighborhood when he killed his friend Tommy Hess for hitting on Ryan's girlfriend. The way he killed him, though, is what garnered him so much attention: Ryan shoved the barrel of the gun into Hess's rectum and fired several shots.

Mac, remembering, shook his head. "I'm no angel, but I couldn't do that. That's…" he paused. "That's not nice. We had codes."

Then came his common refrain: "We didn't ever hurt anyone not in the life. All of those guys, they knew the risks. Just like us. We all knew the risks."

Mac's codes of conduct also included not turning on other Westies. The Italians were one thing: they had to kill a few people they knew. That was always harder. But he reminded himself they weren't his crew. He hadn't grown up with them. They weren't family; they were business.

His other rules: do not whack people in front of their families; do not hurt anyone not in the life. Mac said he made sure no one innocent got hurt accidentally. "If you start doing that, then it could have been someone I loved. It could have happened to me."

Mac had opportunity to test out this principle. Roy DeMeo assigned Mac a hit, and told him he could find the guy at an Irish bar on Queens Blvd. Mac went there disguised as a wino every day for a week, watching the guy, checking his movements, learning his schedule. He figured out the best time to strike.

But the day Mac was about to make his move, Jackie Coonan burst into the bar. The hit was off. It was the wrong guy.

Mac exploded at DeMeo later that night. He got so close to his face DeMeo could feel the spit as Mac yelled each word. "I told you to get your shit straight! Get your shit straight or do it yourself! You almost had me kill an innocent man!"

Mac only killed people who put themselves in the line of fire: other mobsters, gangsters, and union officials who sunk to the level of doing business with the mob. At that point, Mac felt they were like him, and could be dealt with.

"Everyone we went after was worse than us."

This is the justification Mac clung to in order not to see a monster in the mirror staring back at him.

This is the same justification Roy DeMeo's son Albert uses in his book *For the Sins of My Father*. Albert was fifteen when he had to go to identify his father's body. Roy DeMeo, head of the crew called "Murder Machine." Roy DeMeo, the Westies' connection to the Gambino family. Roy DeMeo, who killed Mickey Spillane and cleared the way for Jimmy Coonan to become the head of the Irish Mob.

Despite all of this, even though Albert knew what his father did for a living, he still thought Roy was a loving man and a reluctant killer.

The man I knew was careful and compassionate. I had always believed that my father killed only out of grim necessity, only when there was no other way to resolve the situation, and that those who had died at his hands were fellow soldiers in an internecine war. They knew the rules and played the game anyway.

It wasn't until he read the book *Murder Machine* detailing the actions of Roy DeMeo's crew that Albert began to think of his father as "a professional assassin." Albert writes of the contradictions he had to hold after that, and how it also destroyed him mentally. But he shared that both he and his mother clung to one thing they knew to be true even as they processed so much horrific information about Roy De-Meo: "My father loved us. Whatever outsiders believed, we knew that my father loved us all."

None of this erases the immense damage done: devastation wrought on families and innocent bystanders who invariably seem— no matter how hard one tries—to get caught in the crossfire. At the end of the day, Mac committed murder. Just as at the end of the day, Kakamia was part of a conspiracy to commit murder. Both did so for the same reason: financial gain.

But there are so many different words for murder, depending on who is pulling the trigger, and for what purpose. As I wrote at the beginning of the chapter, corporate executives conspire to commit murder for financial gain, but it is called unfortunate losses. Iraqi cities are demolished in bomb strikes to retaliate against fabricated weapons of mass destruction, and thousands of innocent civilians die. The military term for this is "collateral damage." Often that damage is part of the intent of U.S. military attacks, to "shock and awe" the population into submission—to crush the belief in resisting the most powerful military force in the world.

I have done work with military veterans who have returned from service and oppose the war. Some are individuals who have committed atrocious acts. In order to shift some of the crushing blame, they use the same justification as Mac: "I was just following orders." This is the refuge of being not a person, but a weapon, with no agency of your own: just a tool to be used in the hand of someone with more authority.

Mac never hung out of windows, gun blazing, blasting a street corner bursting with people, hoping he hit his target. He never shot into a village with elders and children, hoping he hit an insurgent. He certainly did not sit back in a command center, pushing buttons that ended countless lives.

Mac's kills were close up, hands on. He looked into their eyes as their life left their bodies. He told himself they had chosen that path. He knew it could very well be him one day, looking into his killer's eyes as the life drained from his body. He made his peace with that as best he could. He, the former altar boy, would pray nightly even though he wasn't sure God even listened to him anymore. He would go to heaven, stand at the gates, and plead his case.

The first real letter I received from Mac was in September 2003. Before that it was cards, short notes. We had talked on the phone and in visiting rooms. But this was the first time he sat down to reckon with himself: just him and a blank sheet of paper.

The letter was eighteen pages long.

He spoke plainly of the murders and extortion. He presented mitigating evidence, what many would say were excuses. But he knew this life he had chosen—this life he had been born into in many ways— was not a healthy one. "I always tried to discourage the younger kids in the neighborhood when they asked me about the mob. I told them tough guys don't last long… I've been lucky in my life. I can't believe the things I did growing up. I guess I never took the time to think about what I had done."

Mac worked hard to never let himself think deeply about what he had done.

* * *

1985 was a year of big changes, both for the Westies and the criminal world in general. Members of John Gotti's crew, then a captain or *capo*, were indicted by the FBI for narcotics trafficking. Again, even though Big Paulie wasn't above taking his cut of money earned from drug sales, having it so publicly tied to the most powerful Mafia family was bad for business. Gotti knew this; he feared Paulie planned to kill Gotti and others of his crew. So Gotti got to Paulie before Paulie could get to him.

John Gotti, along with Jimmy C. and a crew of renegade mafiosi, assassinated Paul Castellano that same year, and Gotti became *capo di tutti.*

His reign as don was a sensational one. The flashy Gotti became known in the media as both "The Dapper Don," because of his eye-catching wardrobes, and later "The Teflon Don," because of his uncanny ability to avoid prosecution.

Jimmy C. met Gotti in prison in the 1970s. Gotti was there for truck hijackings at the Idlewild Airport (later to become JFK Airport), and the twenty-three-year-old Coonan for the murder of two men he had mistaken for hitmen hired by Mickey Spillane during their internecine war.

"I remember Jimmy told me when he was in prison with Gotti that John was going to be the next boss," Mac mused during an interview. "He knew. The rest of those wiseguys, they were phony, but John Gotti, he was a good guy. Solid."

Mac's first time meeting Gotti wasn't until a few months after Gotti seized power. Ironically, it took place at a funeral, Frank DeCicco's. DeCicco, the underboss, or second in command, of the Gambino family, had been killed in a car bomb.

The meeting with Gotti was brief. Jimmy C. led Mac into a back room at the funeral home. Gotti was waiting, dressed in a flashy sharkskin suit, hands and arms swaddled in gold, steely gray hair in a formidable pompadour. He definitely lived up to his legend.

John spent a minute eyeing Mac. He then turned to Jimmy C. and said, "This the kid?"

Coonan responded, "Yeah, this is him. He can definitely do the job."

Gotti extended his hand to Mac and shook it. His grip was firm and commanding.

"I'd like to take you out to dinner sometime," Gotti said, and then he walked out of the room.

"What was that all about?" Mac asked Jimmy C. a couple hours later as they sat at a Soho restaurant.

"You know. They want someone taken care of. We'll get more information when the time is right," Jimmy C. responded. Mac knew this was a big moment for his boss and for the Westies.

A few weeks later, Mac learned the original "job order" entailed handling John O'Connor, vice president of Local 608 of the United

Brotherhood of Carpenters and Joiners. O'Connor found himself un-wittingly on the wrong side of Gotti when he had trashed a Gambi-no-owned restaurant for employing nonunion labor.

Mac and three other Westies were given instructions to "kneecap" O'Connor, or break his legs. They caught him coming out of an ele-vator, and Kelly proceeded to shoot O'Connor four times. The shots went high above the kneecaps, and one of them lodged in O'Connor's buttocks. The Westies found this hilarious, as a taped conversation be-tween Kelly, a friend, and the incarcerated Mickey Featherstone proved:

"He's got a hot ass now," the friend joked, and then they all three laughed.

"Yeah. He's got an extra asshole," Kelly added.

* * *

In the end, it turned out not to be a laughing matter for John Gotti. In 1989, he was tried for orchestrating this shooting. The key witness against him in this case? The stand-up Mac, breaking one of his sacred codes of conduct: don't ever, ever cooperate with the government.

Mac had already served two years in prison at this time for the Westies' RICO conviction. He was looking at fifty-eight more to go. There wasn't much he could get out of testifying. It was not a major case against Gotti—not a murder or a racketeering charge. Ultimate-ly, Gotti was acquitted. Testifying of course involved immense danger: most people didn't live long after snitching out the boss of all bosses.

So why would Mac do it?

"I ratted on Gotti because the Attorney General's office black-mailed my girlfriend. My girlfriend ran when I was arrested and they framed her. After I had been in prison two years, they offered me this deal for her. I took it."

He did not use the euphemisms others do to make themselves feel better: testified, informed, debriefed. No—Mac ratted.

The New York district attorney came to visit Mac when he was in Lompoc federal prison in California. He said they had a wiretap of Mac's girlfriend, given by a Westies member who had also turned rat to save himself. On the wiretap, Mac's girlfriend talked about ten thousand dollars Coonan had given Mac for legal fees when he was previously charged with murder. Mac's girlfriend felt it wasn't enough. Court documents said she felt he hadn't been properly compensated for "the skillfulness with which he applied his craft." The tape has her saying, "When it comes to killing, you tell him about it, you forget about it, and you read about it."

This was enough to make her a co-defendant in conspiracy to commit murder, along with a laundry list of other charges. She was looking at fifteen years, easy—unless Mac came through for the DA in this case against Gotti.

Mac knew he was unlikely to get any reduction in his sentence, and did not make that a condition of his testimony. In fact at court, John Gotti's defense attorneys accused Mac of lying and cutting a deal with the state to frame Gotti.

One of them pounded his hand on the prosecution's table, saying loudly, "You know what gets you off the hook? Your pals at this table."

"They can't get me off nothing," Mac replied in a hushed voice. "Only the federal judge can now."

Mac stared into my eyes unwaveringly as he told me why he turned rat, adding another layer of complexity to this man who refused to snitch when countless racketeering indictments began raining down, the Westies started crumbling, and everyone was looking to get a deal. He broke the first rule of the underworld: never work with the authorities. He held true to another cardinal rule of the underworld that others like Mickey Featherstone did not: never snitch on your own crew. He did not ask for time off of his sixty-year sentence in exchange for his testimony. He put love above his underworld honor.

There was a tiny part of Mac—the part that hopes for torrential rain while living in a desert—that dreamed he might get released because of his cooperation and get into the Witness Protection Program: they would just give him the golden ticket, without him asking.

But the part of him rooted in Hell's Kitchen knew he wasn't getting relocated by the feds with a new identity and a new chance at life. And, truth be told, he honestly couldn't justify that, even to himself.

So at Gotti's trial, when one of the lawyers asked Mac, "Do you think you deserve to come out of jail after what you've done?," Mac replied quietly, "No."

"But you're hoping," the lawyer prodded.
A long pause.
"Yah." Almost inaudible.

* * *

Eventually, even Teflon wears off. In 1992, Gotti was convicted on a long list of charges: racketeering, loan sharking, gambling, hijacking, extortion, and thirteen counts of murder. He was sentenced to life in prison, and that's what it became: On June 10, 2002, John Gotti died in a Massachusetts federal prison hospital from throat cancer.

The code of *omerta*—the vow of silence about Mafia business every made man takes—wasn't what it used to be. This was another reason Mac eventually turned state's evidence against Gotti without fearing much reprisal. Everyone was doing it; the main witness against Gotti was his underboss and best friend Salvatore "Sammy the Bull" Gravano.

For the Westies, it was also the second-in-command. Mickey Featherstone made a deal with the state after he felt he was set up by other Westies to take the rap for a murder he said he didn't do.

Even with Featherstone's testimony, the government took months to gather evidence. It's hard to have such a massive operation without some leaks. There were rumors all over the neighborhood about the feds closing in. It was enough to push some people over the edge like Billy Beattie, one of the younger Westies members. He turned state's evidence. He was the one who got Mac's girlfriend on wiretap. Beattie recorded Mac trying to sell some drugs to an undercover agent Beattie had vouched for.

After the deal, Beattie and Mac had hung out—just two old friends, one of them with a wire. They talked about Mickey, who everyone knew was working with the government by then.

"The cocksucker. If they asked me, if they said they'd let me out if I'd rat, I'd spit at 'em. If I was gonna do twenty-five years in the hole. Fuck it," Mac extorted passionately.

Beattie gave a half-hearted, "Yeah, I hear you," conscious of the tape prickling his chest, holding the microphone in place.

* * *

The government investigation was so long because prosecutors didn't just want to get the Westies on one murder, or even ten. They were building a case under the Racketeer Influence and Corrupt Organizations (RICO) Act.

Enacted in 1970, RICO was one of the big tools the legislature supposedly gave law enforcement to fight organized crime. It was touted as a means to destroy the Mafia.

The problem with prosecuting organized crime is that you can pick off the little guys at the bottom for everything from robbery to murder, but it's really hard to get the don. He kept his hands clean for the most part (though Gotti was a notable exception to that, doing a number of murders himself after he became the head of the Gambino family). The don always had an alibi and the best lawyers. So you arrest twenty of the low-level soldiers, and there were twenty more eagerly waiting to replace them. The don and the organization itself remained untouched.

RICO changed all of that. In order for it to be applicable, prosecutors had to prove not only individual crimes, but "a pattern of racketeering," which added up to a criminal conspiracy. If prosecutors could prove individuals were part of a "criminal enterprise," they could try everyone for the same crimes, regardless of whether a certain individual was present or not. If they're in the organization and someone in the organization did it, they're all responsible.

Prosecutors can also bring in prior convictions to prove a criminal enterprise. If someone was convicted of burglary five years before and it can be proven that burglary was committed as part of this "criminal enterprise," it can be used as evidence. In effect, people can be tried for the same offense twice, even if they were convicted and already did their time.

There have been many criticisms of the sweeping scope of RICO, and the social and political effect on the criminal justice system. Many argue that the ends of "getting" organized crime do not justify the means of bypassing constitutional rights.

According to Attorney Jeffrey E. Grell, who been prosecuting RICO cases for a decade, RICO's original intention to "get" the Mafia shifted after its creation. "Today, RICO is almost never applied to the Mafia. Instead, it is applied to individuals, businesses, political protest groups, and terrorist organizations. In short, a RICO claim can arise in almost any context."

Mac's assessment of RICO was more succinct: "RICO could convict a ham sandwich."

The first time I heard about RICO was not in relation to organized crime. It was in relation to organized resistance. I was doing support work for U.S. political prisoners, most from the Black Panthers and Black Liberation Army, many of whom got hit with RICO charges. They were given much longer sentences than under state charges. Prosecutors were able to use RICO to turn politically oppositional organizations into "criminal" enterprises.

Marilyn Buck, a white political prisoner who worked in support of Black liberation groups, was convicted under RICO of conspiracy to commit armed bank robbery with the Black Liberation Army, and to break BLA member Assata Shakur (successfully) out of prison. Buck was sentenced to fifty years.

Ray Luc Levasseur, another white political prisoner, was found guilty in federal court in 1986 of bombing U.S. military facilities, contractors, and businesses that were profiting from South African apartheid. He successfully defended himself and his co-defendants against a RICO indictment for sedition. He is quoted in *Imprisoned Intellectuals* arguing that actions like his, those of Buck's, and countless other political prisoners could not be construed as "criminal" activities, but must be seen in its proper political context and global struggles for freedom:

> I can't tell you how insulted I am that these prosecutors charge me with being a racketeer. That law was passed in the 1970s and it was specifically passed to be used against real gangsters and real racketeers. "Racketeering Influenced and Corrupt Organizations"—I do not believe has the word revolutionary in it, or political dissident. They're trying to bend the law… You cannot be a revolutionary and be a racketeer. It's a contradiction. It is either one or the other. You cannot support freedom struggles in South Africa or Central America or the Black nation within this country from the foundation of a criminal enterprise…. In twenty-one years of

political activity I've never done anything for personal gain or profit. Nothing.

I did not know all of this when I first heard about RICO. I only knew that people I cared about—people I read about, people I wrote letters to, people I visited in prison for years, people who supported me and kept me strong through the worst periods of my life, people who had endured thirty years in prison for their beliefs, people who were not home with their families where they belonged—were in prison because of this act. From the moment I heard about RICO, it was a sinister presence.

I talked with Mac about my introduction to RICO, so different than his. I told him I always thought of it as a tool of political repression. He smiled and said, "Hey, I'm not a political prisoner."

Thinking of the pictures I had seen in books of the Westies' victims (or the parts of them that were found) there is no way to make a case that Mac and the others were not brutal and dangerous men. They were the poster children that allowed RICO to pass, the bogeymen FBI agents whispered to each other about on late-night stakeouts. In our current rhetoric on crime and punishment, whatever law enforcement can do to get them off the streets and behind bars for as long as possible is worth the cost.

But again what ends justify the means? In an earlier chapter I wrote about Mumia Abu-Jamal's profound commentary after the federal retrial of four officers who beat Rodney King. In their original trial, all four were acquitted. Los Angeles burned in outrage. In the retrial, two were acquitted and two found guilty. Abu-Jamal received much criticism for this piece, because he argued that the police should not have been retried; it was a violation of their constitutional rights.

"While no one would call the writer a cop lover, it is my firm opinion that the federal retrial of the four L.A. cops involved in King's legalized brutality constituted a clear violation of the Fifth Amendment of the United States Constitution, which forbids double jeopardy."

Regardless of emotion, sentiment, or political stance, Abu-Jamal realized the frightening implications of allowing this infringement to stand: if those seeking justice condoned these measures, brutal cops or mobsters would not be the targets of this precedent in the future; it would be those struggling to create new, just worlds.

As someone who has spent over thirty years on Pennsylvania's death row for a crime he did not commit, who has had legitimate legal appeals turned down to the consternation and outrage of legal and governmental bodies around the world, Abu-Jamal realized what a danger it was to call for a compromise on issues of justice.

* * *

Political debates about the legal viability of RICO notwithstanding, the Westies were decimated by massive arrests in November and December of 1986. Ten people were indicted, including Mac, on charges dating back to 1965. There were fourteen counts of taking part in a "racketeering conspiracy" and sixteen murders, attempted murders and conspiracies to commit murder. All told, prosecution argued the Westies were responsible for thirty murders over a fifteen-year period.

Billy Bokun, one of the youngest Westies, was ten years old when the first crime brought against all of the Westies was committed. Yet he was part of the criminal enterprise and therefore just as responsible for it as the people who committed it, according to RICO statutes. In addition to some being charged with crimes committed when they were children, others were charged with crimes committed while they were already in prison.

Coonan had been acquitted by the state of New York in a previous murder case. However, in his RICO case, that case was used as evidence against him.

"He was basically convicted of it ten years later under RICO," Mac snorted.

Mac had considered himself lucky to win an acquittal for the murder of William Walker, for which he was tried in 1980 (a murder he later admitted to). After the charges came down, he wasn't so sure that he'd been lucky. If he had been convicted in the Walker case, he would have been behind bars for much of the evidence being brought against him. Maybe he would have escaped being part of the RICO indictment. As one of the original three Westies, however, there was no escape for him.

On February 24, 1988, all the Westies received heavy sentences. Mac was given sixty years in prison. It was his first conviction. He was forty-two years old.

All in all, Mac considered himself fortunate when I interviewed him about his conviction and time in prison.

"I'm lucky I'm still around, things I've been through. It's kind of a dangerous life," he mused, looking off in the prison visiting room.

"But it was normal to me, I thought it was normal growing up."

It was normal to do whatever you had to do to survive, to expect to be shot dead in the street or do hard time in a penitentiary. It was normal to drown yourself in drugs or alcohol to block out those memories, and less than a year before Mac went on trial, he was admitted to the hospital for pneumonia related to his drug abuse. He relapsed and had to be admitted again, close to death.

Very few young men in Hell's Kitchen expected to see old age. Even fewer expected to see the pearly gates after they passed.

That didn't stop them from praying feverishly each night to God. It didn't stop Mac.

PAPER FLOWERS

I watched Mac's hands on our first visit. They shredded a white paper napkin precisely, almost daintily: folding and rolling. His eyes were locked on mine the entire time as he told me about the murders he had committed and about his life in prison since his conviction.

My interviews with Mac could really only loosely be termed interviews, as most of the time, I didn't ask questions, and made almost no attempts to steer the conversation. I came in, having reviewed my notes from previous talks and research, with a set of questions I needed answered or information I needed clarified. But I rarely asked them outright.

Mac would walk through the ringing metal door. We'd hug and exchange greetings. I offered him a cup of coffee, and he would demur, saying, "Oh I don't want to be any trouble." I always made sure to chug the coffee I bought immediately on my entry, so that by the time he came into the visiting room twenty minutes later, I could say truthfully, "It's no trouble at all, in fact, I was getting up to get myself one anyway." He would acquiesce with a quiet, "Well, if it's no trouble…"

When I came back, we would usually talk about the coffee, then the visiting room: how full it was, who was out, any interesting tidbits Mac knew about the folks in the room. I have found the sexist presumption that women are the only ones who like to gossip to be untrue. Nowhere is this clearer than in prison. These are people (in this case those the state has categorized as "men" in their strict enforcement of the gender binary) forced to live in quarters far too close for comfort. They know everything about one another. When their families write and visit—and when they don't. They know when they fight with their girlfriends via mail—letters crumpled in anger and thrown across a six by eight foot cell as evidence. They know when they cry in the middle of the night—pillows clenched tight between teeth. They know when they shit. Even for those who voluntarily choose to commit themselves to that level of intimacy—like married people in love—it is an incredibly difficult circumstance.

For people ordered to be there—some of them for the rest of their natural lives—it can be a living nightmare. The total lack of privacy leads not to rehabilitation and growth, but to madness and sometimes murder. I have been told stories of cellies being sent to the hospital beaten almost to death because they snored, or ground their teeth, or read out loud. This type of violence is not an everyday occurrence, as popular TV shows and movies would have you believe—a natural part of these people's psyches and makeups. It is, instead, the most extreme manifestation of a simple desire for privacy—for dignity.

So if, in order to relieve this sometimes-deadly pressure, men decide to share tidbits of this hard-won information about their fellow prisoners, it is understandable.

I went on a prison visit several years ago in rural Oregon. A young woman, no more than twenty-years-old, belly overfull with baby, walked hand in hand with a fresh-faced blonde manchild, tattoos creeping up his neck.

"Wow," I said, stating the obvious, "she's really pregnant."

"Yeah." My friend's tone lowered conspiratorially. "All I'm saying is, it's interesting that your girlfriend is eight months pregnant, when you're in your last six months of a three year bid."

His half smile was almost the saddest thing I had ever seen.

* * *

During one visit, Mac made a few comments about folks, none of them embarrassing or invasive. Mac, former hitman for the Mafia, was nothing if not discreet. He mentioned he had done time at another prison with one of the men out on a visit. This led him to the story of being incarcerated in a cell right across from Charles Manson, at Corcoran.

Like most of America at the time, Mac was appalled by the murders carried out by Manson's followers in the late 1960s, directed and orchestrated by Manson himself. He was portrayed in the media as a demented devil cult leader. Mac wanted nothing to do with him.

"I always said I'd chop his head off if I ever met him."

Coming from someone else, this would be an expression of anger and disgust at the situation. But from Mac, it was more a commitment to utilize his skillset for the greater good.

A "funny" thing happened though, in that way that is not funny at all. After Mac was next to Manson for a few months, they began to talk. In prison, without distractions, you find yourself having conversations with people you would have avoided religiously on the outside.

One Puerto Rican prisoner told me he had conversations with white supremacist Nazis, their skin emblazoned with swastikas. "They're not my friends or anything, but it passes the time, and some of those guys aren't all bad. I mean they're morons for what they believe, but they're still human beings too, they have families. This is hard for all of us, you know?"

Former Black Panther and political prisoner Sundiata Acoli told me of alliances forged between the neo-nazis and the prisoners of color during uprisings, strikes, and protests behind the walls.

"I don't believe in this idea that your enemy's enemy is your friend," I said, my privilege shining through. "That person is still your enemy—you don't join ranks with someone you don't agree with. That's compromising your principles."

Sundiata leaned back. "Look, we had to know who the bigger enemy was. We were all in here catching hell from these guards and the administration. They treated the white prisoners a little better, but at the end, we were all just numbers to them, just convicts. So we had to join together for the short term. Sometimes just to survive, and other times to actually win any real changes."

Mac's feelings about Manson were less urgent but equally complicated. While bonding with Manson over their shared Irish heritage,

Mac definitely felt he was "a nut" through their talks, but also found him incredibly creative. "He wrote songs all the time." In fact, he grew to not only tolerate Manson, but to champion "Chuck" as an innocent victim, almost a political prisoner. "Manson didn't do anything, he's a scapegoat. They came back to him and said, 'We did it for you.'"

Mac went from Manson to talking about white supremacists—whom he despises—in prison, of which Manson was one, though Mac didn't discuss that.

* * *

Inside the walls, Mac became a celebrity, especially after T.J. English's book *The Westies* came out. He was at Riker's Island then, in New York. Prisoners asked him to sign their books. Even guards got in on the action.

"If it was the other way around, I wouldn't want these guys' autographs," Mac mused. Our culture makes celebrity of atrocity: inhuman becomes cinematic. For Mac, it was a past he tried every day to find a way to make peace with. Most days he failed.

Mac was originally housed in New York state prisons, close to Hell's Kitchen and to his children, siblings, family, and community. This changed when he testified against John Gotti. Even though Gotti was acquitted, Jimmy was transferred multiple times.

"For my own protection," he scoffed. "I didn't hurt anyone with that testimony. They won't come after me. I mean, everyone's gone. Gotti's dead."

He did not fear repercussions from the Gambinos or from anyone. RICO broke the Mafia's back. They are still operating—specters of their former glory. Like Mac and the other Westies, many of the well-known mafiosos are dead or they are old men staring into cracked prison mirrors and wondering whose face stares back at them.

After several transfers, Mac ended up on the other side of the country, where there are Mexicans instead of Puerto Ricans, where speech is slow instead of clipped east coast style, and where made men are nothing but characters at the movies.

This is part of the reason he bonded so quickly with Kakamia; they could smell the New York on one another—the bodegas, the subway, the crisp bite of a New York winter. The city that never sleeps birthed both of them, set the path under their feet. They found themselves in a place with too much sun and not enough family for shade. They needed each other: Kakamia estranged from his birth family, Mac a continent away from his. For people whose neighborhood was their entire world, California is not just another planet; it's in another galaxy.

Mac met Kakamia when he first got transferred. He was in the day room. Kakamia sat at a table, drawing as usual. One of the other prisoners pointed out Kakamia to Mac and said, "You should meet that guy. He's from New York, too. In fact, that's what we call him."

Mac didn't pay any attention to that. "I figured he was from upstate New York, pretending like he was from the City. I ran into that tons of times, these guys trying to be big tough guys."

But then Kakamia spoke. "The minute he opened his mouth, I knew he was from the City."

Their friendship started tentatively, like most friendships in prison: as a dance, watching the footwork, seeing where it's safe to step. A nod on the yard. A hello in the chow line. Small talk in the day room. One of them tossed out a joke about New York. They were the only two laughing. There it began.

"Me and your brother used to laugh at these west coast guys, trying to be so tough." For Mac, tough was the best compliment he could bestow on anyone. "They didn't know tough. They didn't want to know tough."

Over the years marked off on calendars, they began to understand one another. Both of them charmers, they grew closer, mostly through outrageous stories of life on the streets and life behind bars. They shared the laughter that understands that when everything is deadly serious, nothing can be taken lightly.

Somewhere along the way, Kakamia started calling Mac his godfather. Mac started thinking of Kakamia as his nephew. Kakamia was drawn to Mac's gangster past, the persona he worked so hard to craft for himself when he was younger. But deeper than that, he was drawn to the demons he could see flitting in the corner of Mac's eye: the regret and the fear that maybe there is no forgiveness, in this world or the next.

Mac was drawn to Kakamia's loud New Yorker presence, the City slur because you're moving too fast to pronounce the ends of your words. He was drawn to Kakamia's boundless energy, his commitment to his art, his commitment to something bigger than him. The only reason Mac agreed to an interview with me is because I'm Kakamia's sister.

Mac had turned down interviews before. The Manhattan DA wanted him to write a book. "I told him where he could shove it."

But this was different. It was for his "nephew." Mac thought, why the hell not?

Then my brother got transferred to a different yard. They only saw each other in passing. They wrote to each other through the internal inmate mail system, after receiving permission. The spaces in between Mac's letters kept growing longer. Kakamia worried about Mac, knowing he was sick. He knew it physically hurt him to write. He asked friends he left behind to check on Mac, of course without letting Mac know.

When Mac got transferred after a few years to Kakamia's new yard, they celebrated. Kakamia "cooked" a feast, a concoction out of crackers and ramen and other bits and pieces of food from the commissary. When he told me about it, I grimaced at the thought of putting it in my mouth. Kakamia assured me it was delicious. Kakamia, Mac, and Kakamia's cellie Terra enjoyed it, talking and joking over dinner, almost able to forget the bars.

But Kakamia worried constantly about Mac's health, which was deteriorating rapidly. He stopped by every day, just to chat with Mac. They didn't speak about anything of consequence. Kakamia would invite Mac to "come over" every night for dinner, until Mac was no longer able to get around on his own.

* * *

Mac and Jimmy Coonan were the only ones left in prison. And because the world loves irony, Coonan was incarcerated at the same federal prison as political prisoner Sundiata Acoli, who calls me his "comrade daughter."

The last time I went to see Sundiata in the forests of upstate New York, before Sundiata was transferred down to Maryland, I met Jimmy Coonan. As with most prison visits, I had woken up hours before the sun and driven for miles, a thermos of coffee within arms' reach.

I was the first person to arrive. I wandered into the visiting room in an early morning daze after processing and picked out my seat. I wanted to be far enough from the guards' station and close enough to the cracked patio door to catch a whiff of the autumn air now and again.

In the visiting room with me was a towheaded family. The white-haired grandmother had laugh lines etched permanently into her skin. The mother had piercing eyes and cascading hair. The daughter was a mix of teenage bravado and insecurity. Then I heard the guard yell out, announcing who was here for visiting by the prisoner's last name. "Coonan!"

I whipped my head around. Out came a prisoner in the drab blue of that institution. I craned my neck to see his face, but couldn't.

Soon they called Sundiata. After grins and hugs, and coffee bought from the vending machine, he jerked his head toward the family. "I told you Jimmy's here, right? He's out on visit over there. I passed on the information you shared with me about Mac to him. I'll introduce you when we have to get up for count."

I just nodded, a little overwhelmed at meeting the head of the Westies, whom I had spent so much time researching. It was even more surreal than meeting Mac for the first time, when I'd had time to prepare myself. But here, without warning, was a man who was the head of "the most savage organization in the history of New York," according to Rudy Giuliani.

I felt strange being there and working on this book. What did he think about my book about Mac? Did he think I had no right to do it? How would he feel about how I frame Mac, the Westies, and Coonan himself? Stories are so subjective, reducing everyone to characters, not people, and Coonan's story had been told so many times publicly, none of them by him.

And what did Jimmy Coonan think of Mac in general? Mac, who was his friend from childhood? Who had waded through a river of blood with him? Who had broken the cardinal rule of their world by cooperating with the state?

Sundiata and I continued with our visit. The time raced by. There is never enough time to be in the warmth of Sundiata's sun smile.

The guard bellowed out "Count time!" All of the prisoners in the room stood up and walked toward the front, to stand in line and read out their number as their names are called. This was to make sure they hadn't escaped—from a guarded, locked visiting room.

"No talking during count!" The guard glared at a little girl who asked her mother for a drink.

When it was finished, Sundiata and Jimmy walked over towards me.

"Jimmy, I want you to meet Walidah. The one I told you all about."

I was staring into a face I had only seen in mug shots and surveillance photos. In the flesh and blood version, gravity weighed him down. Some extra weight padded the features, and some lines cut through where there had been none, but the same blue eyes looked straight into me: like an ice pick.

Then a grin split his face. He looked young enough to run out to play kick the can with Mac before supper time. "Nice to meet you. I've heard a lot of great things about you." A firm warm handshake. I mumbled back words of greeting as well, and gave a little wave.

Then he returned to his family gathering under institutional eyes, a man nearing the end of his life holding hands with his wife, kissing his granddaughter on the forehead. Trying to slow time down, just like all the rest of us there.

* * *

Both Mac and Coonan were eligible for parole. There is a chance that Coonan will be released and meet his family on the other side of the gates for the first time. Originally given sixty years, like Mac, he would be almost a hundred if he served all of his time. There is a chance that Coonan will be released. But it is far from likely.

Mac thought he would have the chance to walk through those gates, have another wedding and start fresh, see his daughter's face free of checkpoints and stamped hands. I'm sure Coonan carries the same hope tucked safe in the side of his cheek.

Kevin Kelly was the last Westie released, in October of 2008. The rest stepped free over the last twenty years. Jackie Coonan, the crazy one, the "anarchist" whom I reminded Jimmy of, died in prison in 1988 at the age of forty-four, of AIDS contracted from contaminated needles when he injected cocaine.

Even though Mac felt the feds had a personal vendetta against him and Coonan, he always gave me updates on his legal situation. Whenever I visited or spoke with him, he was always so sure something good was on its way. He should hear back from the federal courts soon. He will be out by Christmas. Then Easter. Thanksgiving. In this way, he sounds just like my brother.

Hope both keeps you alive and kills you slowly.

And what would Mac have done if he got out? There were no job opportunities for him when he was eighteen years old, young and full of energy. What doors would have opened for a sixty-some-year-old, notorious ex-con who most see as a psychopath, whose eyes drift to old horrors when he talked, whose hands traced a faded scar?

The smell of contradictions and atonement.

"We're all done. I'm done. I'm out of that life. I couldn't go back to the life even if I wanted. I'm with them. I'm with the DA's office."

It was hard to interpret the emotion in his voice. Regret? Resignation? Relief? Probably all of the above.

Mac never fooled himself. He knew the price of cooperation. He knew his former associates and childhood friends would walk past him on the street if he ever got out, knew he would carry that to every prison he went to. Mac the gangster. Mac the informant.

"Look I don't think you are hearing me." The last gasp of fall sun hot on my and Sundiata's backs. "There is no grey area with Mac. None."

Sundiata was insistent. You do not tell. Ever. There was never a reason, never an excuse. He repeated it over and over again.

"I understand that," I said, a little exasperated. "I'm just wondering what Coonan thinks about Mac as a person? I know Mac turned state's evidence against Gotti. I know because of that he is shunned, exiled. But I just wonder what Coonan feels about him. Personally. They've been through so much."

After meeting Coonan, I became obsessed with thoughts of Coonan and Mac. What did Coonan feel for Mac? For the little boy who stole candy with him? Who later stole cars with him? And then stole lives? Mac spoke of Coonan only with affection and respect throughout all of our interviews. Was Coonan burning with rage toward Mac for being a snitch? A number of Westies had threatened to kill Mickey Featherstone if they ever got their hands on him. Was it different with Mac, because he hadn't betrayed the gang but the Italians? Because he had done it to save his girlfriend? Did any of that get counted on the mobster's scales of justice?

"Look, this is how it is: if you cooperate that's it. No ifs, ands, or buts. There is no coming back from breaking the code. Mac knew the code and he broke it. And that's that. That's something he put on himself. And he had to wear it for the rest of his life. It's not something you can ever take off."

I had never seen Sundiata so focused, so intense. His usual laid-back, no-nonsense demeanor dried up completely. He was trying to impart something to me, one of the next generation of radicals. He needed me to understand. Sundiata has lived by his principles, giving up over forty years of his life. He has been prepared to die for his principles for even longer. His principles were the thing he had when they stripped everything else away from him. They have cost him so much. They have kept him alive.

And I did understand. I agreed. I believe if I challenge the government, I cannot then turn around and ask the state to solve my problems, even if calling the police meant making a situation better, instead of the worse it means in real life. If you stand outside the system, in opposition to the system, then you cannot (as my mother always told me) have your cake and eat it too.

I knew and respected completely why the answer was black and white for Sundiata. I felt ashamed and vaguely guilty that the answer has some shades of grey for me. After all, the two people I was writing a book about both cooperated. I do not think it was the right thing to do. I do not know what I would have done in their circumstances. In prison culture, and in movement culture, there would be no compromise—they would be outcasts. I wondered, sitting on the metal bench in the concrete yard outside with Sundiata, what it said about me that I could not write off Mac and Kakamia. I wondered what it meant about my commitment to struggle, to change. I wondered what it meant that the complexities of their humanity were not erased for me by one of the titles both will forever wear: rat.

* * *

I wonder if the prisoners asking for Mac's autograph did the tally, saw the losses. Did they understand what that meant? Did they know it meant trying to start up a life that no longer existed, returning to a neighborhood that no longer existed, trying to become a human being again, living beyond a prison number, trying to be human when you are worried that what was human about you died long ago?

To them, Mac was an outlaw, a renegade. America loves the lone man who takes his destiny into his own hands and wrestles it to the ground, forcing its submission. Rooted in this country's fantasy, white supremacist manifest destiny devoured a continent—the indigenous peoples and their struggles, Africans in chains, the lands of Mexico.

This fantasy engrained itself into our American psyche. Rory Dubhdara wrote:

> What is it, really, that causes Americans to cheer on the gangster, despite his or her grisly legacy and blood-soaked trademark? Could it be that Americans have lost faith with the fabled "American Dream," as more working class people lose hope and end up out of work, impoverished or homeless? Perhaps the American gangster captures the spirit of the Robin Hood or Ned Kelly of yore, fighting back against "the Man," and using guerilla tactics to survive as he and his kind are continually disenfranchised and plundered by the robber barons of Corporate America.

This is part of why America as a nation is fascinated by the gangster, while simultaneously being repulsed by the aftermath left by the gangster. But the term itself—gangster—is absolutely racialized: colored white when we talk about the bygone Prohibition era, romanticizing names that live in infamy. It is colored Black when we talk of gangsters (or gangstas) today, portrayed as little more than rabid dogs, super predators devouring their communities and intent on devouring the nation unless they are stopped.

When I tell people I am writing a book about the Irish mob, who worked with the Mafia, they are fascinated, titillated. I tell them my Puerto Rican adopted brother is in prison for conspiracy to commit murder, and they attempt to control looks of horror, sometimes disgust. And yet, while both were involved in heinous acts, Kakamia did not pull the trigger, while Mac did over and over again—for profit.

The white supremacy that is rooted in our society is no less present in underground capitalism than it is in aboveground capitalism. When Italians and Irish came to this country, they faced discrimination and prejudice. But though they were persecuted, they were never on the same level as Black people. This is clear because these illegal economies, created by those locked out of financial opportunity, were dominated and run by the Italian crime families. The Mafia was the pinnacle. They were what Kakamia aspired to be when he was a kid. But the reality is, even if he had been involved in gangs when he was still in New York, he would never have risen in the ranks. His brown skin would have marked his place in the illicit hierarchy as it did in the larger one: at the bottom.

So it is through this racial reality that Mac and other white gangsters who utilize violence are given an air of mystique and intrigue, while people like Kakamia who engage in violence are marked as deviant criminals. This is true today, and has been true historically.

If Mac had been a cowboy, he would have ridden with Jesse James and the like. His name would be legend. If he had been a soldier, volunteered or drafted like so many others, he would have gone to Vietnam. He would have been ordered to participate in the My Lai massacres, and the others we do not know the names of. He would have done it. He would have come home with a chest full of medals and the same exact nightmares. If Mac had been a cop, like his friend Jackie had wanted so badly, he would have received commendations for his use of violence.

America does not abhor violence. The concern this nation has is not people killing for profit, but that it is done in the service of private acquisition of wealth, rather than corporate wealth.

The state does not have a moral objection to murder; it has a monopoly on it.

Mac was a gangster. He lived outside the borders of legality. He showed violence was not simply the purview of the system. In many ways, he had a much stricter code of conduct than if he had been in the military or a police officer. His rules forbade collateral damage. No friendly fire.

For that, he lost everything. He accepted the litany of things lost, parents and child who died while he was incarcerated, then the heartbreak of his own son incarcerated, the sorrow at paths carved and children's feet set down to walk the course. All his children grew without his presence. Friends betrayed him to save their own flesh. His neighborhood was reshaped by economic forces. He was exiled from home in every sense of the word.

Mac carried all of these losses. Penance. Each loss a prayer bead in the hands of a prodigal son.

He did receive one gift while incarcerated: his adopted son whom he simply called his son, had been sent to prison in New York. Mac bowed his head when he first told me, accepting responsibility. It was one more sin to carry. When his son was released, Mac's handwriting was almost illegible with joy. They had spoken on the phone for the first time in years and years.

Like all prisoners, Mac planned his life beyond these walls. He would not go home. There was no home to go home to. He wanted to make a new home. Mac planned to marry his girlfriend. They started dating after he went to prison. She just happened to be Eddie "the Butcher" Cummisky's niece. She used to babysit for Mac's kids.

Life is funny, Mac said.

* * *

Is this the justice we the people were promised? Is this what makes us safe?

Justice for whom? This is the real question. Justice for the state—justice for the community—justice for the victims—justice is not absolute. For the state, justice was a needle full of poison into the veins of Troy Davis, a young Black man executed in 2011 by the State of Georgia, despite overwhelming doubt in his conviction, and petitions signed by half a million people, each (like the Pope) saying Troy Davis should not be killed.

Too often the state uses the word "justice" when it should say "maintain the social order." Justice and order are often not only antithetical but in direct conflict with one another.

For the community, justice can look like the South African Truth and Reconciliation Commission, which was held after the end of apartheid to tell the truth of the atrocities that had happened. It can look like Creative Interventions, a Bay Area organization that creates effective, sustainable, community-based interventions to family, intimate partner, and other forms of interpersonal violence—without calling the police.

And what does justice for the victims look like? For me, for years, it looked like accountability colored with punishment. What I wanted and what I knew were right were often at war. Groups like Murder Victims for Reconciliation have helped frame loss not as an opportunity for vengeance, but a commandment for healing. "Reconciliation means accepting you cannot undo the murder but you can decide how you want to live afterwards."

Hannah Yoo's father was murdered. She joined Murder Victims for Reconciliation. She decided to travel to Korea, to meet with the two brothers who killed him. One killed himself in prison before she got there, but she met with the other.

"I visited the prison and confronted the murderer's accomplice anyway. I have a sense of closure… a sense of peace and satisfaction knowing that I gave him a warm smile. He may be spending the rest of his days in prison, but he knows that I have forgiven him. I hope that will have meaning to him someday if it doesn't already."

It is not my place to tell people who have survived harm themselves, or lost loved ones to violence, what the "appropriate" response is. I do not know what I would do, what I would want, in Hannah Yoo's place.

But I would like for us to start with questions, rather than foregone conclusions. I would hope all of us could start with the question, "What would be the healthiest for the individuals and community involved?", rather than "Who should we make pay?"

* * *

Mac's letters sprouted smiley faces like they were wild flowers. He used to say it was like a little kid hijacked his letter in the middle of him writing it. Mac used them almost as much as he used periods. How are you. Smiley face. Hope you finished your thesis on time. Smiley face. Your brother sends his love. Smiley face.

I asked him about them. "They're silly, right?" he replied. "I don't know why I do it. But don't mind the smiley faces. I'm always smiling."

Mac did not speak of his illness to me. He would make passing reference in a letter. "Sorry it's taken me so long to write. I was in the hospital." "Okay, that's it for now. Hard to write." "Would love to see you when you're here. I hope I'm able to sit with you. I'll try."

The last time I saw Mac was behind glass. He had been placed in the hole. A mistake, he said. It was a mistake. He was soon transferred back to general population, to the same unit as Kakamia. Mac did not know I was coming to visit that day. The letter had been delayed, so my visit was unexpected. We were only allowed an hour through the scratched up worn phones. He took 20 minutes to come out. Unshaven. Eyes hollowed out. He looked older than I ever imagined he could.

He apologized for his appearance so many times I lost count. He was embarrassed to be seen like this, vulnerable.

The light eventually came back into his eyes throughout the conversation. He asked about a recent poetry performance I had done.

"I bet you were great! I bet everyone rushed you like a rock star afterwards!"

I demurred, modesty that was only slightly tinged false.

"When I get out, I'm going to be your bodyguard. So you don't have to worry about anyone crazy messing with you after your shows. If they wanna mess with you, they'll have to come through me." He jerked his thumb towards his chest. The shackles on his hands, tethered to the floor, rattled.

"You know I think of you like family." The seriousness abrupt and brusque. "Like a niece."

Mac signed his letters "Love your friend James Patrick McElroy, Jimmy Mac, Westies, Hell's Kitchen, NY." He told me before that I was an honorary member of the Westies. A "Westette." I was disturbed by this. Then I saw Mac was working, like so many in prison, to build community, to build the family too far away to touch. He was offering me the only thing he thought he had of value: membership with him in infamy.

I stared into earnest stormweather eyes, knowing all the wrong seen and done by them. I remembered hours of stories told by this man, now sick and tired and looking for connections denied him. Rightfully so, Mac would say, rightfully denied. But I had the space not to see a butcher, unlike the families of his victims, unlike the larger society. I had the space to see a human being in pain. I had the space to be able to offer a man, near the end of his life, alone, the gift of forgiveness.

"That means a lot to me, Jimmy."

Sun smile through the storm clouds.

"Great! Hey when you have a kid, I'm going to be uncle to them, okay? I'll be Uncle Jimmy! But you don't have to," he added in the same breath. Keep expectations in check. Don't hope for too much.

I put my hand to the glass. "Uncle Jimmy it is. Just don't expect to be an uncle anytime soon!"

Our laughter was muffled by the plexiglass.

Mac's eyes were serious. "You know you're the first person I really opened up my thoughts to. I never really told anyone my business before. Not about all this."

In a breath the guard rolled the door back and unhooked the chains from the floor. Mac told me to take care, to have a good visit with my brother, and to give Kakamia all Mac's best. I smiled and waved goodbye. He winked at me. We both turned. Out of the corner of my eye, his wink turned to a grimace. He slumped slightly forward, the ever-present pain in his body taking command.

Mac was in constant pain for the last years of his life. It was not just physical.

This project was hard for Mac. For Kakamia. For me. Sifting through one's life, dredging up memories we have worked so hard to lock away. Asking ourselves the questions we had done almost everything to avoid. We all thought we would just be telling a story. Instead, we relived horrors, sins, atrocities, losses, traumas, and heartbreaks. We were forced to see the people we were, the people we have told ourselves no longer exist. We saw them not in photographs but in mirrors, not just in memories but in ourselves.

"I've done so much damage." Mac could not look me in the eyes. "I never sat down and thought about it before. When I look back at the past, it's hard to believe I did all that stuff. It's really, really hard to believe."

* * *

"Here," Mac held out the creation he birthed during our first visit. A white rose, sculpted from three paper napkins. It was delicate, white petals full as lips.

He answered my look of astonishment. "It's something I learned to do here. I learned while I was in the hole. I never would have had the patience for anything like this. It takes so much time. Some of the big ones take hours. But sitting in the hole, you learn. And now, I can do 'em easy. It calms me, you know? I guess it's my meditation."

This was before they stopped letting visitors take anything out of the prison visiting room. I left, clutching my rose, this delicate beauty created from the hands of a killer in a state penitentiary—a killer who used to want to be an interior decorator, who dropped out of school at the age of sixteen when they told him he had to be a shoemaker. Whose palette became human flesh to create monstrous creations out of.

Mac promised to send me a whole bouquet of paper roses—blue ones. My favorite color is blue. I do not think Mac knew the symbolism of that flower; there is no such thing as a naturally-occurring blue rose. In literature, it has long been the symbol for the never-ending quest for the unattainable. A bouquet of blue roses from Mac: an impossible gift of eternal hope from the hands of a killer.

Mac never made me my blue rose bouquet. He grew too sick.

Mac's son once said, "My father was no saint. But people said he could light up a room. He's been away fifteen, twenty years, and you still felt protected by him."

The white rose Mac made me still gives off the faint scent of redemption. And damnation.

* * *

One night, Kakamia was awakened by a flurry of activity in the dorm. He asked everyone what was going on. It was Mac, they said; he wasn't able to breathe. Guards took Mac out, put him in a prison van, and drove him to the hospital. Later, Kakamia found out he suffered a heart attack. They performed emergency surgery on him, but Mac died in the middle of the night on the operating table, his chest peeled open, his heart exposed to the world.

"You have a collect call from an inmate. You will not be charged for this call. This call is from 'Wa, it's me your brother.' To hear the cost of this call dial or say nine. To connect this call dial or say five. To decline this call dial or say one."

I stabbed the 5 button.

"Wa, I have something to tell you." Kakamia's voice was heavier than I've ever heard. "Mac's... Mac's dead. He died two days ago."

Stunned silence hung on the crackling line. My brain revolted at this information. How was that possible? Yes, he was sick. But somehow I had never linked Mac sick to Mac dead. Mac could not die. He had survived shoot-outs and hits, police stings, and twenty-five years in prison. But it was his body, so many years warehoused, that ultimately betrayed him.

"They just let him get sicker and sicker." Kakamia's voice was thick as syrup. "The healthcare in here, it's so fucking awful. People dying who don't have to. Who wouldn't on the outside if they could see a real fucking doctor. But this shit in here they call medicine... Man, it'll kill you." A laugh that sounded like a sob barked out.

"Wa, I'm tired. I'm so fucking tired. I can't take losing anyone else. My son. Mom. My nephew. Now Mac. I can't lose one more person while I'm in here. I'm tired. Tired. Tired." The word was a rosary bead rubbed over and over again between praying hands, hoping for a miracle.

"I don't think I'm going to make it. I really don't. I don't think I can make it through twenty more years. I know I'm going to die in here... what does it matter if it's now or later?"

Kakamia's sobs filled my ears.

My heart ached. I wanted more than anything to hold him, because there is nothing to say. I wanted to wrap him in my arms, to hold him up. But I could not reach him. I could not tell him to come over so he wouldn't be alone.

I know my brother, though. I knew he needed to be anchored, teth-ered down. I had to rope him back in with words of love and obligation, to remind him he was not superfluous, that he had responsibilities.

"I know it hurts. I know you feel all alone. But you are never alone. I have you tattooed on my arm. You are with me constantly. I am over your heart. Protecting it. Never for one second doubt that I am always going to be here for you. And you *will* make it through this. You *have* to make it through this. Because people are depending on you. I am depending on you. You made a commitment to us, your friends, your chosen family, to be here. To stay on this planet. In this fight. And goddamnit, you are gonna honor that!"

"*You have sixty seconds remaining on this call.*" The too-familiar rush of time being torn from my hands cut through my words. I did not know what to say. I repeated "I love you" over and over.

"I love you. I love you. I love you. I love you. I love you. I love…"

Click. The finality of our call being severed, of me being severed from my brother. I sat holding the phone to my ear for a long time. I still don't know what I was hoping to hear.

Then I cried for Kakamia: this brilliant wild child who has a heart too big for his own good.

And I shed tears for this former hit man who made beautiful flow-ers with his hands.

WHACKING GIULIANI

IN THE BEGINNING WHEN I VISITED WITH MAC, I WAS A JOURNALIST; I put my activist identity on the shelf. Mac made jokes about how they used to beat up hippies protesting the war in the early days of the Westies. I figured better safe than sorry. So when I sent him rough chapters of this book, including ones about my political history, I sweated it out for a month until our next visit.

I was cautious when Mac finally sat down. We made small talk. I bought him a cherry soda. Then he jumped in. "Ah, see, I told you you were like Angela Davis, with your big afro. I knew you were one of those radicals." Grin splitting his face.

Relief spread throughout my body.

"So you knew, huh?" My grin in return.

"Yeah, I knew from the minute I saw you in the visit. I didn't know what to expect that first time. I wasn't nervous or nothing. But then I saw your afro. I liked you right away. I knew you were a radical. I admire people who fight for what they believe in."

It's strange how much this gangster's acceptance meant to me.

"When I get out, I gotta go see one of those rallies of yours. I think that would be fun. I remember that one guy, who's the guy you mentioned in your chapter, with the cop in Philly?" he asked.

"Mumia Abu-Jamal."

"Yeah, yeah that's him, Mumia. I heard about him, I remember that. They did him wrong, I'm telling you, he should have already

gone free. But they set him up. They wanted him off the streets because he was telling the truth. The cops. Cops... They'd set up anybody for anything. We always hated them for that." He grimaced.

"Yeah the Supreme Court just declined his request for a new trial,"
I replied.

"Of course they did. They're scared, is what they are. He's too
smart. They're scared of him."

I smiled in amazement. Never in my life did I imagine I would be
discussing Mumia Abu-Jamal's case with a convicted hitman for the
mob—or that we would be in complete agreement.

"I remember another Black Panther, he was on trial the same time
we were. He had a RICO charge against him too. You know him?"

I went through my mental rolodex of Black Liberation political
prisoners, turning to 1987 and RICO charges. There were so many...

"He was a doctor, you know, he stuck needles in people to make
'em feel better."

"Acupuncture! Sure, Mutulu Shakur was it?" I responded, incredulous at the connections.

"Yeah, yeah! That's him! He was on trial the same time we were. We
were housed at MCC [Metropolitan Correctional Center] together."

How could I not have realized that? I knew the legal timelines for
both cases. Of course they were there together. In my head, my work
on this book with Mac and my political prisoner work were light years
apart, connected only by the barbed wire of prisons. I have since come
to realize they are literally a hand's span apart, hands outstretched
through bars giving pounds and support.

"Mutulu did that acupuncture thing on one of my friends there, it
was real good. He was on trial with this little white girl..."

"Marilyn Buck," I supplied, horrified to hear this political prisoner
of decades, accomplished organizer, and poet referred to as a "little
white girl."

"Yeah! Marilyn Buck. She seemed nice. We only saw her on the
elevator rides to the court. But she seemed nice."

"What did you think of Mutulu?" I was curious to see his take on
a Black Liberation Army member who was convicted of robbing a
Brinks armored truck to expropriate funds for revolutionary activities, and convicted of freeing fellow BLA member Assata Shakur and

spiriting her to decades of safety and exile in Cuba. Pretty different than whacking a mafioso and cutting up his body.

"Ah he was a great guy, real nice. Real smart. Like I said, that's why they wanted to get these guys, 'cause they were too smart. We weren't like them. They wanted those guys for different reasons. We weren't political prisoners…" He paused. "Were we?" Mac quizzed abruptly.

I almost choked on my orange juice.

"No." I measured my words slowly. "No, I don't think you guys could be called political prisoners at all."

Mac shook his head decisively. "Yeah you're right, we're not."

I could see Mac's mind working, questioning and comparing the different circumstances of the cases and the punishment meted out. I saw him react as the idea that laws created to catch people like him were employed to stifle dissent. While the Westies were cutting people up for money, others were breaking laws in the pursuit of freedom, with the hope of making the world a better place.

"I like that you're going to be telling all these stories together in your book—the political prisoners, the Irish and the Italian mobs. I was thinking, these political prisoners, you never hear about them. Some of those guys have twenty or more years in prison. But nobody ever writes about them, all they write about is Italian mob guys. Right?"

I nodded, dumbstruck. Was Mac really making these incredible connections about political repression in this country?

"I really don't know too much about these political prisoners. It's like the government don't want anyone to know about them. They need a voice. That's where you come in," he stared at me intently. "Those are the guys you should be writing about," Mac said decisively. "Those are the guys people need to know about 'cause they are being punished for doing what's right. Not a bunch of gangsters like us."

"Well," I smiled, "I think I can do both. You're helping me do both right now."

Mac grinned. We went on to talk about many different political topics. Mac gave me more information on the Westies, items brought to the forefront of his brain by my draft chapters. I scribbled on the scraps of paper the prison provided, using the little quarter golf pencil, just like I had done for the past four years interviewing Mac.

When our hour was up, we hugged. I promised to come back soon and spend more time, when I wasn't rushed to attend a conference on prisons. I walked out quickly. I was already thinking about processing, and hoping it would go smoothly so I would have more time with my brother.

"Ma'am, what do you have in your hand?" a short female officer barked.

I looked down and saw the notes I had taken. "These are nothing, just some notes I wrote to myself. I'm going to put them in my car. I'm not bringing them back into the prison."

"You're going to have to hand those over," she glared.

I did so, and waited, shifting from foot to foot while she called over her superior officer, an older white man with a walrus-sized white moustache drooping down his face. I had one eye on the clock, and one eye on my notes to make sure they didn't go anywhere.

Walrus Moustache called me out of line and over to the side of the bright orange counter.

"And what," he asked victoriously like he already knew the answer, "are these?" He shook the tiny pages covered in my almost illegible scrawl.

Evasiveness was my best route. Since I hadn't officially informed the prison that I was working on this book, I didn't want to start that discussion here. Not with my brother on the other side of the bars, waiting for me, checking the walkway every five minutes for my familiar afroed silhouette.

"They're just some notes to myself. My friend was telling me some funny stories, and I wanted to remember them."

This sounded pathetic even to my ears.

"They're letters, aren't they." A statement, not a question.

"No, they're notes, just notes. They're not going to anyone but myself."

"Well, you're not allowed to bring any written material out of a prison visiting room. You violated one of the rules."

My stomach dropped. I know people who were banned from a prison because they forgot they had a stick of gum in their pocket. They were told they were bringing in contraband. I saw an old woman banned from a prison when a drug test came up positive for her. They later discontinued the use of that test, because they found it gave almost as many false positives as true. She still had to fight for months to lift her ban. If there truly was a rule that I violated, my brother would be waiting a very long time to see me.

"I've taken notes out before on all my visits, for four years. I had no idea there was a rule," I stammered. Panic rose in my chest, straining my voice.

He snorted. "It's on the back of the visiting form you signed when you first came here." He pulled out the form and slapped it on the counter, pointing to small print at the bottom, which read: "It is illegal to bring *correspondence* in or out of the visiting room, or pass it between inmates."

"They're just notes." My voice took on a level of desperation. "I was putting them in my car, I have done it many times before. I didn't know it was a problem. I can just throw them away. But my brother is waiting to see me. I was going back in to see him, can I go… please?"

The please tore at my throat, like swallowing gravel. But prison is all about humiliations. If my brother had his body violated by a body cavity search every time he came out to see me, I could crawl a little in front of this tin-plated dictator.

Walrus Moustache turned to the female guard. "How did she bring this out? Was she trying to hide it? Was she sneaking it out?"

I could hear the hope saturating his voice.

She looked at me coldly for a long minute. "No, she had it in her hand with her ID. There was nothing sneaky about it."

He looked deflated by the answer.

"All right," he begrudged, "you can go back in to see your brother."

"Do you just want me to throw those away then?" I asked nervously, reaching for the papers.

"No, I'm going to keep it here to study it."

My nervousness escalated to full blown anxiety. The notes were all over the place. Since I was writing by hand with a mere nub of a pencil, I just scratched the bare bones—like when Mac told me the story of how he and Jackie Coonan wanted to kill Rudolph Giuliani, then U.S. Attorney General, the one leading the charge to smash the Mafia and the Westies.

"Jackie and I, we worked on the set of *The Days of Our Lives*. We'd be there every morning at 5:30 in the morning. And like clockwork we'd see Giuliani walking his dog. Every morning, by himself, like he didn't have a care in the world. I wanted to take him out so much. But Fat Tony [Salerno, head of the Genovese family] said no, we couldn't. It would bring down too much heat to kill him. Well, Fat Tony got five hundred years when Giuliani was through with him. That's not heat? Man, I wish we had done it."

From this statement ensued a lengthy discussion between us about the political ramifications of Giuliani's untimely death upon the state of the nation. It was sort of like sussing out the plot of a science fiction novel: What would have happened to Mac and the Westies? To the Mafia and organized crime? Would they all still be riding high, instead of limping along, waiting for that final bullet to put them all out of their misery? What about the radical movements of the 70s and 80s? Giuliani was responsible for a number of RICO charges, specifically against Black Liberation Movement. What would have happened to the movement if it hadn't been dealt those blows? What would New York look like now if not for Giuliani's "cleaning up" of the city, his "broken windows" zero tolerance policies, which were really an attack on the poor, the brown, the homeless, the street vendors, the "unde-sirable" in a way that allowed for accelerated gentrification of the city that never sleeps? What if Giuliani hadn't been mayor during 9/11? What would the response of a city under attack have been? Might it have been one of thoughtful reflection? An attempt at healing? Would that have changed America's response to the incident? Would we even be engaged in an endless war on terror around the world right now?

It was obviously all theoretical. It was fun nonetheless to pull the strings of history and imagine what would unravel, what would be unmade.

My notes of the conversation, however, just read, "Whack Giuliani with jackie. Fat Tony. Heat. 500 years. Mornings dog Days Lives. Change everything. Political prisoners freed?"

Visions of me being detained as an enemy combatant who planned to kill a former U.S. mayor filled my head. I could see Michael Cher-toff, then head of Homeland Security, holding up my scraps of paper as evidence, bellowing that I was going to hold Giuliani hostage until they freed all the political prisoners and then kill him anyway.

I pasted a smile on my face and said to Walrus Moustache, "Sure, of course, keep them. Thank you so much."

Through the entire visit with my brother, I stressed and worried. It loomed over me.

Still we had a great time. My brother can turn a visiting room into *Showtime at the Apollo*. We have a good-natured game of dozens, which begins the minute after we get finished hugging hello.

"Damn, scarecrow, what are you on that Kate Moss diet or something?" Kakamia poked me in the ribs.

"Whatever, fivehead," I responded, "with a forehead that big you could land a plane on it."

Usually when I visit prisons, I am my sweetest, most understanding self. I try to leave everything small and petty in the car, along with my wallet and my car alarm keychain.

But Kakamia and I are truly siblings, even if we weren't born that way. It creates a sense of normalcy when we snap on each other. After a particularly good cut, we both can't keep a straight face. Instead we crack up, hug, and move on to other topics.

"C'mon, Wa, let's take a walk." Kakamia meant we should go outside into the "recreation area," which consisted of two metal outdoor tables on concrete surrounded by fencing, more dog pen than picnic. We strolled around the confined space in lazy circles. When we both got animated, arguing or discussing plans for him to come home, we both unconsciously sped up. We lapped other folks walking two by two. On this cement slab, located behind two high walls, with a clear shot of the snipers in the guard towers, I could still feel like we were strolling down a country road with sun on our faces, laughter in our throats.

As always, the visit ended all too quickly. I left, holding back tears I know hurt him more than they do me.

I was ready to face the music.

The female guard was there. Three other guards leaned on the orange counter. She stared down at me—pretty impressive because I had at least five inches on her.

I said in my smallest voice, "I just wanted to make sure that everything was all right from before. As I said, I didn't know the rules and just want to make sure that there's no trouble in the future…"

"If you were in trouble, ma'am," she interrupted, spitting machine gun staccato, "you would already have known about it. Have a good evening."

This, then, is the power of the prison system: the ability to sever and slice, to break and crush bones and bodies, and more importantly, connections and hearts.

REMEMBERING FREEDOM

IT HAS TAKEN ME OVER TEN YEARS TO FINISH THIS BOOK. I STARTED this book before I went to grad school. Then it became my thesis. When I graduated, I sent invitations to Kakamia and Mac. Both said they were so proud of me. Mac said how he wished he could attend. He made me promise to send pictures. He wanted to see me in a cap and gown, diploma in hand.

After the incident with my notes described in the last chapter, I no longer wrote any thoughts down during prison visits. Whether during interviews or just tasks I said I would do after visiting with a prisoner, I didn't want to risk my visits in any institution regardless of the written rules.

So instead I employed a pneumonic device to remember items: I would pick out a word to sum up, take the first letter, string the letters together of the items and then make a word or even a sentence out of it, like so:

1. Print an article on Adinkra symbols - A
2. Follow up on a calendar order – C
3. Ask someone if they received a letter – L

A C L. All Cats Lie.

During visits I would add to this list in my head, repeating mentally every time I added to it over the six or more hours I was inside
the prison. Once I left, I would write quick notes in the car as soon as
I exited so I didn't forget on the short drive back to the hotel. There
I would immediately sit and type up the notes in longer form, with
everything I could remember about them. If the visit had been an
interview, I would send the notes back to the person once I got home,
ask them clarifying questions, and try to make sure I had remembered
all of the information correctly.

I feel like this convoluted, imperfect process is the nature of storytelling in general, and especially the storytelling involved in bringing
voices from behind prison walls. What parts of the story get heard are
based on what is most important to the listener, what makes it into
the notes, what is remembered, what is repeated back, what is told
and retold until it becomes the full and only truth.

This is how we create history. This is how we decide what justice is.

And all of it is mitigated and filtered through structures of power. It is negotiated within the system, limited by it. But the flawed
method I developed, one that relies on clandestine memory, is one
oppressed peoples have had to employ for centuries in this nation.
Enslaved Black people encoded subversive messages of freedom in
songs. Black spirituals like "Follow the Drinking Gourd" are actually
instructions on how to escape enslavement: continue to follow the
North Star, which is part of the constellation the Big Dipper, and they
would be heading north, out of slavery.

This is making a way when there is no way—telling stories never
meant to be told—just like Mumia Abu-Jamal clandestinely writing
his first book on death row and having it smuggled out. It is just
like Marilyn Buck and Mutulu Shakur and the others who breached
prison walls to rescue Assata Shakur, proving the prophetic words of
Assata in her poem "Affirmation":

> And, if i know anything at all,
> it's that a wall is just a wall
> and nothing more at all.
> It can be broken down.

* * *

So much has changed during that time period in my world—in the world of prisons. Personally, I saw dozens of people released from prison. I saw many more people go into prison in that time period. I saw my comrade put to death by the state of Texas. I saw another comrade come within hours of lethal injection and receive a commutation—because of organizing work. My friend Sean, faced with a prison sentence, took his own life. Another friend attempted to kill himself less than six months out of the gate. My nephew was sentenced to eight years in prison.

Kakamia marked twenty-five years in prison. Sadly, he is still counting. He was transferred to a new facility, formerly a women's prison turned into an institution housing those the state designates as male. This is part of California's attempt to reduce the prison overcrowding as ordered by the federal government. Rather than release people, it transferred those previously in the women's prison to another women's institution that was slightly less overcrowded than the male facility. Then it moved male prisoners in to the newly vacated prison. A political shell game, played with human lives. "See if you can find the overcrowding, the constitutional violation!" No matter which shell you choose, it seems as though there's nothing underneath. Unlike a disappearing trick, though, the issue is only masked, not absent. Even if we can't find it, we know it's there.

On the larger organizing scale, in 2010, Georgia prisoners staged the largest prison strike in history up to that point. Over ten thousand prisoners refused to leave their cells until demands for decent treatment were met: echoes of Attica. Less than a year later, an even larger hunger strike took place in California prisons, involving twelve thousand people and lasting for over a month. When the strike leaders ended the strike in 2011 after CDCr agreed to some of their demands (which was unprecedented), the leaders said they were prepared to go back on strike. In 2013, they did just that. Over thirty thousand participated in almost every California prison. They will continue to starve themselves, pushing their bodies almost to the point of death until they achieve justice.

These are some of the most courageous organizers I will ever know.

The past ten years has brought so much more work around prison abolition, alternatives to police and prisons. Organizations practicing alternatives here and around the world have blossomed. Anthologies exploring the principles and concepts of abolition have been published. Abolitionist frameworks have been integrated into other organizing, recognizing that calling for anything that expands the carceral system ultimately makes all of us less safe and less free.

People are exploring and experimenting, both in theory and practice, with abolition. They have answered the question Angela Davis poses in her book's title *Are Prisons Obsolete?* with a resounding yes. Much more complex is the next question, "So what instead?" As I have explored here in this book, there are no neat and clean answers. And we in this society want them desperately. We have been inculcated with the idea that if there isn't a clear resolution where everything comes out perfectly, we have failed.

Through that standard, the abolitionist movement has failed. We have not devised a vacu-sealed and packaged commodity called abolition with slick advertisements that will take away our fears, our heartache, and our brokenness in three easy steps.

But what if the standard for success is not a neatly wrapped-up sitcom ending, as we are told by society? What if it is instead about questioning everything we have been told is true and possible? What if it is about exploring what it is that makes us most human, and elevates our humanity to its highest level?

If that is the case, then the abolitionist movement continues to fulfill its purpose, because even asking the question, "How would we live without prisons?" demands that we step outside of this society and stretch our imaginations to the limit. And this is where all social advancement has come from. If we cannot imagine a different way of existing, then we cannot create real change.

"I think hard times are coming," writer Ursula K Le Guin said during a 2014 National Book Awards speech, "when we will be wanting the voices of writers who can see alternatives to how we live now and can see through our fear-stricken society and its obsessive technologies to other ways of being, and even imagine some real grounds for hope. We will need writers who can remember freedom."

As a writer, I absolutely believe in the importance of those who can reframe issues through literary means, asking questions anew. And I also absolutely believe we need those organizers and changemakers who are doing the work on the ground to pull the literary into everyday reality.

For the past ten years, abolitionists have been exploring many concrete models of alternatives, a handful of which are explored in this book. There are countless others. But I think even more far-reaching is the concept of principles that abolitionists have been exploring: what sorts of ideals do we want to build our societies on? What sort of visions do we want to base new, just worlds upon?

As Alexis Pauline Gumbs writes in her essay "Freedom Seeds," abolition then becomes about realizing that the concept is not just about destroying prisons or eliminating police—not at its core. Those are tactics to get to the central purpose of abolition, which it to re-engage and recenter our humanity, each and every single one of us on this planet. Abolition is not about destroying but about building community, nurturing connection, and growing freedom seeds.

> What if abolition isn't a shattering thing, not a crashing thing, not a wrecking ball event? What if abolition is something that sprouts out of the wet places in our eyes, the broken places in our skin, the waiting places in our palms, the tremble holding in my mouth when I turn to you?
> What if abolition is something that grows?

* * *

The biggest loss for this book in the past ten years was Jimmy McElroy's passing in 2011. He was sixty-six years old. I did not expect Mac to die. Next to the sadness came a consuming guilt. Mac would never get to hold this book like he wanted. He said many times he couldn't wait to show it off to folks on the inside: the book his niece wrote about him. Time passes so differently on the outside. Ten years is a breath. I walked away from the book. I told myself I was taking a break. Life conspired to fill in all the cracks of my time. I kept telling myself I would get back to it.

Then it was too late for Mac.

I told everyone, including myself, that the book took so long because I did not have time to work on it; I was so busy with other projects. True. But the real reason I did not carve out time to work on it was because I was afraid.

I originally planned to write a feature story on Mac, place it in a magazine, and move on. Then he asked me to write his biography one visit. Truthfully, I had already been thinking of it. But in looking in his eyes and saying yes, a tidal wave of uncertainty hit me. How would I be able to tell this story and be true to Mac, to history, to my politics?

Then there were years of interviewing and research. No writing. I need more information, I said. I have to finish gathering that before I can start. The impetus for me to actually start writing was going back to school for my MFA in Creative Writing. The genesis of this book was my thesis.

As I finally began to write, I realized I could not write a traditional biography. As I have said, I believe objectivity to be a fallacy. But I had no distance from this. Kakamia and I had already claimed each other as family. Mac became family throughout this process. I knew I could not even pretend at impartiality.

And so instead I decided to strive for responsibility and accountability: to Mac, to Kakamia, to myself, and more importantly, to the ideas underlying all of our lives. I want to be accountable to the unanswered—sometimes even unasked—questions that demarcate the boundaries of our worlds: the hidden (and very clear) prisons each of us lives in every day. I strove to challenge readers, but more importantly myself, to envision communities based on healing and transformation, not punishment and brutality.

Writing this book stretched the limits of my comfort zone so far that I could not even recognize the original shape. I knew I had to include my story in this book for it to feel true. I had to speak publicly about scars I have worked to hide. If I was laying Kakamia and Mac bare, it seemed only fair.

So I pulled at threads and saw my abortion tied to solitary confinement. I yanked harder and saw my assault intertwined with tough-on-crime legislation. I also saw the pain of my violation inextricably linked to my brother's own redemption. I saw (with the help of a supportive community that challenges and pushes me) that if I could find forgiveness, find hope, for the men in this book and for the hundreds of prisoners I have worked with, then I had to think about Dovid's redemption, something I had not considered up to that point. I had to think about forgiveness for him. Not blanket and blind forgiveness, but forgiveness with memory—forgiveness with accountability. And not for him, but for myself. I dropped so much anger and hurt. I had held it so long that I had forgotten it was not a part of me. I was able to walk forward leading with my strengths and not my pain.

I had to come to a place where I can leave things messy. I could not clean up the narrative around my relationship, neatly labeling Dovid the villain and myself the victim. I could not drop the contradictions of what Kakamia has done, and who he is now. I could not write Mac clean, nor could I write him hopeless. I could not and cannot give easy and definitive answers to the question, "When people do fucked up things to each other, then what?"

That's something we all have to answer together, as communities. As a nation. As a world.

This book is not the book that works to answer the question posed in the beginning, "Sometimes people do bad things, and then what?" There are many other brilliant minds crafting those answers collectively, on and off the page.

I hope, instead, that this book can serve as a bridge to get us to the place where we can even ask that question, because we can begin to see those people who do harm—sometimes immense brutal and irreparable harm to individuals and communities—as human. Flawed, damaged, and culpable, but still human.

The pieces of the larger whole I hope to bring are the stories of angels with dirty faces. The capriciousness of fate. The idea that every person has the capacity to salvage their tattered humanity, even in the moment before they take their last breath.

I want to remind people to say a prayer for all the children who couldn't run as fast as we could.

BIBLIOGRAPHY

"2012 Annual Report on the Extrajudicial Killings of 313 Black People by Police, Security Guards and Vigilantes." *Operation Ghetto Storm/Malcolm X Grassroots Movement.* Accessed July 11, 2015. http://www.operationghettostorm.org/uploads/1/9/1/1/19110795/new_all_14_11_04.pdf.

2Pac. *Dear Mama.* Tony Pizarro, 1995, CD.

Abu-Jamal, Mumia. *Live from Death Row.* Reading, MA: Addison-Wesley, 1995.

Alexander, Michelle. *The New Jim Crow: Mass Incarceration in the Age of Colorblindness.* New York: The New Press, 2012.

Angster, Daniel. "REPORT: New York City Television Stations Give Lopsided Coverage To Black Crime." Media Matters for America. August 26, 2014. Accessed July 11, 2015. http://mediamatters.org/research/2014/08/26/report-new-york-city-television-stations-give-l/200524.

Asbury, Herbert. *The Gangs of New York: An Informal History of the Underworld.* New York: Thunder's Mouth Press, 2001.

"Attica Prison Rebellion." Freedom Archives. Accessed July 11, 2015. http://www.freedomarchives.org/audio_samples/Attica.html.

Baker, Jeff. "Ursula K. Le Guin's Fiery Speech, and the Overwhelming Reaction to It (full text and video)." *The Oregonian.* November 20, 2014. Accessed August 1, 2015. http://www.oregonlive.com/movies/index.ssf/2014/11/ursula_k_le_guins_fiery_speech.html.

Balagoon, Kuwasi. *A Soldier's Story: Writings by a Revolutionary New Afrikan Anarchist.* Montreal: Kersplebedeb, 2003.

Bandele, Asha. *The Prisoner's Wife: A Memoir.* New York: Scribner, 1999.

Barganier, George Percy, III. "Fanon's Children: The Black Panther Party and the Rise of the Crips and Bloods in Los Angeles." Master's thesis, University of California, Berkeley, 2011.

Bayor, Ronald H., and Timothy J. Meagher. *The New York Irish*. Baltimore: Johns Hopkins University Press, 1996.

Beale, Sara Sun. "The News Media's Influence on Criminal Justice Policy: How Market-Driven News Promotes Punitiveness." *William and Mary Law Review* 48, no. 2 (2006): 397–481.

Berger, Dan. *Captive Nation: Black Prison Organizing in the Civil Rights Era*. Chapel Hill: University of North Carolina Press, 2014.

Bisson, Terry. *On a Move: The Story of Mumia Abu-Jamal*. Farmington, PA: Litmus Books, 2000.

Bogle, Donald. *Toms, Coons, Mulattoes, Mammies, and Bucks: An Interpretive History of Blacks in American Films*. New York: Continuum Publishing Company, 1996.

Bonanno, Bill. *Bound by Honor: A Mafioso's Story*. New York: St. Martin's Press, 1999.

Bonanno, Joseph. *A Man of Honor: The Autobiography of Joseph Bonanno*. New York: Simon and Schuster, 1983.

"BOP Statistics: Inmate Offenses." Bureau of Prisons. May 30, 2015. http://www.bop.gov/about/statistics/statistics_inmate_offenses.jsp.

Butler, Paul. *Let's Get Free: A Hip-hop Theory of Justice*. New York: The New Press, 2009.

Censky, Annalyn. "Black Unemployment Rate: Highest since 1984." *CNN-Money.* September 2, 2011. Accessed July 11, 2015. http://money.cnn.com/2011/09/02/news/economy/black_unemployment_rate/index.htm.

Chang, Jeff. *Can't Stop, Won't Stop: A History of the Hip-Hop Generation*. New York: St. Martin's Press, 2005.

Childress, Sarah. "Chicago Drops CeaseFire from Anti-Violence Strategy." PBS. October 17, 2013. Accessed July 11, 2015. http://www.pbs.org/wgbh/pages/frontline/social-issues/interrupters/chicago-drops-ceasefire-from-anti-violence-strategy/.

Chinn, Staceyann. "Marcus, Marley, Morrison and Me." *VideoWired.* Accessed July 11, 2015. http://www.videowired.com/watch/?id=3559870308.

Chomsky, Noam. "Drug Policy as Social Control." In *Prison Nation: The Warehousing of America's Poor*, edited by Tara Herivel and Paul Wright. New York: Routledge, 2003.

Churchill, Ward, and Jim Vander Wall. *Agents of Repression: The FBI's Secret Wars against the Black Panther Party and the American Indian Movement.* Boston: South End Press, 1988.

———. *The COINTELPRO Papers: Documents from the FBI's Secret Wars against Dissent in the United States.* Cambridge, MA: South End Press, 2002.

Coffey, Joseph J., and Jerry Schmetterer. *The Coffey Files: A Man against the Mob.* New York: St. Martin's Press, 1991.

Cohen, Rich. *Tough Jews: Fathers, Sons, and Gangster Dreams.* New York: Simon & Schuster, 1998.

Collazo, Abigail. "Chivalry Must Die: On Women's Expectations and Men's Obligations." *Everyday Feminism.* September 28, 2012. http://everydayfeminism.com/2012/09/chivalry-must-die/.

Color of Violence: The Incite! Anthology. Cambridge, MA: South End Press, 2006.

"Community Accountability." *Community Accountability.* Accessed July 11, 2015. https://communityaccountability.wordpress.com/.

"Community Accountability: Emerging Movements to Transform Violence." *Social Justice: A Journal of Crime, Conflict & World Order* 37, no. 4 (2011). http://www.socialjusticejournal.org.

"Community Conferencing Center - Baltimore." *YouTube.* October 29, 2009. https://www.youtube.com/watch?v=odAecoqIqZk.

"Creative Interventions Toolkit." *Creative Interventions.* Accessed July 11, 2015. http://www.creative-interventions.org/tools/toolkit/.

Davis, Angela Y. *Are Prisons Obsolete?* New York: Seven Stories Press, 2003.

DeMeo, Albert, and Mary Jane Ross. *For the Sins of My Father: A Mafia Killer, His Son, and the Legacy of a Mob Life.* New York: Broadway Books, 2002.

Doherty, Thomas. *Pre-Code Hollywood Sex, Immorality, and Insurrection in American Cinema, 1930–1934.* New York: Columbia University Press, 1999.

Dubhdara, Rory. "America's Mythological Fascination with Cult Outlaw Figures." *America's Mythological Fascination with Cult Outlaw Figures.* June 3, 2010. Accessed July 11, 2015. http://politics.feedfury.com/content/42435309-america-s-mythological-fascination-with-cult-outlaw-figures.html.

Dwyer, Jim. "Saying Farewell to a Gangster of a Bygone Era." *New York*

Times. May 10, 2011. Accessed July 11, 2015. http://www.nytimes. com/2011/05/11/nyregion/a-farewell-to-jimmy-mcelroy-gangster-of-a-lost-era.html.

English, T. J. *Paddy Whacked: The Untold Story of the Irish-American Gangster.* New York: Regan Books, 2005.

———. *The Westies: Inside the Hell's Kitchen Irish Mob.* New York: Putnam, 1990.

Fanon, Frantz. *The Wretched of the Earth.* New York: Grove Press, 1965.

FBI. "Crime in the United States 2012." FBI. July 30, 2013. Accessed July 11, 2015. http://www.fbi.gov/about-us/cjis/ucr/crime-in-the-u.s/2012/crime-in-the-u.s.-2012/offenses-known-to-law-enforcement/ expanded-homicide.

FBI. "FBI Crime Statistics." FBI. 2013. https://www.fbi.gov/stats-services/ crimestats.

Ferris, Amanda. "Announcements & Events from Local Businesses in New York City." *New York City Business News & Events.* May 16, 2011. Accessed July 11, 2015. http://newyork.nearsay.com/nyc/hells-kitchen-midtown/ real-estate-windermere-hotel-mark-tress.

Flatlow, Nicole. "Half Of Wisconsin Inmates Are In Prison Because They Violated Parole." *ThinkProgress.* January 19, 2015. Accessed July 11, 2015. http://thinkprogress.org/justice/2015/01/19/3612985/ half-of-wisconsin-prisoners-are-there-because-they-violated-parole/.

Frum, David. *How We Got Here: The 70's.* New York: Basic Books, 2000.

Gene, Mustain, and Jerry Capeci. *Murder Machine: A True Story of Murder, Madness, and the Mafia.* New York: Dutton, 1992.

Gilbert, David. *Love and Struggle: My Life in SDS, the Weather Underground, and Beyond.* Oakland: PM Press, 2012.

Gilmore, Ruth Wilson. *Golden Gulag: Prisons, Surplus, Crisis, and Opposition in Globalizing California.* Berkeley: University of California Press, 2007.

Goldman, John J. "Gotti Basks in Celebrity Role as Trial Nears End : Mafia: His Lawyers Say He Is a Salesman. Prosecutors Say He Heads the Gambino Crime Family. And Now a Jury Ponders the Fate of the Man Dubbed the 'Dapper Don.'" *Los Angeles Times.* February 7, 1990. http://articles. latimes.com/1990-02-07/news/mn-255_1_john-gotti.

Gumbs, Alexis Pauline. "Freedom Seeds: Growing Abolition in Durham, North Carolina." In *Abolition Now!: Ten Years of Strategy and Struggle against the Prison Industrial Complex,* edited by CR-10 Publications

Collective. Oakland: AK Press, 2008.

Hoffman, William, and Lake Headley. *Contract Killer: The Explosive Story of the Mafia's Most Notorious Hitman, Donald "Tony the Greek" Frankos*. New York: Thunder's Mouth Press, 1992.

Hurley, John W. *Irish Gangs and Stick-Fighting: In the Works of William Carleton*. Philadelphia: Xlibris, 2001.

Imarisha, Walidah. "Hasan Shakur's Last Words Were of the Struggle." *Cleveland IndyMedia*. September 3, 2006. Accessed July 11, 2015. http://cleveland.indymedia.org/news/2006/09/21705.php.

———. *Scars/stars*. Portland, OR: Drapetomedia, 2013.

"Incarcerated Women." *The Sentencing Project*. Accessed July 11, 2015. http://www.sentencingproject.org/doc/publications/cc_incarcerated_women_factsheet_sep24sp.pdf.

INCITE! *Incite!* 2014. Accessed July 11, 2015. http://incite-national.org/home.

INCITE! Women of Color Against Violence, "INCITE! Statement on Gender Violence and the Prison Industrial Complex." In *Abolition Now!: Ten Years of Strategy and Struggle against the Prison Industrial Complex*, edited by CR-10 Publications Collective. Oakland: AK Press, 2008.

Jackson, George. *Blood in My Eye*. New York: Random House, 1972.

James, Joy, ed. *Imprisoned Intellectuals: America's Political Prisoners Write on Life, Liberation, and Rebellion*. Lanham, MD: Rowman & Littlefield, 2003.

Johnson, Kirk. "West Side Gang Linked to 30 Unsolved Killings." *New York Times*. December 16, 1986. http://www.nytimes.com/1986/12/17/nyregion/west-side-gang-linked-to-30-unsolved-killings.html.

Jones, Charles E. *The Black Panther Party (Reconsidered)*. Baltimore: Black Classic Press, 1998.

Hughes, Timothy and Doris James Wilson. "Reentry Trends in the United States." *Bureau of Justice Statistics*. Accessed July 11, 2015. http://www.bjs.gov/content/reentry/reentry.cfm.

Kelley, Robin D.G. "How The New Working Class Can Transform Urban America." In *Race, Class, and Gender: An Anthology*, edited by Patricia Hill Collins and Margaret L. Andersen. Belmont, CA: Wadsworth Cengage Learning, 2013.

Kelley, Tina. "A Diner for Rent, With Many Memories to Tell." *New York Times*. September 13, 2007. Accessed July 11, 2015. http://www.nytimes.com/2007/09/14/nyregion/14diner.html?pagewanted=all.

Landmarks Preservation Commission. "The Windermere." *Landmarks Preservation Commission June 28, 2005, Designation List 365 LP-2171.* Accessed July 11, 2015. http://www.nyc.gov/html/lpc/downloads/pdf/reports/windermere.pdf.

Law, Vikki. *Resistance Behind Bars: The Struggles of Incarcerated Women.* Oakland: PM Press, 2009.

Lawrence, Alison. "Probation and Parole Violations: State Responses." *National Conference of State Legislatures.* November, 2008. http://www.ncsl.org/print/cj/violationsreport.pdf.

Lehr, Dick, and Gerard O'Neill. *Black Mass: The True Story of an Unholy Alliance between the FBI, and the Irish Mob.* New York: Perennial, 2001.

Lubasch, Arnold H. "Prosecutor Says Gang Terrorized Hell's Kitchen." *New York Times.* October 19, 1987. http://www.nytimes.com/1987/10/20/nyregion/prosecutor-says-gang-terrorized-hell-s-kitchen.html.

Lubasch, Arnold H. "Westies Informer Tells How Gang Cut Up Body." *New York Times.* October 21, 1987. http://www.nytimes.com/1987/10/22/nyregion/westies-informer-tells-how-gang-cut-up-body.html.

Lubasch, Arnold H. "Westies Informer Tells of Links to Gambino Mob." *New York Times.* November 5, 1987. http://www.nytimes.com/1987/11/06/nyregion/westies-informer-tells-of-links-to-gambino-mob.html.

Lupo, Salvatore. *History of the Mafia.* New York: Columbia University Press, 2009.

Maas, Peter. *Underboss: Sammy the Bull Gravano's Story of Life in the Mafia.* New York: HarperCollins Pub., 1997.

Maas, Peter. *The Valachi Papers.* New York: Putnam, 1968.

Manhattan Rental Market Report. Report. New York: MNS, 2014. http://www.mns.com/manhattan_rental_market_report

Marks, Claude, and Isaac Ontiveros. "Pelican Bay Hunger Strike: Four Years and Still Fighting." *Prisoner Hunger Strike Solidarity.* July 9, 2015. https://prisonerhungerstrikesolidarity.wordpress.com/2015/07/09/pelican-bay-hunger-strike-four-years-and-still-fighting/.

Mauer, Marc. *Race to Incarcerate.* New York: New Press, 1999.

Milito, Lynda, and Reg Potterton. *Mafia Wife: My Story of Love, Murder, and Madness.* New York: HarperCollins Publishers, 2003.

Mogul, Joey L., Andrea J. Ritchie, and Kay Whitlock. *Queer (In)justice: The Criminalization of LGBT People in the United States.* Boston: Beacon Press, 2011.

Naanes, Marlene. "New York City News: Latest Headlines, Videos & Pictures." *AM New York*. May 21, 2009. Accessed July 11, 2015. http://www.amny.com/urbanite-1.812039/city-lawsuit-saves-historic-windermere-apartments-in-hell-s-kitchen-1.1287594.

"The New York City Draft Riots of 1863." *The New York City Draft Riots of 1863*. Accessed July 11, 2015. http://www.press.uchicago.edu/Misc/Chicago/317749.html.

O'Brien, Joseph F., and Andris Kurins. *Boss of Bosses: The Fall of the Godfather: The FBI and Paul Castellano*. New York: Simon & Schuster, 1991.

Olmeca. *Pieces of Me*. Olmeca & Quincy McCrary, 2011, CD.

"One in 31: The Long Reach of American Corrections." *The PEW Center on the States*. March 2009. http://www.pewcenteronthestates.org/uploadedFiles/PSPP_1 in31_report_FINAL_WEB_3-26-09.pdf.

"One in 100: Behind Bars in America 2008." *The PEW Center on the States*. February 2008. http://www.pewcenteronthestates.org/uploadedFiles/80 15PCTS_Prison08_FI NAL_2-1-1_FORWEB.pdf.

Ontiveros, Isaac. "Hungry for Californian Prison Reform." *Al Jazeera*. July 10, 2011. Accessed July 11, 2015. http://www.aljazeera.com/indepth/features/2011/07/201171073515637475.html.

Padilla, Felix M. *The Gang as an American Enterprise*. New Brunswick, NJ: Rutgers University Press, 1992.

Paoli, Letizia. *Mafia Brotherhoods: Organized Crime, Italian Style*. Oxford: Oxford University Press, 2003.

Peltier, Leonard. *Prison Writings: My Life Is My Sun Dance*. New York: St. Martin's Press, 1999.

"People & Events: The Era of Gangster Films, 1930–1935." *PBS*. Accessed July 11, 2015. http://www.pbs.org/wgbh/amex/dillinger/peopleevents/e_hollywood.html.

Piepzna-Samarasinha, Leah Lakshmi, Ching-In Chen, and Jai Dulani. *The Revolution Starts at Home: Confronting Intimate Violence Within Activist Communities*. New York: South End Press, 2011.

"Plea and Charge Bargaining: A Research Summary." *U.S. Department of Justice*, January 24, 2011. Accessed July 11, 2015. https://www.bja.gov/Publications/PleaBargainingResearchSummary.pdf.

Prashad, Vijay. *The Karma of Brown Folk*. Minneapolis: University of Minnesota Press, 2000.

"Prison and Crime: A Complex Link." *The Pew Charitable Trusts*.

September 11, 2014. http://www.pewtrusts.org/en/multimedia/
data-visualizations/2014/prison-and-crime.

"Prisoner Hunger Strike Solidarity." *Prisoner Hunger Strike Solidarity.* Accessed
July 11, 2015. https://prisonerhungerstrikesolidarity.wordpress.com/.

Raab, Selwyn. "Carrier Museum Called Target of Racketeers." *New York
Times.* April 3, 1987. Accessed July 11, 2015. http://www.nytimes.
com/1987/04/04/nyregion/carrier-museum-called-target-of-racketeers.
html.

Raab, Selwyn. "Witness Says Gotti Ordered A Shooting." *New York
Times.* January 29, 1990. Accessed July 11, 2015. http://www.nytimes.
com/1990/01/30/nyregion/witness-says-gotti-ordered-a-shooting.html.

Sacramento Bee Staff. "2 boys arrested, charged with murder, attempted
murder." *Sacramento Bee.* December 17, 1990.

———. "Sacramento son who killed mom for life insurance due parole
hearing." *Sacramento Bee.* December 14, 2010.

"Safe Neighborhood Campaign." *Audre Lorde Project.* Accessed July 11,
2015. http://alp.org/safe-neighborhood-campaign.

Schneider, Eric C. *Vampires, Dragons, and Egyptian Kings: Youth Gangs in
Postwar New York.* Princeton, NJ: Princeton University Press, 1999.

Servadio, Gaia. *Mafioso: A History of the Mafia from Its Origins to the Present
Day.* New York: Stein and Day, 1976.

Shakur, Assata. *Assata: An Autobiography.* Chicago: Lawrence Hill, 1987.

Shakur, Sanyika. *Monster: The Autobiography of an L.A. Gang Member.* New
York: Penguin Press, 1993.

Simon, David R. *Tony Soprano's America: The Criminal Side of the American
Dream.* Boulder: Westview Press, 2002.

St. John, Paige. "California Prison Officials Say 30,000 Inmates Refuse
Meals." *Los Angeles Times.* July 8, 2013. Accessed July 11, 2015. http://
www.latimes.com/news/local/political/la-me-pc-ff-california-prison-offi-
cials-acknowledge-hunger-strike-20130708,0,3234974.story.

Stanley, Eric A., and Nat Smith. *Captive Genders: Trans Embodiment and the
Prison Industrial Complex.* Oakland: AK Press, 2011.

"Stop the Execution of Derrick Frazier." *Texas Civil Rights Review.* July
20, 2010. Accessed July 11, 2015. http://texascivilrightsreview.
org/2010/07/21/stop-the-execution-of-derrick-frazier/.

StoryTelling & Organizing Project. Accessed July 11, 2015. http://www.
stopviolenceeveryday.org/stop-2/.

Sugg, Diana. "Boy's plot to kill parents alleged; mother dies; father survives." *Sacramento Bee*. 18 December 1990.

"Transformative Justice Love Questions Panel Transcript." Accessed July 11, 2015. https://drive.google.com/file/d/0B5bil8ipXJb2TWtQZk5FWW9fVW8/view.

Traub, James. "The Lords of Hell's Kitchen." *New York Times*. April 4, 1987. http://www.nytimes.com/1987/04/05/magazine/the-lord-s-of-hell-s-kitchen.html.

Umoja, Akinyele Omowale. "Repression Breeds Resistance: The Black Liberation Army and the Radical Legacy of the Black Panther Party." In *Liberation, Imagination, and the Black Panther Party: A New Look at the Panthers and Their Legacy*, edited by George N. Katsiaficas and Kathleen Cleaver. New York: Routledge, 2001.

Valrey, JR. "Danifu Bey Interview." In *P.O.C.C. Block Report Radio*. Los Angeles. November 2005.

Wicker, Tom. *A Time to Die: The Attica Prison Revolt*. Harmondsworth: Penguin, 1978.

Wilde, Oscar. *De Profundis*, edited by Rupert Hart-Davis, and Jacques Barzun. New York: Vintage Books, 1964.

Wilkerson, Isabel. "Mike Brown's Shooting and Jim Crow Lynchings Have Too Much in Common. It's Time for America to Own up." *The Guardian*. August 25, 2014. Accessed July 11, 2015. http://www.theguardian.com/commentisfree/2014/aug/25/mike-brown-shooting-jim-crow-lynchings-in-common

Williams, Kristian. *Our Enemies in Blue: Police and Power in America*. Brooklyn: Soft Skull Press, 2004.

Wilson, Wayne. "Boys charged in plot that left parent dead." *Sacramento Bee*. December 20, 1990.

Zinn, Howard. *A People's History of the United States: 1942–Present*. New York: HarperCollins, 2003.

THE INSTITUTE FOR ANARCHIST STUDIES (IAS)

ANARCHISM EMERGED OUT OF THE SOCIALIST MOVEMENT AS A DIS-tinct politics in the nineteenth century. It asserted that it is necessary and possible to overthrow coercive and exploitative social relationships, and replace them with egalitarian, self-managed, and cooperative social forms. Anarchism thus gave new depth to the long struggle for freedom.

The primary concern of the classical anarchists was opposition to the state and capitalism. This was complemented by a politics of voluntarily association, mutual aid, and decentralization. Since the turn of the twentieth century and especially the 1960s, the anarchist critique has widened into a more generalized condemnation of domination and hierarchy. This has made it possible to understand and challenge a variety of social relationships—such as patriarchy, racism, and the devastation of nature, to mention a few—while confronting political and economic hierarchies. Given this, the ideal of a free society expanded to include sexual liberation, cultural diversity, and ecological harmony, as well as directly democratic institutions.

Anarchism's great refusal of all forms of domination renders it historically flexible, politically comprehensive, and consistently critical—as evidenced by its resurgence in today's global anticapitalist movement. Still, anarchism has yet to acquire the rigor and complexity needed to comprehend and transform the present.

The Institute for Anarchist Studies, established in 1996 to support the development of anarchism, is a grant-giving organization for radical writers. To date, we have funded over a hundred projects by authors from countries around the world. Equally important, we publish the Anarchist Interventions book series in collaboration with AK

Press and Justseeds Artists' Cooperative, the print and online journal *Perspectives on Anarchist Theory*, and our new series of books in collaboration with AK Press beginning with *Octavia's Brood*. We organize educational events such as Anarchist Theory Tracks, talks and panels at conferences and events, and we maintain a Mutual Aid speakers bureau. The IAS is part of a larger movement to radically transform society. We are internally democratic and work in solidarity with people around the globe who share our values.

IAS, PO Box 90454, Portland, OR 97290
www.anarchist-studies.org
Email: anarchiststudies@gmail.com

Support **AK Press!**

AK Press is one of the world's largest and most productive anarchist publishing houses. We're entirely worker-run

& democratically managed. We operate without a corporate structure—no boss, no managers, no bullshit. We publish close to twenty books every year, and distribute thousands of other titles published by other like-minded independent presses from around the globe.

The Friends of AK program is a way that you can directly contribute to the continued existence of AK Press, and ensure that we're able to keep publishing great books just like this one! Friends pay $25 a month directly into our publishing account ($30 for Canada, $35 for international), and receive a copy of every book AK Press publishes for the duration of their membership! Friends also receive a discount on anything they order from our website or buy at a table: 50% on AK titles, and 20% on everything else. We've also added a new Friends of AK ebook program: $15 a month gets you an electronic copy of every book we publish for the duration of your membership. Combine it with a print subscription, too!

There's great stuff in the works—so sign up now to become a Friend of AK Press, and let the presses roll!

Won't you be our friend? Email friendsofak@akpress.org for more info, or visit the Friends of AK Press website: www.akpress.org/programs/friendsofak

BIO

WALIDAH IMARISHA IS A WRITER, ORGANIZER, EDUCATOR, PUBLIC scholar, and poet. She is co-editor of the anthology *Octavia's Brood: Science Fiction Stories from Social Justice Movements,* and author of the poetry collection *Scars/Stars.* She has facilitated writing workshops at schools, community centers, youth detention facilities, and women's prisons. Imarisha currently teaches in Portland State University's Black Studies Department.